TITTERSTONE CLEE HILLS

EVERYDAY LIFE
INDUSTRIAL HISTORY
AND
DIALECT

By
A. E. Jenkins

Published by
A. E. Jenkins,
Bower House, Orleton,
Nr. Ludlow, SY8 4HR

Published 1983
Reprint 1984
2nd Reprint 1988
3rd Reprint 1992
4th Reprint 1998

ISBN 0 9509274 0 6

Printed in England by Orphans Press Ltd., Hereford Road, Leominster, Herefordshire.

CONTENTS

ILLUSTRATIONS

Line drawings by author.

Foreword by Major Adrian H. Coles, T.D.,
County and District Councillor for Clee Hill
and Chairman of the Parish Council

Although a relative newcomer to the Clee Hill, (the Hill, the bonk), one quickly realises that it is steeped in the working history of the last two centuries - even today it has a language of its own that English and Welsh visitors cannot comprehend.

Alfred Jenkins has faithfully and painstakingly recorded and catalogued these "times gone by" for posterity, I do not believe that such a thesaurus for this area has been produced before. I would commend it to all - intellectual researcher and layman alike, it is OUR history.

Knowbury House,
Clee Hill,
Shropshire.

ACKNOWLEDGEMENTS

I wish to say thank you to all those people who persuaded me to put pen to paper. My old history master Mr. Frank Reeves of Ludlow said to me, "You'll never finish collecting information. Put down what you know now, so that I may read it". Sadly my busy life did not allow me to do this before he died.

Thanks to the many people who have provided me with old photographs, to David Law, Ken Grant, Peter Bartlett, John Worthing and Tenbury Photography club for their time and photographic expertise. Thanks too to the many oldfolk of Clee Hill who allowed me to talk to them for hours and tape our conversations. Special thanks to Mr. Ted Chidley, Mr. and Mrs. Lambert Matthews, Zepheriah Breakwell, George Broome and Alf Reynolds for their detailed knowledge of old quarrying and mining methods and Gerald Acton of Studio Press.

Thank you too to friends Beti Lloyd, Mary Williams and Brian and Ann Harris for checking the proofs.

I cannot thank Dennis Crowther too much for the endless hours he has spent tramping around Clee Hills with me and collating dialect words. Finally I must thank my family who have endured the tapping of my typewriter for what must have seemed an eternity.

I wish to dedicate this book to my father because he loved the Clee Hills and the people, so much so, that he often dreamed about the area after he had left it.

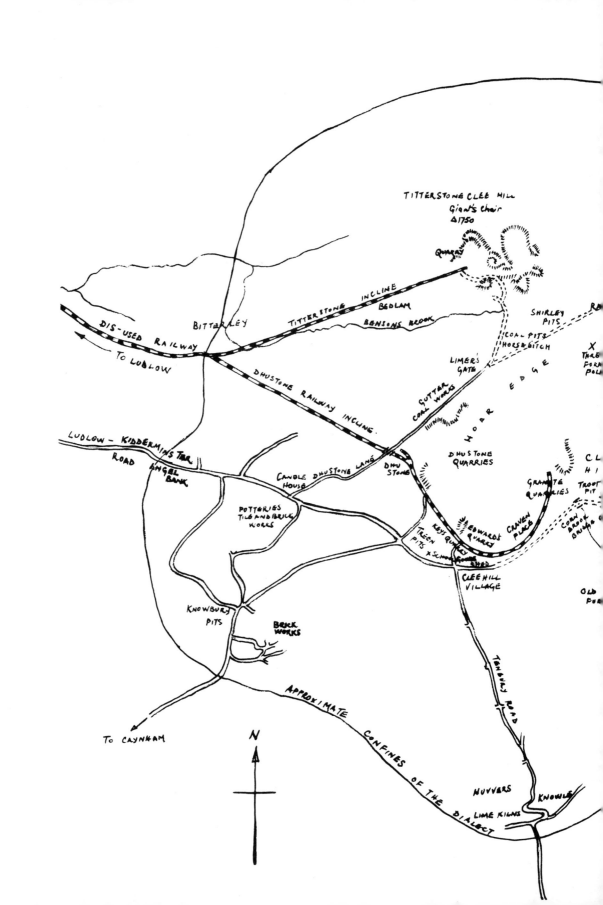

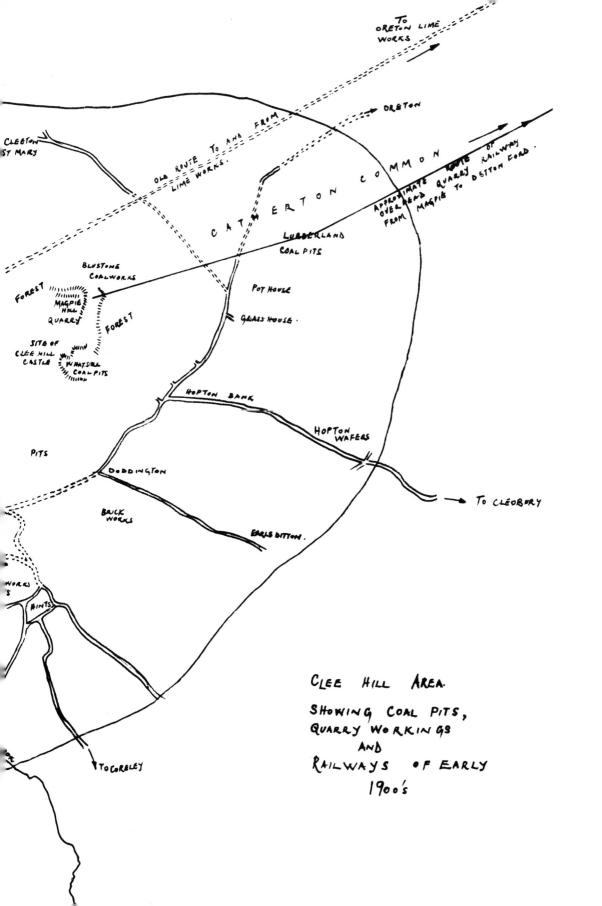

TO ORETON LIME WORKS

ORETON

CLEETON ST MARY

OLD ROUTE TO AND FROM LIME WORKS.

C A T H E R T O N   C O M M O N

APPROXIMATE ROUTE OF QUARRY RAILWAY OVER HEAD FROM MAGPIE TO DITTON FORD.

LUBBERLAND COAL PITS

BLUSTONE COALWORKS

FOREST

MAGPIE HILL QUARRY

FOREST

POT HOUSE

GRASS HOUSE.

SITE OF CLEE HILL CASTLE

WHATSILL COAL PITS

HOPTON BANK

HOPTON WAFERS

PITS

DODDINGTON

TO CLEOBURY

BRICK WORKS

EARLS DITTON.

WORKS

HINTS

CLEE HILL AREA.

SHOWING COAL PITS, QUARRY WORKINGS AND RAILWAYS OF EARLY 1900's

TO CORELEY

Industries of Clee Hill

INTRODUCTION

The Titterstone Clee Hills are situated in South Shropshire within a few miles of the borders of Herefordshire and Worcestershire. Their majestic shape rises to a height of 1,749 feet above sea level and can be seen for many miles from every point of the compass.

The views from the area are varied, beautiful and extensive and in my opinion cannot be bettered anywhere in the British Isles. The area itself is not a place of beauty but its industrial scars give it character and arouse interest in its past.

For centuries its industries of iron ore, lime, coal, glass, bricks and pottery continued along with its peculiar brand of farming.

Poor roads, harsh climate and a localised dialect isolated the hardy independent community and even the population of nearby towns like Ludlow, Cleobury and Tenbury considered the Clee Hill people to be a race apart.

In the 1860s, Clee Hill experienced its own industrial revolution. Stone quarrying became a commercial industry. Hundreds of workers came into the area from many parts of the British Isles. A conglomeration of dialects super-imposed themselves on a Shropshire base to form an interesting mix which confined itself to the Clee Hill area.

Of the industries, by the mid nineteen thirties only farming and stone quarry-ing continued. At that time I was born in a small, rural public house, called the Dhu Stone Inn, which was built primarily for the use of the quarry men.

In the 1930s and 40s many factors including the Second World War, the media, more commuting to work and new housing developments accelerated change. We were persuaded by some that our dialect was not socially acceptable and consequently these and other influences led to its dilution.

Quarrying continues to thrive although it has greater mechanisation and fewer members of the community are involved. I visited the Dhu Stone area recently to find a desolate, forgotten place with only twisted metal girders, rusty steel ropes and crumbling concrete foundations to remind me of the bustle, noise and dust which belched from the crackers and tar-macadam plants during my childhood. The rows of cottages were no longer in the middle of the quarry industry and near a busy railway but perched on the edge of a no man's land.

How unfortunate that as children we do not appreciate our way of life is continually changing, that the things we are used to and take for granted are fast disappearing, never to return.

Every generation has much of value which is worth recording but so often it passes and part of our heritage is lost with it. It is now virtually impossible to find a family who converse in the dialect as we knew it. Clee Hill way of life made it necessary for every family to exploit every situation and pursue many

1

different occupations at the same time in order to survive and provide for its children. There was no escapism or alternative. Now choices can be made.

I was directly connected with this way of life and have talked extensively with many who walked four or five miles to and from the quarries, starting work at 6 a.m. and others who saw day light only at week-ends as a result of life in the Clee Hill coal pits.

Within a decade this link will vanish and the dialect be non-existent. This urgency plus encouragement from many local people has persuaded me to record older members of the indigenous population and recall my own memories.

In my humble way I have endeavoured to illustrate, by photographs and writing, something of the history of the area, my life in a rural public house with a year's events and finally a synopsis of the dialect as I knew it.

My hope is that this book will arouse nostalgic memories but more important persuade others to record in detail everyday occurrences in their localities as and when they happen. This would prevent so much of historical and social interest subsiding into oblivion.

CLEE HILL LIME

Lime was quarried and mined on the Titterstone Clees for many centuries and although the industry was not on the same scale as the stone quarrying considerable numbers of men were employed.

The areas of Oreton and Knowle were well known for the quality of their limestone. Many farms and gardens in North Herefordshire and Worcestershire benefited from Clee Hill. The lime was important too as a bonding agent in the building of stone walls, castles and squatters' cottages.

Ordnance maps of the area show that travelling north, the Dhu Stone lane continues into Limer's lane. Part of this is now the well metalled road leading to Titterstone's radar station. Deviating to the north east is a track which can be traced all the way to Oreton and for many years it was used to transport lime to the Ludlow and Shrewsbury areas.

Locally it was said that the old lane was a Roman road which linked to the Shrewsbury road but I have found nothing to substantiate this. However until the early 1900's the lane was sunken. This was typical of some Roman roads and the high banks on either side could have protected marching troops.

In her Shropshire Word Book, Georgina Jackson mentions the word 'limer', (see dialect section) and its local meaning which was to take unfair advantage. Apparently when the lime burners went to the local public house for some ale it was the practice to pass round a full jug and not for individuals to have a pint each. Older lime burners always made sure they sat in the middle of a group, between younger men. This made sure that if the jug was passed back and forth along a line, the old limer would have more drinks than the youngsters. This was known as coming a limer over someone.

Maps of 1860c show lime works at Studley, between Coreley and Knowle and at the Nuvvers, then spelt Novers. Although lime is no longer quarried or mined in the area, wonderful remains of kilns and tunnels can be discovered with a little effort. If the explorer travels from Clee Hill Village down the Tenbury road he will arrive at the Knowle, notorious in winter for its slippery, hairpin bends.

At the foot of the Knowle bank a lane leading to Hope Bagot can be seen. A few steps along the lane reveals a gateway on the right hand side leading to the lower Nuvvers. With permission from the present owner an exciting hour or two may be spent re-tracing the steps of the old lime workers.

Inside the gateway, a drive leads towards a bungalow, but by following the drive for fifty yards then deviating through the trees to the left, remains of an old cart track can be discovered leading directly to two beautifully constructed arches which are in a surprisingly good state of repair. Close investigation reveals two underground rooms side by side. The walls and roofs are carefully stoned and the fact that they are still in excellent condition is a tribute to the work of past craftsmen.

Some twelve or fifteen feet above the rooms sits a kiln, shaped like a huge egg cup. It must have a capacity to hold at least three tons of lime. Unfortunately a substantial tree now grows from its centre but it has not destroyed the kiln's

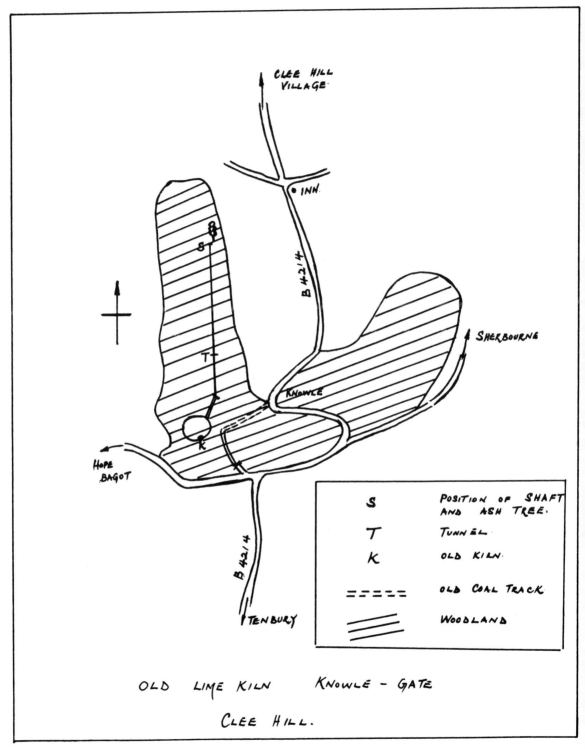

CLEE HILL VILLAGE

INN

B 42/4

SHERBOURNE

S

T

KNOWLE

K

HOPE BAGOT

B 42/4

TENBURY

S	POSITION OF SHAFT AND ASH TREE.
T	TUNNEL.
K	OLD KILN.
- - - - -	OLD COAL TRACK
/////	WOODLAND

OLD LIME KILN   KNOWLE - GATE

CLEE HILL.

shape. Apparently a few years ago a horse fell into the kiln and so the tree was planted to deter further accidents.

In the early 1900's this area was a hive of activity. The whole of the Nuvvers was rented from Hope Court by the father and uncles of Alfred Reynolds, in order to excavate lime. In 1980 Alfred still lived in Lion Lane and was a sprightly, articulate eighty three year old.

Around the old kiln is a large expanse of flat land surrounded by trees. When Alfred Reynolds was a boy he spent many hours here and each Saturday he cut thistles to help keep the area tidy. For this he received 6d (2½p) per week. He recalled quite vividly the lay-out of the works.

Near the kiln there were large stocks of limestone waiting to be burnt and considerable quantities of coal for firing. A grid, similar in size to a household firegrate was fixed in the base of the kiln. On top of this was placed kindling sticks, a layer of coal then a thick layer of limestone. Alternate layers of coal and limestone were placed on top of each other until the kiln was full. Then the fire was lit and the top of the kiln covered with sheet iron, or some other waterproof material.

Slowly the heat increased and over a period of two to three days the limestone decomposed. The fire was allowed to go out and when the lime had cooled sufficiently it was released from the kiln by way of a trap door into the two rooms below. At the top of the central wall the position of the trap door can still be seen.

This storage area kept the lime dry and allowed another kiln load to be prepared. Horses and carts transported the lime to its destination and Mr. Reynolds recalled that he had frequently accompanied his father taking deliveries to the Peacock at Tenbury, Raddle Bank, Kyre and Ludlow, for a cost of 6d (2½p) per hundredweight (56 kilos). Each of these journeys took a whole day which seems painfully slow compared with modern transport.

On arrival at a farm the lime was placed in a large heap and soaked with many buckets of water. Besides its vast quantities of stone, the Clee Hill quarries produced a by product of dust. This was used to seal the field lime heaps and exclude the air. During this time the covered heaps generated tremendous heat and steam could be seen rising from them. As Mr. Reynolds said, "Thaa wun ot enough tu at thi fit/tl on!" (They were hot enough to cook your food on). After two days the slacked lime was raked out and used for field and garden fertiliser.

Local stonemason Mr. Jack Breakwell told me that he had used many tons of Clee Hill lime to make mortar for stone walls. In his younger days, little cement had been available and he used to mix large quantities of lime with a small quantity of cement and the resultant compound was excellent. He reminded me that Clee Hill lime had been used to bond castle walls hundreds of years ago and all the hill squatters' cottages contained lime between the basalt blocks. Everyone locally used lime wash for re-decorating houses, cattle sheds and privies.

By bringing their own teams of horses and heavy wagons, many farmers collected the lime themselves from the kiln. As a gesture they also brought bales of clover for the lime ponies and often a large hamper of cooked beef, bread, cheese and cider. As soon as wagons were loaded and ready for the home journey, farmers and lime workers all sat down to an enjoyable feast. This sort of event was remembered with relish by Mr. Reynolds and it gives an indication of the relationship which existed between people in rural communities.

When descending the Knowle Bank, a cottage can be seen on the right hand side near the first hair-pin bend. Close by is a small gateway through which can be traced the old roadway to the kiln. This was the route used to deliver coal supplies from the Watsall and Barn pits, when the pit head price of coal was about sixteen shillings (80p) per ton.

Back to the kiln. Where did the lime come from? By turning one's back on the kiln and walking to the N.E. direction across the old storage area, a gap will be seen between the trees. Here, a distinct bare track some five yards wide runs straight up the wooded hillside. This was the position of a railway incline built purposely to transport lime down the hill to the kiln. Two pairs of railway lines ran side by side, one pair for the full truck descending and the other pair for the empty truck ascending. Each was similar in construction to those seen in the quarry photographs.

At the top of the hill suspended on two stone pillars was a large wooden drum around which wound a wire rope. The one end was attached to the empty truck and the other end to the full one. The weight of the full truck descending easily pulled up the empty one and to control the speed a brake was fitted to the drum.

When a truck reached the top of the incline it passed under the drum where a set of railway points channelled the four rails into two. The exact spot where the tracks narrowed can be ascertained because they converged through a cutting which still continues along the hill top for a few hundred yards.

Before the beginning of the century, limestone was levered by crow-bars from the quarry face but later a drift was made into the hillside. Just beyond the cutting a tunnel lined and roofed with stone will be discovered. This extends for at least half a mile into the hillside but now it is not possible to explore far with safety because the roof has collapsed in places. But one can wonder at the tremendous amount of time and expense needed to construct such a drift.

When Alfred Reynolds was nine or ten years of age, (1905) his mother often sent him with his father's 'snappin' (lunch) to meet him at the top of the incline. Here he would share the sandwiches and a bottle of cold tea before his father hooked his pony's traces to an empty wagon. Then Alf would jump in and enjoy a ride along the cutting to the tunnel. He was always apprehensive when the truck rumbled into the entrance because as the reverberating sound of the wheels echoed around the tunnel so the darkness grew. The only glimmer of light was that from a tallow candle carried by his father. He had to pick his way by the side of the track, stepping between the sleepers. It was not surprising that occasionally he stumbled, causing the candle to go out. In eerie blackness the boy would wait while his father re-lit the candle.

Travelling for half a mile at slow walking pace with frequent interruptions and little light seemed to take an eternity but eventually the face was reached.

Here the workmen fixed numerous candles to the rock walls to provide sufficient light by which to use picks, shovels and crowbars. Conditions of working were better than a coal face because there was plenty of area in which to move, ample head room and a good air circulation.

The roof was supported by leaving thick pillars of limestone at frequent intervals, not unlike the method used in the bell pits. Explosives were expensive and only small quantities were available. Therefore little was used; the main of the limestone being hewn by hand..

Near the face was a short shaft. This served two purposes, one to enable air to circulate and secondly for workmen to be able to reach the limestone quickly by descending a ladder attached to the side of the shaft. This avoided the time consuming walk through the long, poorly lit tunnel.

The Tenbury Road cottages were very near but the exact location of the shaft was obscured by coppice and scrub. An ash tree was planted near the shaft. As it grew it became a clear landmark enabling workmen to walk quickly to the face from any direction. The old lime shaft has long caved in but the ash tree still stands proudly to mark the spot.

The bottom Nuvvers kiln closed in 1910 because the supply of lime was interrupted by a large fault and the Reynolds family were getting too old to be bothered to excavate for further supplies. They did however continue to operate other kilns in the area until the 1920s.

I have not been able to ascertain whether the industry ended because accessible supplies of lime were exhausted or because the last of the Clee Hill coal pits closed at about the same time so robbing the kilns of a local, cheap source of fuel.

Loading bays beneath the lime kiln.

Alf Reynolds showing trees growing in the old kiln basin.

On the opposite side of the storage area from the kiln an opening between the trees where railway incline ended.

The position of the old incline down which the the lime passed.

The railway cutting which led to the lime tunnel.

The old ash tree which still marks the position of the old lime shaft.

The position from which the old coal road led to the Knowle lime kiln.

Aerial photograph showing how near to each other the old pit shafts are at Lubberland.

1930s. Unloading coal at the top of the Goods Shed lane near Clee Hill village.

About 1904. Miners and Managers at the Watsall pits.

1926. Removing slack from near the Barn Pit during the General strike.

1926. Slack tip at the Potteries, opposite the Dhu Stone lane junction.

Carver boys and miners at the Barn pit in the 1920s.

Miners at the Barn pit 1912. In the centre partially hidden by the dog is Mr. George Broome.

The Three Forked Pole

This is situated near the site of the old Watsall Pit and near Random Farm. It has been a land mark for many hundreds of years and stands where three parishes and three estates meet. This photograph shows the Price family having just re-erected a new pole in the 1920s.

CLEE HILL COAL MINING

Older generations who live in mining areas are familiar with the sight of men making their way home, faces grimed with coal dust and streaked with persperation. Baggy working clothes, collarless shirts, protective helmets and steel toe capped boots complete the picture.

As I came home from primary school, across the old Treen Pit Ground, I met similar groups walking from Clee Hill village to the Dhu Stone. They had earlier completed an afternoon shift at Highley Pit. But they had no luxuries such as changing rooms and pit head baths and were forced to travel a distance of twenty miles in their dirt before being able to clean themselves.

Womenfolk must have been grateful for the free coal deliveries of one ton each month. Without the facility of a bathroom they had the endless, back breaking task of carrying and preparing vast quantities of boiling water ready for when husbands arrived home.

Out came a long, narrow tin bath to be placed in front of a roaring kitchen coal-fire. Worker doffed his clothes and jumped into the knee deep water attended by a considerate wife who washed his back and continually added more hot water to maintain the heat in a draughty, steam filled kitchen. How we take our modern centrally heated, convenient homes for granted.

However, the dirty dangerous job brought better pay than that received by the neighbouring quarrymen, so much so that many miners could afford to occasionally miss a shift and enjoy a boozy market day at Ludlow. This was traditionally a day when the public houses remained open all day and the miners called it pig Monday.

Many years later I discovered that some of these men were descendants of owners of pits and miners who had played an important part in a thriving Clee Hill coal industry which had existed for centuries. Edwards is one such family that still exists.

Murchison the 19th century geologist recorded, 'coal has been wrought from these hills from time immemorial', and the earliest recording of coal mining in the area was 1235 when Wigmore Abbey received five shillings from the sale of coal from Titterstone Clee.

By 1727 coal produced in the area was valued at £1500 but it was said that the coal and seams were not excavated in a systematic way. However aerial photography does not always support this and where there is evidence of haphazard mining, I am told that limited resources and geological reasons left little alternative.

Notes seen in Coreley church state that Thomas Botfield established a blast furnace, using coal as fuel in 1765. The blast was produced by a very large water wheel turned by Corn Brook. Walls and clinker heaps still remain to mark the site.

My geological section map reproduced from an old Dhu Stone Company booklet shows the basalt cap on Titterstone and Dhu Stone with the coal measures lying below. Miners I talked to had never seen such a map but were able to tell me very accurately, by looking at the physical features, where coal was likely to be. They showed me the fault which runs around the Hill from the Magpie to

Dorrington, on to Dhu Stone, out to the Hoar Edge and back again to join up at the Magpie.. It coincides very accurately with the geological map.

In the 1760s a tremendous number of shallow pits were known to have existed on Catherton Common at an area known as Lubberland. According to Murchison some cottagers kept horses to carry lime and coal and were able to earn 2 shillings to 3 shillings (10p to 15p) per day. But there is much evidence to suggest that the miners were very impoverished and in order to maintain their families in decency they had numerous occupations including farming, carrying lime and mining coal. This necessary pattern existed until the time of my childhood. My own father who had himself been a miner years earlier in the Midlands, sold beer and cider, was a wheelwright and undertaker and kept a small holding of pigs, sheep, cattle and poultry.

I met Mr. George Broome, from the Pot House Catherton for the first time in 1978 when he was 80 years of age and a very successful farmer with over 200 acres. But this was a great contrast to his earlier existence. Like most Clee Hill people his life had been an extremely hard one and it amazed me how articulate, clear thinking and fit he was after having spent much of his life in appalling conditions working in the Clee Hill pits.

I questioned him about the miners of the 1760s and he was quite convinced that their lives had been very hard indeed. He said, "When I was young, Clee Hill people had to work before they could eat and I am sure that the Catherton miners were the same. Now you all eat before you work."

A photograph provided by the Committee of Aerial Photography Cambridge, shows very clearly the close proximity of the pit shafts at Lubberland to each other. Mr. Broome had mined in that area himself and although he admitted the mining looked haphazard insisted there was no other economical alternative. The coal seam in this area is very thin and in fact disappears completely slightly further east because of a fault. This is substantiated by the Dhu Stone Co. geological section. Coal is only a few yards below the surface and could be reached, by sinking a very shallow shaft. Miners did not bother to excavate any great distance along a seam from a shaft because the time involved in carting coal along a tunnel, the laying of track and necessary equipment would have cost disproportionately far too much compared with the ease of sinking another shallow shaft nearer to where the coal was being hewn. Hence the mole tump effect seen on the aerial photograph.

Some pits on the Clee Hills were positioned above 1300 feet in isolated, bleak spots. Visitors walking the area may question how on earth coal was transported down the steep slopes, because in the early 1800s there were still no roads. Pack horses definitely helped with transportation but more frequently the backs of cottagers' wives were used. In Archaelogia Cambrensis Vol 89 (1934) B. H. St. J. O'Neil said that Richard Jones of Ashford who attended Titterstone wake in 1846 recalled the young women, "fine and handsome upstanding wenches they were, and well dressed too; but you wouldna' know 'em the next day with a bag of coal strapped on their backs, for in them days coal from the Clee Hill pits were carried down the hill on women's shoulders."

On the other side of the hill a track still exists ascending from near Hopton

Bank Filling Station to the site of the old Watsall pits. There used to be a large, flat slab positioned on the side of the track which was called a resting stone. Here women paused to rest their loads without having to remove them from their backs, before continuing down to the mud track road where their burdens were lifted onto carts and transported as far afield as Hereford.

During the mid 1800s coal became much more important in the area because stone quarrying developed into a tremendous, commercial business.

To move and crush stone a great deal of machinery was needed, all of which had to be powered. Coal was the only suitable local source of energy, therefore quarry owners encouraged the rationalisation and extension of the existing coal industry. Larger, deeper pits were developed.

The coal was a good quality, being hard and bright. As a result it was requested for household use in South Shropshire and North Herefordshire although this meant slow transportation by road.

Plumley observed, 'the inhabitants purchase at great expense the land carriage coal from the Clee Hills.' No doubt the industry would have developed more and lasted longer had plans drawn up by Telford to join the area to the Severn by canal been implemented.

By 1860 a necklace of pits had developed around the Hill and even if you study carefully a map of this time the quantity is almost too numerous to count.

To the east of Titterstone were the Shirley Pits. Moving south the Horse Ditch Pits and Gutter Coal Works near Hoar Edge could be seen. Very little of this area is left because of advancing quarries. When I was a child this was a favourite whimberry picking area, but all that remains of the bushes are bare stalks because of over stocking of the common land with sheep. Continuing south the Winthills pits and Knowbury Coal Works could be located near a private house which was formerly the Crown Inn. Moving east one could see the Treen Pits in the area now known as the Pit Ground, where as children we unsuspectingly skated across ice which covered pools formed in the hollows of some of the old pit heads. Nearby Treen House still stands to remind this present age of the area's past importance. This house was formerly the home of Mr. Fred Edwards who during my childhood owned the Clee Hill Transport and Rolling Company. His grandson Michael Plant is still concerned with Clee Hill Plant Ltd and the photograph of the gentlemen of Watsall Pit includes Mr. Edwards, the great grandfather of Michael. Further east past the Clee Hill village were the Cornbrook Pits. Three of these, the Top Trout, Bottom Trout and Barn Pit were still in use in the 1920s and The Barn Pit was the last one on Clee Hill to close. For safety reasons the shaft was filled and capped with concrete in the 1940s. Its position can easily be located by climbing the hill for a few hundred yards from Cornbrook Bridge. The area covered by the slack heap around the shaft is quite impressive and it makes one realise that this was an important pit which had been in use for a considerable number of years. The Watsall pits were shown near Chatterpie Hill and Clee Hill Castle. The hill is now known as the Magpie but Clee Hill Castle no longer exists. The position of the largest Watsall Pit can easily be found by the prominence of the pit head slagheap not far from the Three Forked Pole and Random. The lesser known Kilkenny Pit was near this point too. It is interesting to note that the Blue Stone Pits were considered part of Herefordshire in the 1860s in an area known as the Farlow Enclosure. The necklace of pits was completed by those known as Lubberland.

Everytime I gaze from Watsall to the main road far below, I contemplate what sort of existence it must have been for women who had to carry considerable loads on their backs, day after day, down that rough, bleak, rocky slope to awaiting heavy horse drawn and steam traction wagons. Lighter wagons were taken to the pits, where there was much jostling and careless driving in order to get to the front of the coal queue. This competition and recklessness led to accidents one of which was reported in the Ludlow Standard on Saturday August 22nd, 1840 as follows:-

ACCIDENT AT CLEE HILL

'To the editor of the Ludlow Standard.

Sir, I have often regretted the want of a Local Newspaper whose columns would be open to the complaints and suggestions of the neighbouring country, and it is with great pleasure I hail the commencement of your journal feeling confident that our occasional contributions will meet with at your hands a rejection or a welcome as their merits may deserve. I have often witnessed with great anxiety the racing of various carters when near the coal pits at the Hill, a practice that is most certainly punishable being dangerous to men and brutal to the poor animals. On Saturday last an accident occurred which I trust will be a sufficient warning, a boy unfortunately was thrown under the wheels of one of the carts when at its greatest speed, and for some time the Medical gentleman H. Maymott Esq., under whose care the boy was placed, doubted much to his ultimate recovery, which can only be effected by slow degrees. I shall trouble you occasionally with a few lines from this quarter and wishing you every success, I remain sir, your obliged. O.R.'

I mentioned this to Mr. Broome and he said this practice continued years later. The reason was insufficient coal was produced to supply everyone's needs because the Quarry Company required most of the coal and slack to drive its machinery. Also the Company was anxious to supply orders to many parts of the country by way of the railway spur from Belfry to the Dhu Stone and Bitterley.

Coal was allocated on a rota system and in order to qualify, each person wanting a load had to go along daily with horse and cart to register his name. This meant standing in a queue for hours. But more frustrating was the fact that it was often necessary to repeat this exercise for four or five consecutive days before qualifying for a load. Mr. Broome had often experienced this procedure himself.

The place where they waited was known as the joggins, a modern equivalent would be a lorry park. At the site of the Top Watsall pit the slack heap covers a tremendous area but on the south side is a low rectangular shape. Here stood large buildings filled with coal in front which was the joggins occupied daily with mules, horses and carts from as far afield as Hereford. Frustration often led to quarrels and irresponsible driving. In order to obtain a prominent position in the queue it was necessary to leave home hours before daylight. An official known as the banksman noted everyone present and allocated coal accordingly.

I knew another gentleman known as Zephaniah Breakwell who had personal experience of collecting coal from the Top Watsall Pit before becoming a miner. He lived in the Cross Lane, Clee Hill Village for many years and finished his days at Teme Side, Ludlow.

Mr. Breakwell's mother had a coal round business and used horses and carts for this purpose. In 1916 at the age of fourteen, Mr. Breakwell was employed by his family to collect loads from Watsall regularly. He certainly remembered the carters' reckless driving but what impressed him most was the vast quantity of drays and wagons, far more than the number of cars seen on Clee Hill today.

Charlie Jones, who lived opposite Tommy's Bakery in Clee Hill Village was in charge of the weighing machine at the pit. Mr. Breakwell was always given a gold sovereign by his mother to pay for each ton of coal and from that coin he received three shillings and four pence change. This meant that a ton of coal cost sixteen shillings and eight pence, (83p).

He recalled a story, which is of interest to local people, concerning a gentleman called Jacky Turner who lived at Horseditch. One Sunday evening he went to Tea Kettle Alley public house, which was situated near the top of Hopton Bank, and consumed his usual quota of pints before walking home. His route was up the coal carrying track to Top Watsall Pit, over the Hill past the Three Forked Pole and on to Horseditch. What an extremely difficult journey to make without the help of street lights and having to negotiate hazards such as jagged rocks, rabbit holes, pit shafts and quarry faces.

This particular evening was darker than usual and rain was falling heavily. At Watsall Pit there was an engine heated by coal for operating the winding gear. Beneath it was a large stoke-hole.

When Jacky reached Watsall he crept under the stoke-hole to shelter and rest. He must have dropped off to sleep. Hot ash fell from the fire onto his body and he was burnt to death. The following morning Mr. Tom Webb arrived as usual to stoke the fire. He put the wheelbarrow in position to rake out the ashes and as he did, discovered Jacky's body. Mr. Breakwell arrived to collect coal just as the dead man was being carried and laid in an office by the side of the pit. With a chuckle Mr. Breakwell said, 'I dun/nu want tu sim disrespectful, but I ad tu loff, kos there wus poor odd Jacky, burnt tu dyuth, still ooth is ard at on, and it wun/nu touched.'

There have been numerous pits at Watsall but the Top Pit was the last one on Clee Hill where a maiden seam was worked. There are three seams of coal around the Hill. The first and shallowest is known as the Great Coal. It is six feet thick and lies at a depth of one hundred yards. When a pit first opened this was the seam first worked. In 1918 all that remained of this seam at the Watsall were pillars of coal which had been left at regular intervals to stabilise the workings. Some twelve feet below, a second seam known as the Smith Coal was reached by way of a sump hold. Yet another twelve feet deeper was a third seam known as the Four Foot. This was inappropriately named because it is only two feet thick.

The two Watsall Pits were run by the Granite Company for many years. Pit props were supplied from the Magpie Hill forest, an area owned by Major Woodward. Gradually all the timber was felled but tree stumps still remain and give an indication of the extent of the woodland.

In the early 1900s the pits began to run at a loss and were handed over to Mr. William Edwards, whose son Dragon Edwards lived at the Miner's Arms Public House at Coreley. The pit became a family concern but eventually like most pits in the area it was forced to close because of flooding.

Many miners wanted to break through to a new shaft which had recently been sunk but which could not be worked because it was against a fault. Mr. Lee Roberts was the quarry manager and he would not give permission for a further new shaft to be sunk. Time passed and when he eventually consented, private funds had been exhausted and work could not continue.

Ventilation problems were extremely acute at Top Watsall because the ventilation shaft was only thirty yards away from the main shaft. This was too close to create sufficient draught and so workmen had to carry an airline. Candles were used for lighting. As men passed Magpie pool on the way to work they gathered a handful of clay which they rolled to make a pliable ball as they walked along. At the coal face a candle was pushed into each ball and pressed firmly onto the sides of the tunnel as near the working area as possible. But, workmen told me that the current of air was so weak that usually the candles had to be suspended in almost an inverted position to keep them alight. On reflection miners marvelled how they tolerated such conditions. Inadequate light added to dangers and led to many accidents. Boys pushing coal tubs in the main tunnels frequently crushed their fingers.

Mr. Breakwell was one of a gang of four employed to drive an airline vent from Barn Pit to Bottom Trout. Because of the gradient, water was continually pouring down the tunnel, and in the semi-darkness the gang worked in a chain fashion throwing stones to each other. This caused broken and damaged limbs. Mr. Breakwell's right hand was smashed against a boulder so ruining his fingers for life.

The Four Foot was so narrow in places that it was impossible to use a tool freely. To quote from Mr. Broome, "We were on our stomachs or our sides continually and had to scoop and shovel the dirt and coal back to men behind us. They did the same and the process was repeated many times until a bigger, higher space was reached. Here, boys known as donkeys, because it was donkey work, dragged loads along the tunnels."

As youngsters both Mr. Broome and Mr. Breakwell worked as donkeys or 'carvers.' They said, "We used to have straps fitted over our shoulders connected to a wider leather strap down the middle of our back. Attached to this was a chain about a yard in length. This was hooked to a carv, the name given to a large, shallow box with wooden skids beneath it. The space was so confined we spent most of our time pulling with our hands and knees submerged in mud and water. We started at 7 a.m. and finished at 2 p.m. having very little time for rest. Although this was a long spell for boys to work in those conditions, we considered ourselves lucky compared with the men. They began work at 6 a.m. and did not

DONKEY STRAPS WORN BY A CARV BOY

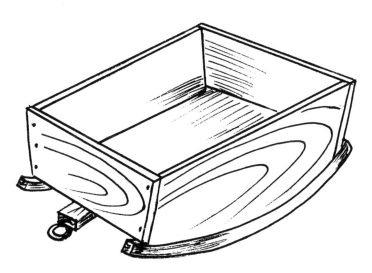

A CARV. THE NAME GIVEN TO A BOX WITH WOODEN
SKIDS, USED TO MOVE COAL FROM THE FACE TO THE
MAIN TUNNELS

finish their shift until 6 p.m. This meant they only saw daylight at week ends during wintertime."

In 1911 when Mr. Broome was thirteen years of age, he worked in Magpie Quarry for 2d, per hour, less than 1p. He decided to work in the pits because his father and grandfather had been miners, working hours were a little shorter and he assumed he would earn more. However it proved to be an Irishman's rise, for when he went to the choltermaster, or cashier, at the end of the week he received one shilling and eight pence, approximately 8p per day.

Mr. Breakwell began working at the Barn Pit in 1916. He walked from Knowbury and had to be down the pit ready to begin work at 7 a.m. The working week was six days for a wage of fifteen shillings (75p) or half a crown daily (12½p). He said, "We had fifteen minutes break in the morning, between eleven and quarter past. This meant we worked four hours before a break. The charge hand came round and said we'd got fourteen minutes for snappin and no more. He watched and made sure we obeyed the rules. We were always so ravenous that this was ample time to eat and nothing was ever taken back home."

At first he often cried because the conditions nearly broke his heart. The cage in which he descended the main shaft had no protection and the sides were open. This and the noisy blackness terrified him. Some boys were lucky enough to pull loads down hill to a main road but Mr. Breakwell had to do the reverse from a lower level to a higher one. He said, "The air was warm in the pit and we tolerated our sodden clothes but, in wintertime when we stepped out of the cage at ground level the air was often freezing. In these conditions when I arrived home my trousers were frozen stiff."

Not surprisingly, Mr. Breakwell contracted pneumonia and on doctor's orders was not allowed to resume work underground for some considerable time.

There were three eight hour shifts to ensure continuity of production. The day shift involving about thirty men, moved the coal whereas the afternoon and night shifts, repaired, cleaned, packed rubble in the used areas and maintained the roofs. The total employed at Barn Pit was about eighty.

Flood water was a tremendous problem there, so much so, that a group on night shift was continuously employed ladling out water to keep the level sufficiently low to enable coal to be mined each day. Even then, men often stood waist deep in water. On the main road mid-way between Cornbrook and Doddington Church, a track called Furnace Road leads down to Fairy Glen. Here near the remains of the old furnaces is a bricked arch, opening into the hill side. This 'footrid' is the entrance to a long complicated network of tunnels which was connected to many pits as far as the Three Forked Pole. Their purpose was to assist ventilation and drainage.

Mr. Breakwell described the tunnels as being six feet high and beautifully bricked for considerable distances. In places the tunnels continue through solid rock where no support or brickwork is needed. While working in this maze, he discovered many tools inscribed with the name Thomas Botfield. These had obviously been left many years previously by those extracting raw materials for glass making, the production of pig iron and coal. The Botfield family owned glassworks and this was quite an industry. Gold and silver sand was transported from Knowle Wood and water which poured from the footrid emptied into Cornbrook where it was harnessed to create power.

Many years later, during my childhood, this power was used to generate electricity. Local people took their 'wireless' accumulators there to be re-charged, while industry used the energy to re-charge larger accumulators too.

Until a connection to the Rhayader/Birmingham pipe line was made in 1970, water was pumped from the brook to supply all the houses in Cornbrook area and part of Tenbury Wells too obtained its needs from the lower reaches of Cornbrook.

In an attempt to ease flooding Mr. Broome and others were sent up the footrid to clear it out but they failed. The fireman ordered the same group to drive a new flood tunnel from Barn Pit down to Cornbrook in an attempt to join it onto the footrid, but the angle was very steep. He said, "We managed to excavate some fifty yards but the water continued to increase because we could not get rid of it. Nowadays it would not be tolerated, but we knew no better and had no choice in the matter. Finally the water increased to shoulder height and we had to abandon the project."

Before workers became qualified miners they had to pass through numerous recognised stages. The first one was carving. Many boys could not tolerate this job and left before being able to graduate to wagoning. The carvers dragged the loads along tunnels which were only inches high until they reached areas where standing was possible. Here they met the wagoners, the name given to boys in charge of small wooden wagons known as tubs. Four carv loads were required to fill a tub before it was pushed to the main tunnel. Once there, a pony was used to pull it to the base of the shaft. The tub tunnels were little wider than the loads and every wagoner expected to have damaged hands. It was difficult to avoid these injuries because as they moved forwards the loaded tubs swayed from side to side and bumped the tunnel walls.

Successful wagoners became fillers. Their work was packing slack, stone and poor quality coal into worked out areas. This served two purposes, one being to avoid roof collapse and the other the necessity of hauling all the waste up the shaft to the surface.

Stage four was a holer or pickman. Before any coal could be removed from the working face the holer had to lie on his side or kneel down to use a pick to grout out a hole beneath the coal, one yard deep and five yards wide. This was known as a stint. Although this job necessitated lying on one's stomach all day while trying to use a pick, at a coal face dimly lit by an almost inverted candle, contending with a hot and humid atmosphere with little air to breathe, younger men really felt promotion had been gained when they had the opportunity of this work.

Stage five was the mature miner or collier. He had a wide variety of jobs but his first one was a buttaker. This was removing the coal from above the holer's stint. A day's pay for a holer was four shillings (20p) and a buttaker four shillings and sixpence (22½p). A miner could be promoted to fireman and so be in charge of thirty men. Only managers were in charge of more than this number.

Local coal was an important, necessary source of fuel to operate stone crushers and winding gear for the railway inclines. In spite of this requirement, pits continued to close because of flooding and ventilation. Conditions were impossible and efficient equipment which could deal with those problems was too expensive.

Barn Pit closed and remained so for about five years, but because of its proximity to the quarry and the industry's need for coal, it re-opened again in the early 1920s. To begin with only three men worked below ground namely, George Hall, Sam Hall and Arthur Cleeton. Above ground were Jim Steadman, Jack Carless and his son. Mr. Breakwell joined the group when men from Knowbury's closed pits were encouraged to come to Clee Hill. Mr. Broome joined Barn Pit at the same time.

Working conditions did not improve, for within a short space of time the operators received fourteen summonses for lack of safety. Numerous explosions occurred and Mr. Breakwell remembers losing his clothes in one blast but his injuries were no worse than concussion and a good shaking.

Blasting the coal was dangerous work. The one in charge of the operation was the shot man. He used loose gunpowder rammed into a deep hole and connected to a fuse. This was ignited and he retired as quickly as possible; not an easy task considering inadequate light and the natural hazards surrounding the face.

Only 'top and gaub' coal remained. Four of the six feet of Great Coal had been removed years previously and two feet of the coal remained as the roof. In previous years there had been no demand for small coal and slack, therefore it had been packed tightly behind the working miners to fill all spaces beneath the remaining two feet and so save expense of hauling it to the surface. Hence the name 'top and gaub'. The removal of this small coal and maiden seam of two feet was the last commercial mining to take place on Clee Hill. Soon eighty men were employed and a fireman called George Williams came from Highley to take charge. The cage held half a ton and full loads came to the surface as fast as they could be handled. Part of the output drove the quarry's machines whilst most of the remainder was taken by horses and carts to Belfry where it was tipped from the wharf into trucks and transported via the Dhu Stone railway to distant power stations.

Many private people were employed as full-time hauliers and two well known names often mentioned were Owen and William Davis. In fact anyone who could provide transport was welcome to the work. '

Because naked lights were used, the fireman was the first person to enter the pit each day to check whether the atmosphere was safe, but water again became the major problem. Night after night men ladled it into a large barrel which was continually hauled up the shaft and poured away. This process was painfully slow and not surprisingly the flood water increased. Mr. George Broome said that someone hit on the bright idea of making a large 'bowk' the name given to a box shape. It was fitted with a hinged base. As it was lowered into the water, the pressure pushed up the hinged base and allowed the water to enter. As soon as the

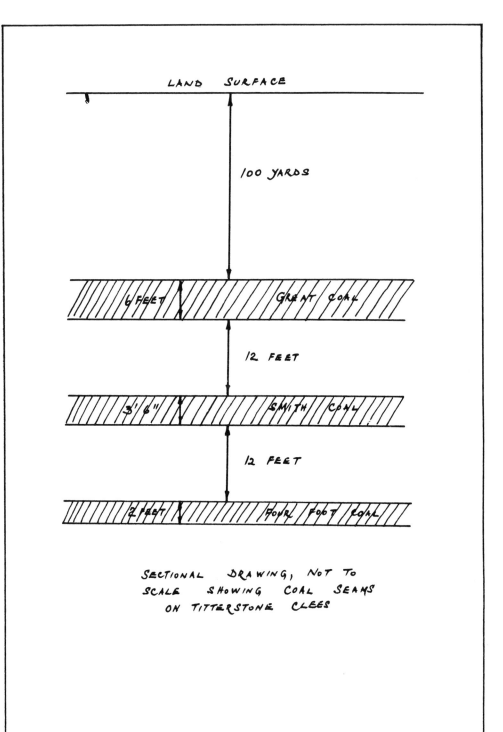

LAND SURFACE

100 YARDS

6 FEET   GREAT COAL

12 FEET

3' 6"   SMITH COAL

12 FEET

2 FEET   FOUR FOOT COAL

SECTIONAL DRAWING, NOT TO
SCALE SHOWING COAL SEAMS
ON TITTERSTONE CLEES

bowk was submerged, it was withdrawn. The weight of the water pushed the hinged base against a rubber seal and large quantities of water were raised quickly and effectively to the surface. Extensive wooden troughs carried the water away from the shaft and down the common land. The use of the bowk kept the water at a level which allowed work to continue.

THE LAST MEN UNDERGROUND ON CLEE HILL

It was the accepted practice at most pits to leave many yards of coal around the base of the shaft to give it stability, and for there to be a number of tunnels deviating from it. This was the system at the Barn Pit.

For easy access to coal and to incur little expense, the fireman gave instructions for quantities of coal to be removed from near the base of the shaft. This had disastrous consequences and when Mr. Broome went to work one morning it was discovered that the shaft had 'toed in', i.e. closed in a little at the bottom. Mr. Williams, the fireman, asked two volunteers to go down in the cage and assess the situation. George and Tim Broome obliged. To quote from Mr. George Broome:-

"The cage was lowered very steadily but became jammed before we were able to reach the insets, the name given to the tunnels leading from the base of the shaft. The cage guide ropes which hung about a foot over either side of the cage were wedged tightly on the shaft walls.

We clambered out and by hanging from the cage discovered we were only about a yard from the shaft floor. Suddenly it dawned on us that the cage was wedged so fast that we could not be hauled up again. Our only possible way out was to endeavour to negotiate the air way to Trout Pit. This road had not been used for sometime. The timbered roof as a result of neglect had caved in in numerous places.

At these spots we had to climb over mounds of rock and broken timber and as we did so, were extremely concerned about disturbing debris, and creating further falls. As we clambered over the first rock fall we found ourselves in water so deep we had to swim. Long, deep pools had been created between the mounds of fallen rock. On reaching the next fall and struggling over, we had to navigate another pool. In all we had seven similar recurrences. It was an ugly, terrifying experience. The distance to Trout shaft was about two hundred yards but on this occasion it seemed endless and took us what seemed an eternity to cover.

Eventually we reached our goal and it was the greatest relief of my life to be hauled up Trout shaft into daylight.

The Barn Pit closed for good and so it can be said that Tim Broome and I were the last men underground on Clee Hill. The coal mining had finished. In my opinion modern drainage and ventilation equipment would not have extended the life of Barn Pit because its resources were practically exhausted, but there is still an excellent seam of Smith coal at Top Trout Pit which would make a viable, commercial proposition.

Dole money was available and I received seven shillings and sixpence per week (37½p), but our families could not have existed on that amount indefinitely and so most of us sought work at Highley and Kinlet Pits".

The final closure took place at about the time of the General Strike in 1926. The huge amounts of slack coal were in great demand and because there were no organised unions on Clee Hill, many miners continued their employment for sometime by moving the slack coal to Belfry railway wharf to be transported via the Dhustone railway incline to Ludlow and beyond.

Other forms of power were now available to drive the quarry industry machinery. The Company had no real need to keep the declining Clee pits open and so the industry ceased. Small pockets of coal continued to be used for domestic purposes and many miners could not resist the thrill and adventure of excavating old shafts.

On marrying, Mr. Broome lived at Moral Cottage on Catherton Common. The property had three and a half acres of land which contained no fewer than four shafts. The older folk of the family knew that coal had been excavated there and continually encouraged George to seek for more. He went to see Major Woodward's father, the Lord of the Manor to ask permission to sink a new shaft, but he advised against it, because many had started and failed. However after continued pressure, consent was given to re-open an old mine with the proviso that Major Woodward should receive royalty on all coal produced.

Directly below the garden hedge the bricked up head of an old pit shaft was removed. A vertical post was positioned on either side, a cross bar fitted and a winch positioned some ten yards back across the field. A cage was made from a thirty six gallon barrel reinforced with iron hoops made by a local blacksmith. With this primitive equipment Mr. Broome and friends began investigating the old shaft during the evenings.

To quote, "We lowered ourselves into the pit. There was no ventilation and we took a great risk because of gas. The shaft was cleaned out and we came to an arched gutter or footrid which was bricked up. On removing the bricks we discovered it was silted up and full of water inside.

The footrid emptied at a spot lower down. We opened it out. Water and silt gushed out in a torrent onto the Cleeton road. With the water cleared we made an inset up the hill towards the coal. With great excitement we soon found a seam.. However our elation was short lived because we had discovered only a 'crop out'. The coal soon disappeared again. We were in fact too high and should have started at a lower level. That was the end of our mining adventures. It was a wonderfully exciting experience but not a paying proposition."

REFLECTIONS

Old miners remembered with sadness and bitterness the tremendous number of workmen who had huge tummies caused by ruptures from lifting and pushing enormous weights. These men never had operations but just tolerated their

21

misfortune. Men had to mine coal to earn cash to live, but even so their earnings had to be supplemented by other occupations. This impoverished state created great family unity and determination. Women folk and children kept the home and ran the smallholdings. Their help to the menfolk was invaluable.

Transport was primitive and slow and road surfaces no more than tracks. It was a day's trip for Mr. Broome's mother to take the parson to Ludlow by horse and trap. This she did in addition to her other chores. Men walked to work before sun rise and did not return until late evening when they were confronted by gardening and farmwork. Now we have machinery. We can travel from Clee Hill to Ludlow in minutes, complete our business within a couple of hours, yet the pace of life is such that we have no time.

Life in those days centred around the community. There was no opportunity and no need to travel. The majority of the time was spent working. Ludlow and Cleobury were foreign lands. People through ignorance and fear preferred to shoot themselves if very ill, rather than be forced to go to Kidderminster hospital. And so they never went until 'one foot was in the grave, and very nearly the other one too.' It is not surprising therefore, that of those who ultimately went for treatment, very few returned home. What a dramatic change today! When a family person or farm animal died, the community raised money to help or replace the stock. This neighbourly fund was called a brief. As times improved and there was less relying on each other the brief disappeared.

"Urban people now look for properties in our community as week-end cottages and commuting homes. We don't know them, they don't know us. Unfortunately they come along and endeavour to tell us how to live. We know the area and what it can provide and with respect outsiders should adjust themselves to our methods."

CLEE HILL QUARRYING INDUSTRY

Nearly one hundred and thirty years ago, stone quarrying developed into a thriving industry on the Clee Hills, but there is no doubt that their physical and geological features gave them importance many centuries before that.

Those interested in cathedrals will know that the ancient Mappa Mundi in Hereford Cathedral was the work of Richard de Haldingham and de Lafford. His real name was Richard de Bello and he held the Prebend of Lafford in Lincoln Cathedral up to AD 1283, after which he held the Stall of Norton in Hereford Cathedral.

As he held staff in Hereford in the year 1305 the date of Mappa Mundi is probably AD 1300. The President of the Geographical Society of Paris, Mons D' Avezac minutely examined the map and fixed it at 1314. It is on a single sheet of vellum 54" wide and 63" high.

I have included a key map as well as a reproduced photo of the map itself. On the left hand side figures 19, 20 and 22 show the British Isles. To the right is France. Great Britain, 19 and 22, is laid out in considerable detail and twenty six towns are shown in England including Hereford. Twenty rivers are also shown but the only hills shown in England are the Clee Hills. Why is this? I believe that even in those days the minerals of the area played an important part in the lives of the townspeople and country folk of North Herefordshire and South Shropshire.

GEOLOGY OF CLEE HILL

The very conspicuous physical features are due to the particular geology of the area. A paper written about 1911 by the Rev. J. D. La Touche for Field and Mackay, the owners of the Titterstone quarries describes the geology very well and reveals why the stone quarrying industry still thrives. He says, "Go back to a time when the Silurian and all the preceding strata, an enormous thickness of rocks had been deposited.

A gradual upheaval, stretching from South Wales to central England, had interposed a barrier of dry land between the ocean towards the west and what was now becoming a vast inland fresh water lake, comparable to the Caspian Sea.

Into this, as it deepened, the waters of the surrounding higher ground carried the material from which the old Red Sandstone was constructed, and which in some places attained a thickness of 4,000 feet, or about three-quarters of a mile, such being the astonishing depth which this great lake must have attained.

Subsequently, through the depression of the intervening barrier, the ocean again encroached upon the land, and a new state of things commenced. Firstly the Carboniferous Limestone was deposited in the deep water and over it, as it became more shallow and shore conditions prevailed, the Millstone Grit, and lastly, over the dreary waste of the slowly rising land, in the estuaries of the sluggish rivers and vast expanse of marsh, the beds of coal were laid down that extend over these hills and northwards into Staffordshire.

You will observe that throughout the changes that have so far been mentioned we find no indication of any violent convulsion, no sudden dislocation of strata. All seems to have been the result of a gradual imperceptible oscillation in the level of the earth's surface, altering from time to time the boundaries of land and water, and thus bringing about the deposition of a succession of sedimentary deposits.

But here we have evidence of a mighty change. At the close of the carboniferous epoch the long quiescence of the previous ages was for a time interrupted. Through fissures in the previous strata, streams of lava issued forth and covered large tracts of land.

Possibly in some places these ingneous outbursts took the form of active volcanoes, but so far as this district is concerned there is no evidence that such was the case here. Professor Geikie has observed that in very much more recent times Western America was the scene of similar eruption, a vast territory being covered with eruptive rocks which welled up through the cracks of faults in the strata beneath. Such was evidently the origin of the basalt which caps the Clee Hills. What the extent of this outflow may have been originally we have now no means of ascertaining. No sooner had the fiery stream ceased to pour forth upon the land and become consolidated into hard rock, and the district had settled down to its previous quiescence, than the usual process of denudation set in.

There can be no doubt whatsoever that at one time the beds of coal which are found on the Brown Clee Hills were continuous with those of Titterstone, upwards of seven miles to the south; and that the whole of the intermediate valley has been eaten away by the gradual process of denudation, each winter's frost disintegrating some portion of the rock, and each shower that falls on its surface carrying off to the ocean its quota of the soil thus formed.

Thus the surface of all the surrounding countryside was gradually lowered, leaving these hills protected by the cap of igneous rock that covers them.

Around the Titterstone the regular succession of strata of Old Red, the Carboniferous Limestone, the Millstone grit and the Coal Measures may be fairly made out in their relative position, but here, the extreme disturbance to which the district has been subject has resulted in such an amount of faulting that the sequence is much less distinct.

And now a few words on what is perhaps the most striking feature in the geology of these hills, the eruptive rock which severs their surface.

On Abdon Burf this does not exist in situ, but on Titterstone the clearest evidences have been established of its origin.

It had long been known that in sinking pits for coal the miners encountered a sheet of Dhustone of a thickness in some places of 64 yards, proving that it must have been erupted subsequently to the deposition of the coal measures, but the source of this antiflow was finally determined, and has thus been described by Sir R. Murchison: "To prove the width and nature of the basaltic dyke or Dhustone fault ... a shaft was sunk close to the side of the wall of basalt which there (on the Titterstone) rises to a height of 50 to 60 feet above the lower ground where the mouth of the shaft was placed ...... After penetrating about 20 feet of rotten Dhustone, various measures were passed through and three or four beds of coal well known in these hills were proved."

On following up these seams of coal in the direction of the basalt mass they were found "to change their character, to become lighter and of little value, *and still nearer the basalt they were completely changed into a sort of dull, sooty substance, in which the dull structure of coal was lost, but in which were disseminated many small flakes of anthracite.*

These seams of coal were more over found to be slightly turned up as they approached the eruptive rock, which is just what might be expected from the protrusion of this mass through their substance. The width of the basaltic dyke was ascertained to be about 150 yards and thus the existence of a subterranean core of solid basalt, which in its heated condition charred the coal seams which it penetrated was well established."

Sir Roderick tells us that though similar evidence has been obtained of a like core of igneous rock at Abdon Burf, there is every reason to believe that beneath the summit of the hill there exists a solid unfathomable mass of this rock, that "this was a funnel eruption, and that from this point the igneous matter flowed over and covered the coal measures of Clee Burf, for there the basalt is a mere sheet which has been repeatedly penetrated in search of coal. If such were the case, however, vast changes must have taken place since the emission of the basalt, for there is no longer any continuity between the mass on the summit of the Clee Burf and the point of the eruption on Abdon Burf the higher and lower summit being separated by a depression occupied by the old red sandstone.

The relative altitude however of the two hills tend to favour the belief that the basalt capping the lower hill originally descended from the higher point of eruption, the intervening or connecting mass having since been denuded.''

LOCAL KNOWLEDGE OF THE BASALT'S CHARACTERISTICS

Clee Hill people have excavated coal for centuries and by 1790 more than forty pits were working. In order to reach coal, tunnels had to be made into the side of the Hill or as Rev. Touche mentioned, vertical shafts had to be sunk right through the basalt cap.

Tremendous determination and effort were necessary to sink such a shaft because only comparatively primitive tools were available to penetrate this exceptionally hard rock. The method used was called 'jumping holes.'

An iron rod was pounded until a hole about six inches deep was made into the rock. Laboriously a circle of holes was made, each hole being about six inches from its neighbour (see fig. 1)

Fig. 1.

A plug and feather were then used. The iron plug was a cylindrical bar, flattened on one side. (see fig. 2)

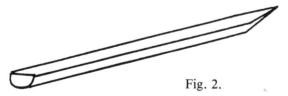

Fig. 2.

This tool was driven in turn into each hole and by its side a metal wedge called a feather was forced. This caused a split to form from one hole to the next. (see fig. 3.)

Fig. 3.

By sheer hard slog and experience these miners learnt that this durable rock would split laterally and by using crowbars, chains and horses, six inches depth of rock could be moved at a time. This was the method used to penetrate as much as 100 yards of rock. Therefore years before the stone quarrying developed as a commercial industry local people understood the stone and utilised it to build their cottages. Hill farmers built stone walls to enclose land in which to retain their sheep and cattle. Local churches and villages were built from the stone too.

If one looks carefully at the bracken strewn hillsides from a suitable vantage point, numerous small cottages with their fertile enclosures make a striking contrast with their sparse, rugged surroundings. The enormous stepped chimneys are quite a feature and no doubt the early squatters exerted their rights knowing that by building a chimney, through which smoke could pass within twenty-four hours, they could claim that land. A cottage was then built onto the chimney and little by little small paddocks were enclosed and a holding created. The availability of stone and the knowledge of its properties acquired by miners encouraged this progression.

But as the stone and coal industries developed I am told by older local residents that Lords of the Manor who had industrial interests actively encouraged squatters to develop properties and charged them a rent of a shilling (5p) or so.

THE NAME, CLEE HILL DHU STONE

How did the Clee Hill Dhu Stone get its name? Vivian Bird in his book, 'Exploring the West Midlands' says that Cleo derives from Old English Clifu, which means group on a slope. This certainly makes sense. Bill G. J. Copley's book 'Names and Places' states that Claeg means clay. Those without knowledge of the area may say clay bears no relation to the large basalt cap which dominates it, but many different coloured clays have been found on Clee Hill and when taking test borings to decide the future of the Belfry Quarry, Mr. Lambert Matthews discovered beautiful clay more than sixty feet thick. What is more obvious is the way locals pronounce Clee as Klá.

Essy Lane runs from Clee Hill main road near the Royal Oak public house and joins Caynham Road near Knowbury House. At the top of the lane's steep hill there was a coal pit. Regular loads were transported to Knowbury's Brickyard. This was situated in Bennett's End road at the bottom of the first steep hill where there is now a housing site. Essy Lane's hill caused great problems. On more than one occasion when cart-horses stumbled and fell, their loaded wagons slipped over the top of them, crushing them on the road.

An incline railway brought clay from a lower level to the Brickyard, where it was pulverised in a large, shallow container. Inside, paddles beat the clay, knocked out all the air and with the aid of water, made it pliable. (see fig 1).

26

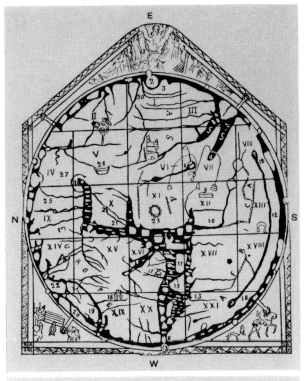

A key to the Ancient Mapa Mundi. Numbers 19, 20 and 22 depict The British Isles.

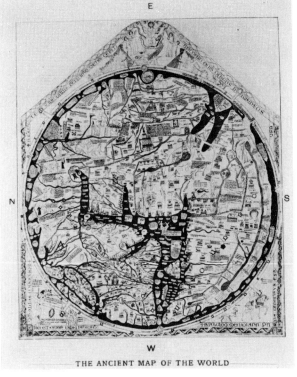

The only hills shown on this ancient map of Britian are Titterstone Clees.

THE ANCIENT MAP OF THE WORLD

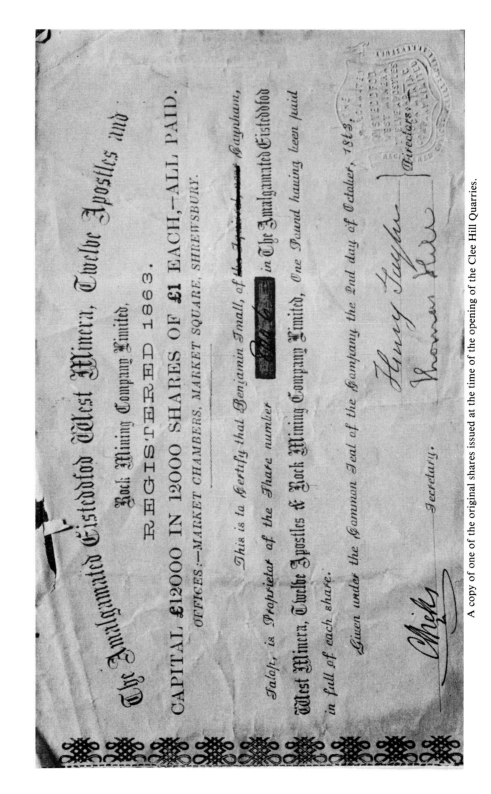

A copy of one of the original shares issued at the time of the opening of the Clee Hill Quarries.

The Dhu Stone Quarry between 1890 and 1900

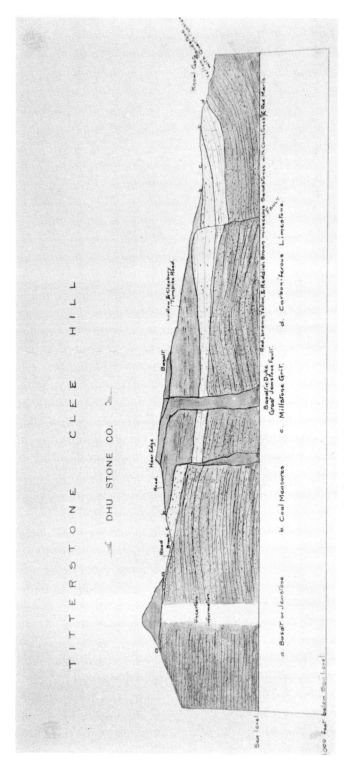

TITTERSTONE CLEE HILL

DHU STONE CO.

Titterstone Clee and Dhustone.

Geological details of Titterstone Clee and Dhustone.

Owners of Clee Hill coal mines and those who developed the Quarrying Industry encouraged potential workmen to squat on the common land. This aerial view shows how the squatters' properties gradually expanded

Mr. Clarke, the gentleman who designed the Bitterley/Dhu Stone incline and was responsible for the development of the Dhu Stone sett making industry.

The railway incline viewed from the Dhu Stone bridge. 1958.

LUDLOW ROAD, CLEE HILL.

Clee Hill Village 1903.

Rouse Boughton Terrace, Dhustone, Clee Hill.

Raphael Tuck & Sons L^d
London.

Dhu Stone Village early 1900, showing Rouse Boughton Terrace and the Village Hall on the left.
Both of these Villages and Titterstone Cottages were built to house quarry workmen.

Sett Making: Using a 28lb hammer to break boulders to manageable sizes.

Stones roughly prepared for sett making.

Sett makers' sheds

Loading setts for Scunthorpe.

A load of setts for Cheltenham

Outside the old Clee HIll School in 1950s, showing the use of setts for edging pavements and building walls. Criterion cafe in the background.

Having a well earned rest. Note the bandage around the left hand. Hands were continually cut and scarred by sharp chips of rock.

The Foreman Mr. Morris. Finished setts on the right and waste chips on the left.

A sett maker's hammer and finished sett.

The last sett makers on Clee Hill. 1958.

The making of a sett. The rock to be shaped is held and turned by the left hand while the chipping hammer is controlled by the right. 1940.

Dhu Stone Quarry early 1940s. In the centre is foreman Mr. Charlie Lucas. Incline winding gear can be seen behind the men and horses. To the left on the hill top is the 'bell house'. Its bell was always rung before blasting and knocking off time.

Dhu Stone early 1900s. The Grand father of Dennis Crowther stands on the left of the picture. He is wearing a small leather apron which protected the body and clothes when lifting a 'reek un pon'.

Dhu Stone. Most quarrymen tied their trousers below the knees with leather straps or string, known as 'Yarks'. Note the mufflers, or Clee Hill collars and ties worn by the workmen.

Dhu Stone. These wooden trucks were in regular use before the triangular metal ones were introduced. Groups of men are seen 'nappin' stone in the background.

Dhu Stone. The stone face. The cracks are a clear warning that rock may fall at any time, especially during frosty weather.

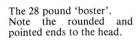The 28 pound 'boster'. Note the rounded and pointed ends to the head.

A new fall of rock being broken into manageable sizes. Note that none of the workmen wore protective headgear.

Dhu Stone 1930s.
Loading stone.

Dhu Stone 1930s.
Loading stone.

Dhu Stone 1930s. General
view of quarry. The horse
driver had to collect stone
from each group of work-
men on a rota basis.

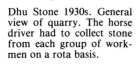

1930s Dhu Stone Quarry. Working beneath the face.

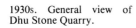1930s. General view of Dhu Stone Quarry.

Dhu Stone 1930s. Loads of stone on their way to the crusher.

Dhu Stone Quarry incline 1930s.

Dhu Stone. Tipping stone into the crusher. Note the wooden 'sprag' inserted into the wheel to act as a brake.

Clear view of a 'sprag'.

CLEE HILL BASALT.

Railways over which Clee Hill Stone travels to its destination.

Titterstone Quarries, Bitterley, Ludlow.

This railway network on an England map in 1910 shows the distribution of stone from Clee Hill Quarries.

CLEE HILL GRANITE QUARRIES

Granite Quarry in 1903.

Crushing Plant & Loading Bins,
Granite Quarries

HARPER. PHOTO. LUDLOW.

Granite Quarry early 1900 showing stone crusher and full trucks leaving the loading bins.

Granite Quarry railway sidings and 'nappin' stone area situated just by the Craven Arms public house near Clee Hill Village. 1900.

Granite Quarry 1903, showing the same area as that of the previous photograph. Clearly seen are the neat piles of setts waiting to be loaded onto the Dhu Stone/Bitterley railway, railway inclines, crusher and shunting engine.

Granite Quarry railway sidings early 1900s. On the left a traction engine can be seen and in the background, right Craven Place. On the wall of this building is a plaque showing when the quarries began. For many years since the building has been the quarry offices.

Granite quarry sidings 1910-20.

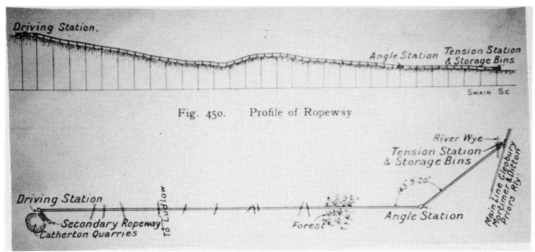

Fig. 450.   Profile of Ropeway.

Aerial Ropeway from Magpie Quarry to Detton

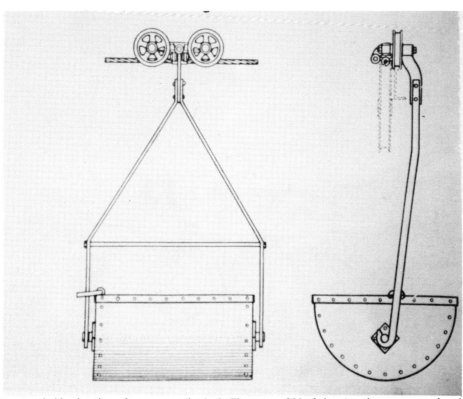

Front and side elevation of a ropeway 'bucket'. There were 256 of these on the ropeway and each carried half a ton of stone.

Crusher and machinery at the beginning of the ropeway.

The Secondary Ropeway which took the stone from the quarry to the main ropeway and loaded the buckets or skips onto the main line too.

Ropeway driving station. A loaded bucket can be seen moving onto the ropeway. In the background right, some of the fifty-five trestles which carried the ropeway can be faintly seen.

Ropeway angle station. (see ropeway profile).

Ropeway bins near Detton Ford which could hold 1800 tons of stone.

How the steel rope was delivered to the ropeway site. It weighed 35 tons and was 3½″ in circumference.

Clee Hill Ropeway. From the Hill

Showing pylons and buckets looking towards Cleeton Road.

The engine house at Magpie Quarry which supplied power for the ropeway. Photo 1900.

Ropeway terminal at Detton showing loading bins and sidings. Photo early 1900s.

Fig. 1.

Clay, in this condition was passed through a channel where it was shaped into an elongated, rectangular prism. A thin wire was brought down at regular intervals so cutting the clay to the required brick lengths. These were placed on pallets, then piled into kilns ready for baking. Two kilns shaped like enormous bottles were in operation. Each had a neck at the top to allow steam to escape. One kiln was firing while the other was being packed. Coal was used for heating and to drive the incline engine.

Knowbury bricks were in great demand and Mr. Askey, the Brickyard owner had his name printed on every one.

Notes seen in Coreley church state that in the 18th century local clay was used for properties, and the building of the church itself. Some of the old clay pit sites and brick works can still be clearly seen and others are indicated by field names as in the case of Duggan's pit, Hints Pit, Brickfields Farm, Chimney Meadow and the Brickyard. The arrival of the blast furnace led to the establishing of a large brickworks nearby at Shutfields. The site is now known as Brick-kiln Floor.

Opposite the Dhu Stone Lane junction there is a holding still known as the Potteries. When I was a child the farm belonged to Mr. Ernie Everall and the Dhu Stone quarry horses roamed freely over its fields at nights and week-ends. Earlier maps show it as The Potteries and foundations of the works may still be seen. This pottery specialised in making bread and milk steens. Ewers, cider jars and gallon stoneware bottles were also made. Mrs. Martin of the Row on Angel Bank used tall jugs for mulling cider and these were made at the works too.

Vivian Bird also talks of a place in Ireland known as Cleenish because it has twin lakes. The name is from a Celtic word meaning cloven or cut in two. Readers will recall that my geological information states that the Brown Clee and Titterstone Clee were one continuous cap of basalt before the central area between the twin peaks was eroded away, so cutting the area into two.

Dhu Stone took its name from a word which has long been used to describe the stone. Dhu is the Celtic word for black. The weathered stone lying on the Hill side is black but I have noticed that when freshly quarried stone is split, it reveals a lovely crystaline blue. However after a short period of exposure it gradually becomes much darker in colour.

DHU STONE COMPANY

When this company was formed, road surfaces were atrocious and horse and cart was a very slow method of transportation. Therefore there were sensible reasons why Clee Hill stone had only been used locally. However for more than three centuries coal and iron had been transported by this method to places as far away as Bringewood and even Hereford.

As the railways developed the Great Western became interested in capturing the coal trade and they looked into the possibility of building a spur from the Hereford-Shrewsbury route.

A Mr. Clarke was appointed to plan and build the spur from Ludlow via Bitterley to the Dhustone and on to Craven Place in Clee Hill village. The project began in the late 1850s and was completed about 1860.

With the help of local knowledge Mr. Clarke discovered that the dhu stone would split and he employed numerous men to shape it into cubes called 'setts'. These he used to build retaining side walls, bridges, loading wharfs and a sound foundation for the railway.

It was possible to construct a railway from Ludlow to Bitterley on a gradual gradient which could be negotiated by an engine and train, but from Bitterley to the Dhu Stone an incline had to be constructed. It was an ingenious, effective piece of engineering. For practically its entire length it had three rails, but halfway down the hill there was a turn-out of four rails. This enabled the descending full trucks to pass the ascending empty trucks. Not only did the three rails reduce cost but they also reduced the width of the incline to a minimum, necessitating the least possible amount of excavating into the hill side.

Just above my home a 'drum house' was built to house a huge wooden drum and metal wheel around which was wound a wire rope, the ends of which were attached to the ascending and descending trucks.

The completed incline for which Mr. Clarke received a designing fee of £50 did promote the coal industry but it also encouraged the rapid growth of the stone industry.

Up to that time the very small quantity of stone which was used for roads in the immediate vicinity mainly consisted of boulders taken from the slopes of the hills, from pit shaft excavations and from a few places which were little more than slight excavations or burrow holes here and there. The transportation to Ludlow was very expensive and as a consequence the stone had little more than a local reputation. Suddenly trains could transport large quantities of stone great distances at a very reasonable cost.

Mr. Clarke's attention had been directed to the suitability of the Hill stone for road and building purposes and he knew that although it was terribly hard it contained minute jointing cracks caused by the rapid cooling process which occurred during its evolution. These cracks are not always visible on the surface, but the fact that they exist enabled men to break the stone either by using huge hammers or by lighting fires near huge boulders. The heat generated turned the moisture within the cracks to steam. Expansion took place and the cracks burst open. In my childhood I noted that at the end of the quarrymen's working day they still lighted fires for this purpose. This enabled them to use wedges next morning to prise open the boulders.

In 1855 tenders were offered for the building of Cardiff docks. Mr. Clarke agreed to attempt the task provided he could use Clee Hill stone. With others including a Colonel Patchett, Mr. Clarke secured the Hill running from Limer's Gate, a length of some one and half miles. At once the opening up of the Dhu Stone quarry commenced.

Men were imported from Wales, Scotland, Ireland and many parts of England and by 1860 between 1500 and 2000 men were working in the quarrying industry.

Bitterley and Clee Hill villages increased in size. The ascending trucks on the Bitterley, Dhu Stone line carried barrels of stout, bags of corn, meal and a wide variety of goods for workers and families.

By the Golden Cross public house in Clee Hill village, the Goods Shed lane leads past nearby houses up the hill side. Here, by the side of the railway a large store shed was built to house delivered provisions, and so the railway spur exported the stone rapidly for quarry owners and imported necessities to local business - men and houses.

A network of lines leading from the quarry face was constructed to transport large stones to the sett makers' sheds. Horses pulled trucks loaded with finished setts to inclines which descended to a tipping wharf near the newly developed Dhu Stone village.

A little further along the Dhu Stone line near the Pit Ground and Spring Field Farm a very large wooden shed was built to house a locomotive engine. Its job was to shunt trains of full size railway trucks from the loading wharf to the top of the main incline where they were hooked onto the drum house rope and gently released down the slope.

The lowering of a train of full trucks and the pulling up of a train of empties was locally known as a trip. A special truck with a braking mechanism known as a dummy was linked to the front of each group of trucks.

Trips ran at regular half hour intervals from early morning until dusk and a few years later oil lamp stands were placed along the track to enable work to continue until late evening.

THE SETT MAKING CRAFT

When Cardiff Docks were completed, Clee Hill stone had earned an excellent reputation. Soon vast quantities were being used for road surfaces and town and city centres all over England. The demand continued to increase until about 1920 when other less dusty surfaces were developed. The stone sett industry of Clee Hill Quarrying did not end until the late 1950s; this was much later than any other area in Britain.

I was fortunate in 1958 to see the last six men working at this craft. They were between fifty and seventy years of age and each one had been perfecting his skill since leaving school at the age of thirteen.

Why did the industry die? The reasons were that better methods of road surfacing developed, reinforced concrete blocks were used instead for edging pavements and finally no young man was prepared to learn the craft. This did not surprise me because sett makers' hands were not a pretty sight. Nevertheless these old craftsmen were extremely proud of the near perfect cubes and rectangular prisms they produced from the terrifically hard stone.

Near the quarry face from which the stone was obtained, four men were employed to crack stones, three feet high and five feet wide, into suitable sizes from which setts could be made. They used 28lb (13 kilo) hammers.

By knowing the nature of the stone, listening to the ring of the hammer and striking the stone two or three times, it could be miraculously cracked. After endeavouring to emulate them I respected their ability. I raised a hammer above my head, brought it down with all my strength only to see it bounce uncontrollably off the stone.

The face men shaped the boulders into very large, rectangular prisms which were transported to the sett makers' sheds. Around these, considerable stacks of finished setts measuring 3″ x 4″, 4″ x 4″, 4″ x 6″, and 3″ x 5″ were piled. Other sizes were made for special orders.

The craftsman I observed, frequently sat on the shed floor with a wooden block infront of him. In one hand he held a roughly shaped sett on the block and with the other hand he used the appropriate hammer. His hands were bound with scraps of cloth which covered gnarled and cut knuckles. The sett was rotated with the dexterity of a gambler's die and chipped with the precision of a sculptor, although comparatively clumsy hammers were used.

Firstly the sett maker used a large hammer to split the stone, then a dressing hammer, which had two sharp edges. With this tool he chipped one face until it was flat and true then another side at right angles to the first. What takes a few lines to describe took many minutes for an experienced craftsman to achieve. All subsequent stages were worked from those two prepared surfaces. The required width and thickness were marked with a cold chisel and the waste areas carefully chipped away to complete the sett.

A craftsman's easy relaxed working rhythm always makes a task look easy, but at my first attempt I found that I either missed the stone or hit it awkwardly so jarring the hammer out of my hand. I was told that if I looked directly along the edge of the hammer I would have more success but I could not maintain the steady rocking movement which these men effortlessly achieved.

Having seen cold chisels being used to mark widths and thicknesses, I asked why they were not used to cut the stone instead of a hammer. I was told because the stone was so hard it blunted the chisels very quickly. It was much easier to manipulate the sett with one hand and use a hammer with the other and if a chisel was used the sett could not be held rigidly.

The sett maker had two dressing hammers. Whilst one was in use the other was at the quarry blacksmith's shop because the craftsman had to have a freshly ground hammer each day.

I watched the sharpening process. Firstly the head of the hammer was removed and heated in the forge. From there it was placed in a snuggly fitting mould and held firmly. The edges of the head were beaten and burred over and this process was continued until the burr was weak enough to be broken off. The hammer head was cooled and the edges ground sharp.

A good sett maker could produce a ton per day and according to the manager at that time, it would have been possible to have sold greater quantities if more could have been produced. The last day I saw these men working, loads of six tons of setts were leaving for Cheltenham and Scunthorpe. They were to be used mainly for kerbing stones but many went regularly to line mills which ground silica for the manufacture of pottery. Dhustone was also used for the making of Charnwood safes.

At the Dhu Stone, while the sett making industry developed and declined, other forms of stone were produced for road surfaces and other uses.

Mr. Clarke believed that the toughness of Clee Hill stone could not be equalled by any other in the kingdom. Crushing experiments had been carried out at Kirkaldy where a 3″ cube crushed only under pressure of 1808 tons per square foot. Further tests were made by Messrs. Robertson and Coltman which gave a crushing pressure of 3147 tons per square foot. Sandstones and limestones readily crushed and were considered virtually useless for road surfaces but these few facts illustrate the tremendous strength of Clee Hill stone.

The Clee Hill railway spur enabled the stone to be transported at reasonable cost to counties 200 miles away. After long trial periods under the most severe conditions in London, Windsor, Ealing, Crewe, Manchester, other large towns, and at railway approaches where there was heavy and continuous traffic the stone was in regular use. It had asserted its supremacy. By 1910 the output of Clee Hill quarries was over 400,000 tons per annum. There were still approximately 2,000 men and boys employed and indirectly, many more benefited by the industry.

As much as twenty shillings (£1) was paid in those days for railway carriage, and this excluded after cartage to the sites, often in districts where stone, gravel and pebbles etc. were available at a trivial cost.

Between 1860 and 1900 the Dhu Stone demonstrated its superiority as a road surface. Demand increased and new quarries began in the area. In 1867 Mr. Thomas Roberts, who had been associated with Mr. Clarke in railway construction in India, opened up the Clee Hill Granite Company and in 1881 Mr. McKay commenced work at Titterstone; and so there were three companies working in friendly rivalry developing the stone trade.

CLEE HILL GRANITE CO. LTD.

The Clee Hill Granite Co. quarries were situated quite near to Clee Hill Village at an altitude of about 1,300 feet above sea level. There were two separate works called the Granite quarries and Catherton quarries, nearly two miles apart with a series of workings at various levels.

The business started in 1867 by Mr. Thomas Roberts of Ludlow and continued in turn by Mr. Thos. Lee Roberts and grandson Mr. R. Lee Roberts. For forty years the Clee Hill Granite Co. devoted its energies to quarrying on the Western side of Clee Hill but in the early part of 1908 a beginning was made with extensive works which transformed a large barren waste on the Eastern side, into a mineral producing station throbbing with life and industry. An aerial ropeway three and a half miles long to connect these new works with Cleobury Mortimer and Ditton Priors Light Railway, was opened in February 1909.

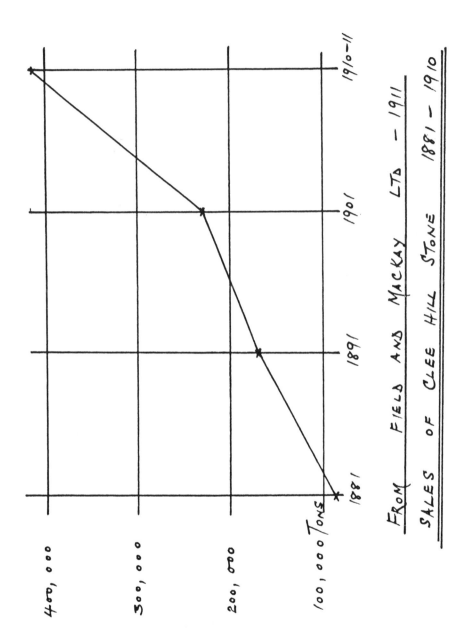

FROM FIELD AND MACKAY LTD — 1911

SALES OF CLEE HILL STONE 1881 — 1910

The Clee Hill basalt is one of four varieties and the hardness of this stone gave rise to the term granite in the Company's title. The Clee Hill granite is described by the geological Museum Authorities as follows:-

'Olivine - diabase or dolerite, or rather coarse-grained, and fairly fresh. The olivine appears in clusters of rounded grains, the augite is smaller, irregular grains, and the plagioclase felspar in long, lath-shaped crystals.'

The rock is a distinct bluish-green colour which gave the quarry face a most picturesque appearance. It extended right through the Hill from the Granite Quarries to Catherton workings and it was thought that the supply was practically inexhaustible.

The output of the Granite Quarries in 1911 was over 125,000 tons a year and the Catherton Plant was capable of dealing with 600 tons a day for 300 working days. Despite the great output annually, there were hundreds of millions of tons available in the Clee Hill for road making.

Many may be interested in the properties of the stone which are:-

Silica	-	48.80 per cent
Aluminium	-	13.00 per cent
-Lime	-	7.52 per cent
Magnesia	-	2.46 per cent
Ferrous Oxide	-	8.19 per cent
Ferric Oxide	-	11.27 per cent
Potash	-	2.54 per cent
Soda	-	4.12 per cent
Moisture	-	0.45 per cent
Combined water	-	1.25 per cent
Magnesium, Titanium		
Fluarine and loss		0.40 per cent
		100.00 per cent
Specific gravity -		2.8.67

As did the Dhu Stone Quarries, the Granite Company supplied setts for tramway work, channelling and paving, rough stone for concrete drives, footpaths and binding material.

The Clee Hill stone, owing to its toughness and weather resistance properties, had great wearing qualities, and formed, according to the experience of many surveyors, a perfect road metalling. It was an extremely economical road stone and had the further advantage of producing little dust in dry weather, or mud in wet. There were between 400 and 450 men employed at the Granite Quarries at the time of the opening of the Catherton extension and the numbers were considerably augmented as a result of the opening of this important development.

The main problem which the Company had to face in opening the Catherton extension quarries was not so much the method of quarrying or crushing the stone, as the transporting it from a precipitous hill across bog and wood, road and river, rough commonland and cultivated ground, to the nearest line of railway. The problem of haulage, apart from the engineering difficulties inseparable from the hilly district, had been fully solved at the Granite quarries. These workings were connected by the six mile Dhu Stone spur and incline with the GWR and London and NW Railway Company's Shrewsbury and Hereford Line at Ludlow.

However, earlier the Railway Companies had refused to extend their line beyond Craven Place and the Granite Company had to build a network of rails from the quarries and build a loading wharf. This was costly work, but when completed it was capable of holding 27 railway trucks at one time and the Company had three main locomotives and further smaller ones nearer the quarries, constantly traversing the network of rails from the various faces. These fed the numerous mineral trains which left the Clee Hill daily for the paved and tarmacadam outer world.

THE CATHERTON EXTENSION

Since 1865 quarrying methods had developed considerably. These new workings contained several features of interest including the ropeway and crushing machinery.

The bottom of the rock was 1325 feet above sea level and a platform was constructed at 1300 feet level giving a natural fall from the quarry face to a secondary line.

The crushing was performed by Marsden's Lever machines erected on pedestals of concrete blocks 20 feet high. They were driven by a vertical engine made by the builders of the ropeway. After being crushed the stone gravitated down through screens and bunkers at the foot of which were shoots for filling the enormous buckets of the ropeway.

Each machine had three bunkers, taking 2¼ inch and 2½ inch broken stone. The setts and rough or unbroken stone each had a separate loading dock.

THE ROPEWAY

A much more difficult and complicated position had to be faced on the Catherton side of the Hill. To connect the new workings with the nearest line railway, 3½ miles of country had to be bridged by different means from those usually employed in British quarries. The nature of the ground was wholly unsuitable for the building of a railway. Several schemes of traction were examined and discarded in turn, before the directors decided that a ropeway would best meet the requirements of the Company and the district.

Direct communication with the great trunk lines of the United Kingdom was by that time available to the district by a light railway running from Ditton Priors to the little town of Cleobury Mortimer, where a junction was made with the Great Western line.

The nearest point on the light railway from Catherton Quarries was Detton Ford, on the River Rea, which tumbles down from the Brown Clee in a wild race to the Teme, which is itself swallowed up in the Severn eventually.

One of the chief difficulties in constructing a ropeway from the quarries to Detton Ford was the impossibility of getting a straight line between the two points. This difficulty was overcome by the building of an angle station 3 miles from Catherton to divert the ropeway from its primary direction into a new straight line leading direct to its destination. There was a train to guide the pulleys at each side of the angle station. These were placed on their sides and were arranged so that the rope could take an easy sweep of 143 degrees. The ropeway was apparently one of the longest, and most remarkable in construction of its kind in the United Kingdom. It was 3½ miles in length and was built throughout by Messrs. J. M. Henderson and Company of Aberdeen, under the superintendence of the Company's engineer Mr. G. F. Grover of Southampton Street, Bloomsbury.

The system of the ropeway may be defined as that by which a single endless running rope performed the dual functions of supporting and transporting loads. The rope 3½ inches in circumference was 7 miles long and was made by a well known local firm Messrs. Edge and Sons of Shifnal. It weighed 35 tons and was delivered to the site in four lengths coiled on large wooden drums, off which it was run directly into position on the line. The four sections were joined together by long splices. These were each 50 feet in length. Tension gear was necessary to keep the rope taut, but stretching due to climatic changes and wear was allowed for. In fact it could stretch 75 feet before it was necessary to cut out a portion and splice both ends. The driving station was at the highest point of the ropeway and was constructed of steel sections. The driving wheel was on a vertical shaft 17 feet 6 inches above the ground and was between 10 and 12 feet in diameter. The rim of the wheel was provided with two grooves lined with teak which enabled the rope to run with perfect evenness. It lay directly in one of these grooves. The driving station was surrounded by a platform.

The ropeway was driven by a 30 nominal horse-power vertical engine, constructed by Messrs. J. M. Henderson and Company. Between the driving station and the lower terminal at Detton Ford the rope was borne on 55 trestles. The average distance between them was 300 feet and they varied in height from 58 feet to 30 feet, and gave the minimum clearance of 14 feet at any point. The stone was carried down the rope in buckets, of which there were 256 on the rope, 128 on each side, and 14 spares for loading. Each bucket had a capacity of 10 hundredweight and with its full load, its clip for automatic fastening on the rope and pulley wheels for passing round the shunt rails at the terminals and the angle station, weighed about 15 hundredweight. The buckets were placed about 50 yards apart.

In order to obtain the greatest economy in cost of loading the stone into the skips, a short line was built from the driving station to the quarry. This extension was about 230 yards long and was called a secondary ropeway. On it there was a series of short rails or short sidings. These enabled the skips to be released from the rope where required and taken to various points to be filled. They then passed along the short rails back to the rope then round the end of the secondary ropeway to the driving station and back onto the main ropeway.

On the loadside of each trestle were four groove pulleys and on the unload side two, carried on compensating beams. The bucket clips glided evenly over these pulleys, and in about three quarters of an hour after loading at the quarries the stone reached the lower terminal ready for unloading into wagons in the Company's siding at the light railway. The rope travelled at 5 miles an hour, and was capable of bringing a ton a minute to the unloading terminal.

The lower terminal had an altitude of 40 feet. The shunt rails here ran round to the top of great bins where the process of unloading the stone was carried out. The bins formed a huge steel structure capable of holding 1,500 tons of Clee Hill stone. This receptacle was divided into six compartments and fitted with Broadbent's hopper doors, to hold the different sizes of stone sent down in the buckets from the quarries. Each bin capable of holding about 250 tons was 60 feet long, 30 feet high and 30 feet wide. The framework and partitions were lined with spruce 3 inches thick. A platform encircled the whole structure which enabled the men to pass along by the shunt rails and tip the stone into specified bins.

The buckets were then set on the return shunt rails to the endless rope where they again began their journey for the quarries. The stone was practically untouched from the time it left the quarry until it was automatically loaded through the hopper doors into the trucks, which were arranged in the sidings underneath the bins. Three extensive sidings, connected with the light railway, had been laid down, two passing underneath the bins and one outside them, for the purpose of loading direct into the trucks. When the Clee Hill stone train was finally made up it passed to the Cleobury Mortimer light railway. This had been opened just before the ropeway had been completed.

TITTERSTONE QUARRIES

When viewed from Ludlow the old workings can clearly be seen on the left of the mountain near to and above the villages of Bitterlcy and Titterstone Cottages.

The quarries were opened by Messrs. Field and MacKay on May 1st 1881 and on February 27th 1911, for family reasons, the firm was registered as a private, limited company. The quarries were on the edge of the Titterstone Clee range and adjoined the 'funnel of eruption'. But before the quarries could begin a railway had to be laid from Bitterley to Titterstone. A reservoir was built to retain water in Benson's Brook near Titterstone Cottages. This was used to drive turbines which generated power for a stone crusher. This enabled stone to be crushed to the necessary sizes for the laying of the Bitterley - Titterstone incline railway.

It may be asked why coal was not used to generate power, because the Dhu Stone Company had supplies near at hand which it already used to power winding gear etc. The reason was that Field and MacKay would have had to have purchased coal from the Dhu Stone or the Granite Company and it was preferred to use the natural water available to their own company, and so this system continued until Titterstone Quarries were fully operative.

Then the Titterstone Cottages were built by Field and MacKay to accommodate quarry men and soon acquired the nickname Bedlam. This is not a name the locals appreciate because it does not reflect the quiet atmosphere of the community. In the early 1920s when a Mr. Aves was head of Bitterley Grammar School, he stated that if you walked from Titterstone Cottages towards the hill top, through the common gate, you soon arrived at the end of enclosed land. If you turned left and continued along the common land hedge, it was possible to find the remains of a building. This was originally a hospital for those with disturbed minds. The wailing and anxious cries from this establishment created bedlam and this is the source of the continued nickname.

When Titterstone quarries became operative Clee Hill stone was already famous and by the 1900s it had increased its reputation amongst surveyors as being the best stone in the country for road metalling.

In 1904 reliability trials for small cars were carried out in Herefordshire. Over thirty vehicles competed in the runs of one hundred miles daily for a week. The drivers, observers and newspaper correspondents were very enthusiastic in their praise of the roads made of stone from Clee and Titterstone, both on account of their excellent surface and their freedom from dust.

The floor level of Number 1 quarry at Titterstone was 1,520 feet above sea level whilst the floor of the East Quarry, which was opened in October 1910 to cope with increased demand for stone, was 1558 feet above sea level.

The stone was sent down the self acting incline railway, which was over a mile in length, to a wharf at Bitterley some 800 feet below the level of the quarries. The quarry wagons carried 2½ tons and each train carried 15 tons. The incline had a capacity for 600 tons of stone per day. The wharf at Bitterley afforded easy tipping into the main line wagons and when Titterstone, Dhu Stone and Granite Quarries were all operative, two locomotives were in continual use from Ludlow to Bitterley.

A large number of men known as hand breakers were used to break stone at the top and bottom of the incline and large quantities of hand broken stone of different sizes were always available.

At the beginning of the 1900s two new stone breaking plants were erected and in 1911 a crusher of improved design was completed. This machine cleverly broke and screened the stone to produce samples equal if not superior to that broken by hand.

The original crushers had one stone breaking machine in each plant, and this did all the work, reducing the stone from the size it was quarried to the size required, and the product was screened by a short revolving screen 2 feet diameter and 18 inches long. This improved method passed the stone through a series of three machines in each plant, gradually reducing it from 12 inches to 2½ inches; then through two screens; the first one took out all the larger pieces, whilst the second one, 4 feet diameter and 30 feet long sorted it into its component parts, ranging from dust to 2½ inches as required. The stone was subjected to less crushing by this process and was broken into a more cubical form.

37

At that time Field and MacKay Ltd listed the following materials in stock:—

MACADAM

Handbroken stone, 2½", 2¼", 2".

Machine broken stone, 2½", 2¼", 2", 1¾", 1½", 1¼".

23 cwt of broken stone measured 1 cubic yard. Other sizes were available to order.

SCREENINGS

Clean 1", suitable for light patching

½", suitable for pathways and binding.

⅜ ", suitable for pathways and binding.

¼", suitable for pathways and binding, concrete and granolithic paving.

The ½", ⅜ ", and ¼" could be supplied perfectly cubical if desired.

MIXED

Dust to ¾", dust to ½", dust to ¼", suitable for pathways and bindings.

Large rough stone for breaking. Small rough stone for foundations and new roads.

SETTS

Size	Length	Area covered by one ton	
3 x 4 "	4 to 6"	5¼ square yards	
3 x 5 "	5 to 8"	4¼	,, ,,
3 x 6 "	6 to 9"	3⅓	,, ,,
4 x 4 "	4 to 6"	5¼	,, ,,
4 x 4	4" cubes	5¼	,, ,,

A great deal of research was being done to ascertain the best materials for road surfaces at this time because it was only poor, pot holed surfaces which minimised road transport. Mr. Thomas Wright FRS wrote a very interesting article about Clee Hill Stone in the Cheltenham Examiner. He obviously had great respect for the stone's qualities but others were not as enthusiastic, as the article reveals. However it was impressive enough for Field and MacKay to use in their publications booklet in 1911. It does make apparent too that although road rollers made surfaces far more compact, pedestrians, shopkeepers and vehicles experienced many difficulties which have disappeared since the introduction of tar macadam.

To quote, 'Several years ago I was asked by two active members of the late Board of Commissioners, "What kind of stone would you, as a geologist, recommend as the best and most durable rock for use as a road making material?"

In compliance with the request I made a careful study of the subject and visited several different localities to examine certain rocks on site. During my investigation I recollected that when a boy, I had learned that the Basalts and

Dolerites of the Campsie Hill near Glasgow, the Melaphynes of the Gleniffer Braes, and Neilston Padd, Renfrewshire, all varieties of basalt were famous rocks, then locally known as "whenstone" and "whin-sill" in the north of England with which most of the adjoining highways were repaired.

This induced me to turn my attention to some specimens of basalt I had obtained from Clee Hill Quarries in Shropshire, and which upon examination, I found to resemble very closely the Scottish whinstones I so well remembered. I had therefore no hesitation in recommending the Basalt of Clee Hill as by far the best rock I had met with in my enquiry, as a good, hard, tough, and durable road material, at the same time informing my friends that this was an igneous, eruptive rock, composed of crystals of several different minerals, and would require to be fragments not too large and of an average size, and such would readily pass through a ring gauge of a certain diameter, that when the stones were laid on the road, they must be set in place by chippings and debris of the same hard Basalt rock, and which could be obtained in any quantity from the quarries. So the Clee Hill stone was introduced to Cheltenham, and if I recollect aright, first used in repairing the promenade.

But, mark the blunder that was then made - instead of employing, as I cautioned them to use, the chippings of the same material, they mixed Bristol stone (carboniferous limestone), and broken ragstone and oolitic limestone, from the neighbouring hills, with the basalt.

At first all went well, but in a short time the road became uneven and bumpy, and so the Clee Hill stone was condemned, and the geologist likewise. I told my friends it was not the fault of the Basalt, but their own obstinacy in persisting to mix the soft limestone with a hard Basalt, as the limestone would soon wear down and be washed away, and the hard basalt would stand forth like little hills among the plain. However arguments were useless; one of my friends believing himself to be a born engineer, had also a great contempt for scientific knowledge, although always eager to avail himself of it, and so the Clee Hill Basalt was ostracised, and the Bristol stone again employed.

With the advent of the Incorporation of the Borough, came soon likewise the steam roller, and now that the Town Council had acquired increased crushing power there arose a desire for a harder and tougher material for our roads than the limestone then in use, so the Clee Hill Basalt again came to the front.

The second experiment was now made, but it appeared to me that the fragments used were too large, and after a first crushing with the steam roller, fine sand from Carlton Pits was thrown freely over the surface and washed into the interstices with a deluge of water.

I saw that another mistake had been committed which would also end in failure, seeing that the sand ran off the surface by water action. In the process of rolling, it found its way into the sewers and would silt them up, whilst the loose particles lying in the interstices of the Basaltic fragments during rainy weather, would work up to the surface by the weight of friction and continuous traffic, and thereby make a sludgy road which must be constantly scraped, or it would become impassable. All these events have happened of late simply because men will not take lessons from the teaching of natural laws.

The behaviour of the rocks to each other is a subject for experiment and observation and not for theory, so by all means when the Promenade is next to be repaired with Clee Hill stone let the chippings of the same rock be used and crushed into the interstices of the stones without any other material, and wait and watch the result, when, I think, a very desirable even surface will be obtained as the whole structure will then be of the same mineral ingredients, and be found to consolidate and wear down together. We shall then have a Basaltic road, which in the course of time, if kept properly in repair with the same material, will give us a smooth surface, in great measure free from the clouds of dust derived from the erosion of the limestone, with which we have been pestered in the summer, and with much less sludge if regularly cleared, than we have been accustomed to in the winter. But, like all other experiments the work must be thoroughly well done, and not executed in a perfunctory manner, if we expect to obtain the desired results. The practical conclusions from the foregoing remarks on the Clee Hill Basalt may be thus summarised:-

Firstly:- That the cost of the roads made from rock, and set in chippings of the same material will be at first more expensive than an admixture of basalt and limestone or sand is true, still in the long run, the work will be much more economical, and the roads permanently far superior in evenness and durability.

Secondly:- The hard, tough Basalt is very little affected by water and atmosphere, because it is a kind of glass, so that less road detrities will be produced and consequently there will be less dust in summer to the comfort and saving of the shopkeepers, and less sludge in the winter, to the delight of pedestrians and street traffickers.

Thirdly:- A Basaltic road, when once well made and kept in good repair is easily cleared, so there will be a saving of scavenger's labour, and less work for horses employed in all kinds of street vehicular traffic.'

Thomas Wright F.R.S.

No doubt Mr. Thomas Wright would have been delighted to know that in more recent times the wearing properties of Clee Hill metalled roads were so superior, that they became the yardstick by which the durability of stone from other parts of the country were compared.

WORKING IN THE QUARRIES

I mentioned earlier that the output of stone from the quarries gradually increased until the annual output between 1900 and 1910 topped 400,000 tons. This is not surprising because hours of work continued to be very long and because the coal industry was declining there was little or no alternative employment in the area; consequently wages were suppressed.

The working day for quarry face men began at approximately 6 a.m. and ended at about 5.30 p.m. In winter this meant starting at day break and finishing 'When thaa kood/nu sa,' (When they could not see). Saturday times were slightly shorter, from 6 a.m. until 4 p.m. However after 1918, week work days were reduced to 8 hours with a specific beginning and ending time and on Saturday they finished at 2 p.m.

Tom Jones from the Titrail who was 80 years of age when I talked to him in 1975, recalled that he was first employed as a tool carrier in 1908 at the age of thirteen. This meant carrying heavy hammers, shovels etc after they had been repaired and sharpened, to the face from the blacksmith's shop. It was a considerable distance. He often had to drag the heavy tools and have frequent rests along the route. He was paid 1 shilling a day (5p). This helped the family income a little but it could not have been sufficient because his mother went to extraordinary lengths to acquire more. When corn had been harvested in late summer, she walked to Tenbury Wells, obtained permission from farmers to walk through the corn fields and pick up the grains of corn. When she had collected as much as she could carry she walked home to the Titrail and by hand, ground the corn into flour before making it into bread. She clothed and fed her family, looked after the home and by candle light made smock frocks for farm labourers. These she carried to Tenbury Wells the next day to sell, then she gleaned more corn before returning home.

In the season, Tom's father travelled by horse and cart to go hop picking. When weather prevented work in the quarry, Tom accompanied him. It was too far to make the return in one day and so they slept in the barns. There were no toilets but large metal buckets were provided. When these were used in the night, the reverberating sounds woke the children. Little Tom was given the task of placing a small quantity of hay in each receptacle daily to deaden the sound. When weather was fine and the hops of good quality, children were frequently 'christened' by being thrown into a hop crib.

There were four days holiday a year, one in August, Good Friday, Easter Monday and Christmas Day, but of course there was no pay.

Like many more, Tom had to leave the quarries in 1914 because of the First World War. He was seriously injured in 1918 and considered himself lucky to return to the quarry to a much easier job of horse driving. Later he became a locomotive cleaner and finally a driver. After 50 years service he was awarded a long service medal. The locomotive he drove became obsolete and was cut up for scrap, but Tom had rescued many bits and his little cottage was festooned with them.

Wages varied according to the work. Boys of 12 and 13 who broke stone all day received 1 shilling and 2 pence per day (6p). They had to be on the site at 6 a.m. If it was raining, they waited in huts, but by 11.00 a.m. if the rain had not abated they were sent home without pay.

There was no national or local sickness arrangements and no trade union. Anyone who was ill relied on the support of neighbours, the community and local organisations, such as the Oddfellows, to which many paid a small weekly subscription.

Local remedies for cuts, bruises and wounds were regularly used. One often mentioned was Okwel Soov. This was homemade sticks of ointment which had to be heated and applied as a poultice.

Even at the beginning of the century some of the rock was removed from the quarry face by blasting. Heavy drifter drills mounted on bogies (trucks) and generated by coal heated steam boilers, were pushed on rails to the required positions. Very little gunpowder was available. Therefore only sufficient was used to dislodge boulders from their position at each blasting. The huge stones which fell from the face were too large to move by hand, therefore fires were used in the same way that the sett makers did. Great quantities of coal from local pits were used for this purpose, to ensure that there was sufficient, manageable pieces of stone available every day. Each morning face men used wedges, crow bars and hammers, known as bars and bosters to force the cracks apart and reduce the rock to smaller sizes.

Further breaking was done with 28 pound hammers (13kg). This must have been one of the most exhausting, back-breaking jobs in the industry. Many stone breakers told me that on arrival home each evening they fell asleep through exhaustion, even while having their tea. However, they must have been resilient because they recovered to dig enormous gardens and pursue other work, not because of choice usually but because of financial necessity.

George Turner began working as a wagon greaser, then he was 'promoted' to stone breaking. It was considered a skilled job. The hammer he used had a specially designed head. One side was sharpened for splitting the stones and the opposite one was rounded for bursting them open.

Like other fellow workers he began at 6 a.m. and finished about 5.30 p.m. Half an hour was allowed for breakfast and one hour for lunch. George lived at the top of Limer's Lane where the stone walls give way to open common land. His cottage, which was demolished in the 1960s, was near the lane on the Dhu Stone Quarry side and had one acre of land, plus common rights. His wage was insufficient on which to live and like everyone else in the area he had to supplement it by working all the hours which God sent. His one milking cow grazed on the common land during the day and was housed in a shed at night. George milked the cow before and after work. The animal produced manure which was used to enrich the small field and vegetable garden. Surplus skimmed milk and potato peelings were used to feed two bacon pigs. At week-ends George collected young ferns from the common. These were boiled in a furnace, washed and added to the swill tub for pig food. All the potato haulm was chopped up and fed to the cow and pigs too.

The cow supplied enough milk to help rear a calf, produce cheese, butter and milk to drink. The family kept a few poultry which provided some eggs but when they were worth one old penny each the children were not allowed to eat any of them, 'Thaay wun too de/er tu yut,' (They were too dear to eat) and so they were sold to bring in badly needed cash. George purchased sugar, considered by him a luxury and occasionally bread, but most of that was made at home.

A field gate was fixed where the Limer's Lane joined the common land. Local people supplied the materials and it was the Turner Family's responsibility to keep the gate in good repair and shut, to ensure that animals did not stray into the lane. This spot was where three parishes and more estates met. To the north and east was the land of Lord Craven; on the Bitterley side Windsor Clive, to the south i.e. the Dhu Stone area, belonged to the Rouse Boughton family and the wedge shaped area to Titterstone belonged to Earl of Plymouth. These geographical complexities could have created problems for the three quarrying companies and it was credit to them that they worked in harmony.

It is incomprehensible to realise that in addition to working ten hours a day, the majority of quarrymen walked terrific distances to and from work, from places such as Hints, Coreley, The Knowle, Knowbury, Gate Hangs Well, Hope Baggot, Bitterley, Cleobury Mortimer and even Leominster. One man named Arthur Martin walked from the Rugpits near Tenbury. He was often asked when he arrived at work, 'How are you Arthur?' His reply was 'Midlin.' No small wonder considering he had walked five miles before 6 a.m. for six days each week. He too dug a garden at night and was asked how he could possibly do this. He replied that a spade was little more than a spoon after using a 28 pound hammer.

Walking in the early morning darkness and often dense fog too was extremely hazardous. No lights were available but the well worn tracks were marked regularly by the men dropping pieces of broken crockery, known locally as 'pitch/uk'.

Once you became a stone breaking quarryman, there was little chance of further promotion, your working life finished more-or-less as you began. They were paid boy's rates until the age of eighteen then full quarrymen's wages; but if it was possible the quarry authorities dismissed young men of this age to combat rising wage bills and re-employed younger boys. Therefore those above the age of eighteen who had the opportunity to continue, considered themselves very lucky and did not complain about the wages.

Mr. Lambert Matthews, who was a quarry foreman for many years, began work in the quarries at the age of thirteen in 1911. His first job at Titterstone was to look after a small gas engine which drove a stone crusher for reducing stone to ½ inch size. Stone passed over a screen and the small dropped through while the 2½ and 3 inch was rejected. This came down a chute into a wheelbarrow and Mr. Matthews had to wheel it away and put it into piles, either to be broken further or be used as base materials for roads. Doing this job for hours on end made his limbs ache and his hands blistered to such an extent, that he often sat on the wheelbarrow and cried. But there was no escape; he had to muster more energy and think of the 9 shillings (45p) he would be paid at the end of the week.

At 16 years of age he became a horseman. This meant maintaining a steady supply of empty trucks to the men working at the face, and return the full trucks to an area called the turnout. Here the trucks were collected by a small loco which took the train either to the crushers or the railway inclines. The locomotives were in such constant use that they could not be spared for maintenance during the daytime. Instead men like Jim Griffiths from the Tank, worked throughout the night from 10 p.m. until 6 a.m. preparing them for the next day's work.

At the end of the working day during inclement weather, horses were housed in stables at each quarry, infact at Titterstone a cottage was built for the horse 'fettler', but when conditions allowed they were taken to nearby fields. It does not take much imagination to realise how early men had to catch the horses and lead them two or three miles to work by 6 a.m. Mr. Matthews found horse driving easier work and it was supposed to be better pay. However at the end of his first fortnight he received half a sovereign (50p) and this he unfortunately lost through a hole in his pocket. But his luck returned. Edwin Lewis was watching the stone working through the crusher and catching inspection samples in his hands, when miraculously the half sovereign was spied amongst the dust and stone.

Most horsedrivers became quarrymen, breaking and loading stone. They worked in groups of three at the quarry face. Stones broken into manageable sizes were stacked in piles and the many splintered chippings stacked separately. Each trio of men was paid according to the quantity of stone produced. Each gang of men comprised of ten, three groups of three and a ganger in charge. Every Friday he drew the pay for the gang and distributed it. A day's wage was approximately 5 shillings (25p). A railway track was laid to each working position. A horse driver and tram, the name given to a wooden or steel truck, carted the stone either to the crushers, the sett makers' sheds or to 'nappers', the name given to the men who broke the stone into piles of smaller stone. The horseman tried to organise his trips so that an equal number of loads were taken from each group of workers, because the gangs were paid on a piece work basis.

The loading onto trams was just as arduous as breaking stone. Each block had to be lifted by hand and smaller stone was handled with a 'reek un pon', (rake and pan). The rake had strong metal tines and was used to pull stone from the piles, onto a large dust pan shape which had two handles. When full and weighing about 25 kilo, it was hoisted to the waist and then by using knees and arm muscles, a further snatch tipped the stone into a truck. To protect their clothes, most men wore thickly woven or leather aprons. It was hard, back-breaking work and extremely difficult to maintain all day. Hands were deformed and disfigured as a result of constant battering and minor accidents. During the Second World War I remember Italian and German prisoners working in the quarries. It was significant that no matter how much pressure or persuasion was used, they refused to lift the loaded pans. Their opinion was that the pans had two handles to enable two men to lift them when full and this is what they insisted on doing.

Canteens were not provided in those days. Men built huts from the material which was easily accessible - turf. This was cut into slabs about seventy centimetres long, and used to build the hut walls. Planks were placed across to form a roof. More layers of turf were placed on top. Inside, planks were positioned around the sides on pillars of turf to form seats. When completed, these buildings were warm, sound proof and a good protection against flying splinters of rock. When canteens were introduced some years later, the men did not like waiting to be served meals and many found them too expensive. The authorities encouraged the development of canteens because it was thought they would avoid workmen having to carry food from home. Tea was provided too, so as to discourage men from drinking cider during working hours. However the canteens were forced to close after a few years because the meals, although excellent, took a disproportionate amount of wages. The men preferred the short dinner time to relax in their huts, eat their 'snappin' and consume cider. This did not please the authorities but they turned a blind eye to the fact that some young employees spent most of their time during the working day, carrying cider in earthenware jars from the Dhu Stone public house. Their great concern was of course for those who worked near the quarry face because they were in constant danger and alcohol dulled their reactions, perhaps making the difference between injury and death.

Accidents occurred frequently, especially at Titterstone. The face there was very high and often adversely affected by frost. One member of each face gang kept a constant watch on the rock and as soon as any movement was noticed everyone dropped tools and scattered as far away as possible. When boulders fell from a great height, they bounced on projecting rocks and splintered into lethal chips before reaching the ground. No one wore protective head gear and many like Ted Garbett from Random had their heads split open by such flying missiles.

Because it descended so quickly, developing mist and low cloud were more treacherous than frost. This obscured the face, and accidents often happened before work could cease. Israel Breakwell, the grandfather of local comedian Dennis Crowther came home safely from the First World War. On the first day of Spring in misty conditions, he was standing on a large boulder bursting it open with a wedge when he was killed by a sudden fall of rock.

The drinking continued and many humorous stories relate to it. One lad occupied as cider carrier became very thirsty. The temptation to have a swig became so great that he sat down and consumed a fair proportion of a jar full. Of course he was soon completely drunk. When he recovered he decided to break the base of the jar and told the workmen he had accidently tapped it while climbing over rocks. However on seeing his condition, they guessed what he had done and so he was sacked on the spot.

While waiting for weather conditions to improve, the card playing, joke telling, singing and drinking continued. Teddy Bytheway was often paralysed with cider and on one occasion when he was oblivious to his surroundings, his gang dug him a grave, turfed it around and placed him in it. They also erected a headstone. When Teddy recovered, he was understandably bewildered to find himself in a grave. He stood up and read this epitaph on the stone, 'Here lies a man, and who do you think, old Teddy Bydi, give him more drink. A drink for a dead man, for we'll tell you why, for when he was alive he was always dry'.

Persistent drinkers were threatened with dismissal but the harsh working conditions and meagre pay sometimes made them adopt a couldn't care less attitude. For instance Enoch Tennant when tottering back to work after consuming a 'skin full' was told by the foreman, "You'll have to be very careful with that drink Enoch otherwise you'll kill yourself under the face". The curt reply was, "Well I work for bloody nothing. I may as well die for the same."

Most of the rock face drilling for blasting was done by hand. Jumping tools were rotated alternately clockwise and anti-clockwise, while a partner hit the tool regularly with a hammer. Wedges were forced in to split open cracks into which the shotmen inserted explosive.

Carpenters had varied work including repairing wagons and making sprags. I have watched men use these with tremendous speed and dexterity to halt moving wagons loaded with stone. To give them sufficient strength, sprags had to be made from cleaved timber. They were about a metre in length and tapered at each end. Horse drawn, loaded trucks had no braking system. Therefore when they reached their tipping position they had to be stopped by 'spragging'. As the trucks and horses picked up speed the spragman ran alongside. It was difficult to see the spokes of the steel truck wheels as they rotated rapidly, but with tremendous skill and accurate timing a sprag was thrust between them. This wedged against the truck body, locked the wheel and brought the truck to a halt. A spragger had to be quick, fit and very alert to stop the truck at the required position and avoid injury to the horse.

FUNNEL OF ERUPTION

This distinct fault caused great problems in 1914. An ominous crack appeared in the quarry face and along the top of Titterstone. As it increased in size there was fear for the men's safety. A decision was made to try and break away the huge mass of stone in front of the crack. There was no road to the summit as there is today, so teams of men laboriously carried drums of water from the quarry floor and poured them down the crack. Over a period of weeks thousands of gallons were used but there was no response.

One beautifully fine, calm morning while the workmen were in the cabins eating breakfast, there was an almighty roar. It was a tremendous, reverberating sound which petrified everyone. They rushed outside to be confronted with a terrific cloud of dust. The face had given way and thousands of tons of stone and dirt had buried all the tools, workmen's jackets, wagons and other equipment. Everyone had wanted this to happen but there had been no indication of its imminency. It was a miracle men had not been buried too. When the men approached the huge fall after the dust had subsided, they felt a mixture of relief and pleasure. They assumed that there was an infinite supply of stone for future work, but, after many months the removal of the great fall was completed. Sadly, it was discovered that the face had been worked back to the edge of the funnel of eruption and there was no more stone at that level.

For every ton of stone that was removed from the quarries, a royalty of 4 old pence (slightly less than 2p) a ton was paid to the estate owners. Some quarries crossed estates. In those cases royalties had to be apportioned to different people. Thanks to these royalties, rows of houses were built to accommodate workmen. At the Dhu Stone one group clearly displays the plaque Rouse Boughton Terrace.

In spite of the income Lady Rouse Boughton would not allow the skyline shape of the hills to be altered. Therefore no more stone could be taken from Titterstone summit, but it could have been removed at a lower level. Fortunately however another quarry had already started at the New East End, very near to where the Radar Station now stands and so quarrying at Titterstone was able to continue, but workmen often reflected in their turf cabins how lucky it was that a major disaster had not occurred at the Funnel of Eruption.

Workmen sitting under the quarry face at Titterstone in the 1930s. The waistcoats and light shirts resemble a football strip. In the foreground, left, is a 'reek un pon', (rake and pan), for loading stone and in the centre are two sprags, tapered pieces of timber used for stopping trucks.

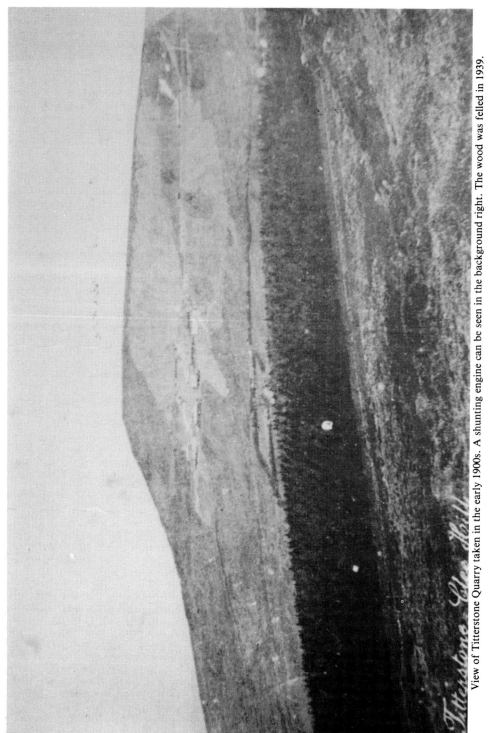

View of Titterstone Quarry taken in the early 1900s. A shunting engine can be seen in the background right. The wood was felled in 1939.

Titterstone about 1940. Crushers and machinery still fully operative. The quarry bungalow can clearly be seen where Mr. Millichip, horse fettler and shop keeper lived. The wood has been felled. No radar scanners on the sky-line.

This photograph of Titterstone Quarry taken in 1914 shows the Funnel of Eruption very clearly.

TITTERSTONE QUARRIES

Titterstone Quarry 1903. Each evening workmen lit fires beneath large boulders. The heat made moisture in the fine cracks expand to such an extent that the boulders would burst open by next morning, enabling men to break them further into manageable sizes. One such fire can be seen on the right hand side.

Titterstone incline. Dust rising from Bitterley crusher and tarmacadam can be seen in the distance. Photo 1930.

Titterstone 1930s. Workmen outside the canteen.

Sett Makers at Titterstone late 1930s. Mr. Clark is holding a sett maker's hammer. To the right are their working sheds and to the left the quarry shunting engine.

STONE BREAKING PLANTS.—LOOKING SOUTH.

Titterstone 1923.

STONE BREAKING PLANTS.—LOOKING NORTH.

Titterstone 1923.

Titterstone 1910. An older wooden wagon and newer metal ones can be seen. In the background left a group of men are 'nappin ston' (breaking stone).

At the top of Titterstone incline 1910. In the centre are the sidings and turnout; to the left are 'ston nappers' and in the background the 'cracker' or crusher.

Titterstone turnout 1910. From this point loaded trucks were gently released down the Titterstone/Bitterley incline. In the left background is the drum house from which ran the wire rope to be attached to the trucks.

Busy Bitterley Sidings 1910. To the right is the road which still leads to Titterstone and to the left can be seen the G.W.R. spur which led to Ludlow.

The Quarries' Railway at Bitterley Siding in 1910.

Bitterley Siding 1940s. Less busy and slightly overgrown.

Looking up the Titterstone incline from Bitterley. 1940s.

Bitterley Siding 1940s. In the background is the Ludlow Bitterley engine and the tarmacadam plant.

Broad Street Leominster 1923. Illustrating a good tarmacadamed
surface made of Clee Hill stone laid in 1909.

Church Street Tenbury Wells 1923. A Clee Hill road surface
after eleven years wear

Angel Bank Clee Hill laid in 1914. Photograph taken in 1923.

Bromfield Road near the site of the Ludlow Comprehensive School. Taken in 1923 to illustrate the Clee Hill road surface laid in 1911.

Laying Clee tar and road surface on the Hay on Wye Road 1921.

Clee Hill road surface at Stockton Cross near Leominster. Laid in 1912. Photo taken in 1921

Aerial view of Dhu Stone and Granite Quarry. 1950s.
To the left is Dhu Stone Village, and the railway continuing to Clee Hill Village. Extreme left, running West to East is the Limer's Lane, now the road to Titterstone Radar station.

Son of the original founder of Clee Hill Transport, Alderman F. G. Edwards. (1966). He lived at Treen House, Clee Hill.

Clee Hill traction engines in the early 1900s.

Clee Hill Transport road rollers (1940s).

Clee Hill road gang working at Caynham in the 1930s.

Clee Hill Road Gang (1930s).

Road Gang at Cayrham (1930s).

Remains of a stone crusher at Dhu Stone. The 'glory hole' on the right of the picture still remains but the railway lines have been removed. This crusher was one of the many man handled into position before lifting equipment was available.

A bungalow built from blocks made from Clee Hill stone dust. This building still stands near the top of Hopton Bank.

Reinforced concrete pipes made with Clee Hill stone chippings. (1922). These were used to build the Birmingham water supply line from Rhayader.

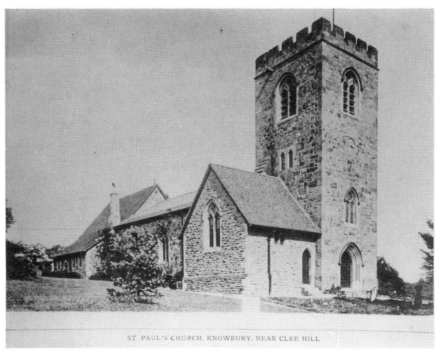

ST. PAUL'S CHURCH, KNOWBURY, NEAR CLEE HILL.

Made from Clee Hill Stone. Photo taken in 1903. The building remains the same but its shape is obscured by tall fir and yew trees.

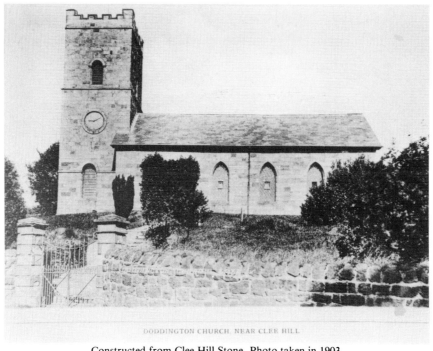

DODDINGTON CHURCH, NEAR CLEE HILL.

Constructed from Clee Hill Stone. Photo taken in 1903.

HOPE BAGOT CHURCH

Clee Hill stone. Photo taken in 1903.

Dhu Stone incline. This accident occurred in the 1950s. Soon afterwards the line closed. The accident accelerated this but the main reason was faster road transport which took stone directly from the quarries to its destination.

A stone breaker in late 1800s.

Back row from left to right
Messrs. Wiltshire, Key, Beeston, Millichip, Martin, Matthews,
Jones, Jordan, Roden, Morris, Mantle.
All these local men received medals for 50 years service in Clee Hill Quarries.

Alongside the major quarries, smaller private ones operated too. A Worcestershire County Council lorry collecting stone from Mr. Edward's Quarry which was situated above the top of the Goodshed Lane.

Workmen dressed in Sunday best at Key's Quarry. This was in Treen Pit Ground. In the 1940s it was used as a Corporation rubbish dump and finally covered with soil.

LOCAL ROADS

In spite of the fact that thousands of tons of stone were leaving Clee Hill annually by rail, local requirements still had to be collected from the quarries by horse and cart.

Parish Councils had permission to obtain some of their stone free off the common land, providing they did not dig down to a depth of more than three feet. The maximum size of stone they were allowed to remove was 9" x 6". Small-holders were employed to bring their horses and carts to collect loads of seven or eight hundredweights each time. These were transported into the bye-ways where men broke the stone into usable sizes. Councils employed 'roadsters' for this work or anyone who was unemployed. Due to weathering, the surface common land stone was semi-broken and over the years its accessibility and low cost must have saved the Councils thousands of pounds.

Mr. William Edwards who built the property known as Pool House which stands above the Craven Arms Inn, could see that there was a need for local commercial transport. He bought traction engines and began delivering to such places as Shifnal, Ironbridge, Bridgnorth and Kidderminster. Two trucks were attached to a traction engine, one carried stone and the other large quantities of water and coal to satisfy the enormous appetite of its boiler. Delivery journeys were extremely slow and very rough. Every pot hole and ridge was accentuated because the traction engines had solid steel wheels.

Mr. Ted Chidley from Cornbrook recalled that the tedious, bumpy journeys were made even slower because the boilers frequently overheated and this necessitated stops to allow them to cool. The roads were little more than tracks in places. Shovels were used to lay the loads of stone because road rollers did not exist. Then traction engines and trucks were driven over each section to level the surface.

In 1914 Captain Lee Roberts who was unable to continue active service due to illness, became Managing Director of the Granite Quarries. Great numbers of quarrymen were conscripted. However, Mr. Chidley had received a serious knee injury and was sent to the Magpie Quarry. Here he found that many women had replaced the men and were operating the overhead railway to Detton Ford. Later that year Mr. Chidley was sent to Kidderminster to be an apprentice mechanic but he was quickly recalled to maintain three company cars and to be Mr. Lee Roberts' private chauffeur.

These were the first cars on Clee Hill and Mr. Chidley remembered how difficult it was to drive them straight because the wheels followed the ruts. He was ridiculed terribly by local people because he looked so ridiculous fighting to control the steering wheel.

Shortly after this, Mr. William Edwards brought the first road rollers to the area. The centre of every road was 'sker/if/id', i.e. loosened up then flattened, to produce an even surface before being rolled. So began the well known Clee Hill Transport and Rolling Company which was continued in my youth by Mr. Fred Edwards, son of William. Craven Place housed the main quarry offices. There was a small residence at the rear where the caretaker lived. Today the same buildings house the Clee Hill Plant Ltd which is managed by Mr. William Edwards' great grandson, Michael Plant.

Behind these premises the first Clee Hill tarmacadam plant was built soon after the rollers arrived. Many teething problems were experienced, the greatest of which was the tar continually catching fire. Most of the time the workmen's faces were as black as charcoal from the swirling black tar smoke because they did not have an effective method of extinguishing the flames. The more they poured water on the burning tar the more it spread. It was quite a common sight to see burning tarmacadam running all the way down the hill on which the plant stood.

The tar had to be heated in a large pot. It was extremely difficult to control the boiling. A little too much heat caused the tar to boil over the sides and so be ignited by the fire beneath. Later however the workmen discovered that fine dust which is generated by the ton when stone is being broken in the crushing machines, would kill the flames immediately it was thrown on them and so the men found they could control fires easily, provided a supply of dust was always at hand.

Within a few years more sophisticated tar plants were installed at the Granite and Dhustone which mixed the tar and fine stone to make excellent road surfaces but at Bitterley they did not have one. Instead, ducts were constructed which ran below large iron plates. These were kept hot by maintaining fires in the ducts. Stone was tipped and spread on the plates. Tar was poured from barrels and men used shovels to mix the two together. For local use the mixture had to be shovelled into carts and delivered by horse and cart to its destination. A flux consisting mainly of creosote was added to delay setting. The tarmacadam remained malleable until the creosote had evaporated. Nowadays it is kept in heated hopper bins overnight and easily dropped into lorries next morning. Once the macadam was spread on a road surface, the creosote evaporated rapidly and the mixture solidified very quickly to form an excellent surface.

Even the early stone crushers installed weighed many tons. Sophisticated lifting equipment was not available. Men had to use simple jacks and steel rollers for days in order to ease the crushers onto sleepers and into railway trucks, before heaving them into a working position. Many quarrymen were ruptured or had injured spines in the process.

The crushers efficiently reduced tremendous quantities of stone to the required sizes, but their operators frequently began work at 4 a.m. and crushers did not become silent until 10 p.m. The stone dust created, may have been useful for extinguishing tar fires but it settled on mens' lungs, produced bronchial problems and I suspect more serious consequences too. Fortunately dust extractors were developed and these minimised the health hazards. In later years cranes and hydraulic jacks avoided unnecessary lifting injuries. More uses were discovered for the dust and it became the main ingredient for vast quantities of pipes which were constructed to convey water from Rhayader Dams to Birmingham. The laying of this line created much local employment when Highley pit closed and more mechanisation reduced the number of labourers in the quarries.

THE INDUSTRY AT PRESENT

With a workforce of about 25 quarrymen, 6 staff and 5 lorry drivers the remaining active quarry produced approximately 125,000 tons of stone in both 1979 and 1980; a very impressive quantity compared with past statistics.

The majority of the workforce live in the vicinity and come from Dhu Stone and Titterstone. In fact they live in the cottages originally built to house their quarrying ancestors. Only one person comes from Ludlow and the Manager lives in Craven Arms. Transport is available to and from work if employees get to the main routes.

Protective clothing is provided. Everyone is encouraged to wear helmets at all times and safety footwear is replaced once or twice a year. Gloves and coats are allocated and overalls washed to ensure a clean supply weekly. A canteen with warmth, tables and chairs and a subsidised vending machine are provided, also hot plates to enable soup to be warmed and plenty of hot water; not luxury but all very acceptable. Compared with other industries of course the quarries are not ahead in this field by any means, but these notes do reflect the considerable improvement which has become at least the norm during my lifetime.

During the early 1900s it was often not possible to drill blasting holes at a rate of more than one inch in one hour. Now with more powerful drills, sixty feet in one hour is possible. All blasting is electrically operated and of course no one is allowed to leave the quarry and consume alcohol during working hours.

Fog does not create the problems it used to because individuals do not work under the face in great quantities. The whole extraction operation is carried out by one driller and shot firer. One excavator driver does all the digging and moving of stone into lorries while a drop ball operator smashes the oversized boulders into manageable sizes. The excavator has powerful headlights enabling the operator to see the face from a distance of at least 15 yards in considerable fog, and as long as the lorry headlights detect the road, work continues. All drilling is done working from above and not from the foot of the face. As a result of these changes only two or three fog stoppages occurred in 1980-81.

Unfortunately, Clee Hill stone is not now considered the best for road surfaces. Problems began to arise when the polished stone value was introduced, i.e. a measure of the speed at which stone polishes under traffic conditions. this is ascertained by mounting samples of chippings in resin on pads. These are fitted near the perimeter of a wheel covered with rubber which just touches the chippings when it is rotated. This simulates road conditions and the effects of traffic and skidding. Tests for five, ten or fifteen years of normal road wear can be simulated in a few hours. For a stone to have an acceptable aggregate it has to have a P.S.V. of about 50. Clee Hill stone is about 45 which conditions its use to C roads, country roads and estates. Its tremendous hardness has become its major drawback. Poorer stones break a little as they wear so forming a continual key for tyres. Clee Hill stone does not even wear to any degree. Its fantastic strength made it wonderful for concrete, but new techniques, and reinforcements make strength less necessary in its construction.

Because of the demise of parts of the railway system and the time involved in transporting by remaining routes, road haulage is now used; but this cost is very high. The viable market is one of about thirty miles radius from most quarries. Therefore the stability of the future depends on what happens within this distance from Clee Hill. The industry survives mainly because local councils, the electricity board, gas board etc. continually come for 100 ton lots, but this is no new situation. Admittedly in the past, thousands of men were employed and hundreds of thousands of tons of stone produced. But, wages were always poor and conditions harsh because profits were very low and the future always precarious and unpredictable. Many times I listened as a child to quarrymen discussing the future and asking, 'Would the industry continue?'

Modern management's concern therefore, is nothing new. The reserves of stone in the Clee Hill quarries are ample, but monopolies, the prosperity of the country and modern trends make the future even more precarious. How long have managers told men, "Things are hard; we shall have to tighten our belts. We have to be more productive."

The industry continues to make a profit but for how long? The cry of 'wolf' has for many years been true but to me it seems that he is now much nearer than ever before. The future will depend far greater on both production, effective management and selling.

My wish, partly because of nostalgia but also because of my concern for local people, is that this industry which has shaped these hills and influenced its community for so long will have a valuable place in our society's future.

My Childhood on
Clee Hill

LIFE IN A RURAL PUBLIC HOUSE

My home, The Dhu Stone Inn existed because of the quarries. My parents provided a very necessary service for those who worked and lived in the area.

The quarrying of stone was a very dusty, thirsty process and there was little or no time allowed to walk to the pub during working hours. Therefore boys were employed to carry cider to the men. These boys had earthenware jars which usually had 'whiskets' to protect them. If a 'whisket' was not used the jars were frequently broken accidently by catching them on jagged rocks. The bottoms fell out and the cider carriers had the unfortunate problem of telling the workmen what had happened.

As each lunch-time approached my mother drew twenty or thirty pints of cider and placed them on trays. As the door bolt was drawn back the quarrymen rushed into the public bar and sat down. The trays of cider were taken to them and the money collected afterwards. This method of service was necessary because after deducting walking time to and from the quarry, lunchtime was very short. The landlady could serve individuals more quickly if they sat down than when they were crowding around the bar.

The furnishings of the public house were bare and rough because the workmen's clothes were always covered with dust and tar. After each lunch hour, it was necessary to wash all the seats and tables to ensure protection of the clothes of evening customers.

Many quarrymen, especially those working in the stone crushers, were not recognisable because of the fine dust sticking to their faces. A few strands of stiff hair protruded from beneath their caps and their bright red lips and shining eyes contrasted greatly against their dull, grey skin.

Most men wore a 'Clee Hill collar and tie'. That was a knotted handkerchief, known as a muffler. Everyone too had string tied around their trousers just below the knees.

Beneath the wooden seats there were piles of cast iron spittoons. These were partially filled with sawdust and in constant use.

Although a disgusting habit, I often admired the accuracy with which these men could spit great distances. On hot summer days they often had contests to see who could spit on a target such as a fly or stone. Many chewed twist tobacco to keep their throats moist, while others constantly coughed as a result of fine stone dust settling on their lungs.

Most men brought their lunch tied up in a coloured handkerchief. The contents were plain but substantial. It was common to see a loaf revealed with its centre pulled out. In its place was a lump of butter and cheese and often a large onion. The essential tool was a well worn pocket knife. I was always intrigued to see how the bread was cut into small accurate cubes. They reminded me of the stone setts made in the quarry. I often asked my mother's permission to join the men with my own knife, bread and cheese.

On a cold day someone would bring in a shovel, clean out the heel, crack an egg on the side, pop it into the heel and fry it over the fire. Not terribly hygienic by modern standards but certainly eaten with relish.

In those days draught cider was four old pence a pint (less than 2p), beer was one shilling and two pence (6p) and porter one shilling and six pence (7½p).

During winter a favourite occupation was to insert the poker in the fire until it was red hot and swirl it around inside a pint of cider. This 'mulled' the contents and made a warm, pleasant drink. Some liked to add ginger too. Occasionally however the poker touched the side of the pint pot with disastrous results.

During the evening the public house became a community centre. Very few people had motor transport and a walk to the local was quite an ordeal. Street lights were unheard of and no one had electricity.

One elderly man by the name of Ted Roberts specialised in the making of candle lamps. He used large jam jars which had metal, screwed on tops. He cut the base of each jar away and attached two metal strips to the sides. A circular piece of wood was used for a base onto which was placed a candle holder. The base, with lighted candle clipped into the jar. The result was certainly not a bright light but it was better than wandering in absolute darkness.

How ever these locals found their way across common land, often having to skirt the quarry's edge, on a starless, foggy night always amazed me. The return journey home after more than a few pints must have been even more hazardous. But make the journey they did and they certainly knew how to create their own enjoyment.

The local football matches or impending elections caused heated arguments in the bar and my mother would sometimes blow a whistle and shout 'Half time.' This de-fused the situation and everyone good humouredly laughed. But occasionally flash point occured and I have seen my small, courageous, wiry mother stand between glaring eyes and clenched fists to prevent a fight. I never remember anyone hitting her or pushing her out of the way. Very infrequently however, these remedies did not prevent an explosion and the two, seething opponents fought on the green behind our house. Grandma reported progress from a bedroom window, saying, 'He above see-eth all.' Eventually common sense or exhaustion prevailed. The combatants returned to the bar and mother proceeded to place a dab of butter around a developing black eye.

The area had a tremendous tradition and enthusiasm for football, although the sporting facilities were very poor. The old quarrymen frequently related the experiences of the Bar and Bosters team. These men worked all the week in the quarries and after many years negotiation were allowed half day off on Saturday. This was football time. Team and supporters travelled by horse and cart down Angel Bank, through Ludlow and on to places as far afield as Craven Arms, fifteen miles from Clee Hill. It is difficult to appreciate that after this time consuming ordeal they played a match, called at a public house on the return journey and eventually reached Clee Hill during the early hours of the following morning. What a transformation in transport has taken place and how easy life is for us nowadays.

As a child I often saw two thousand people watching a football match on Clee Hill. Magazines and cardboard were used as shinguards and it amused me to see paper flying in all directions after a tackle. Much to the disgust of the referee, one trainer stood on the touch line, intermittently insisted that individual players came off the field, had a quick drink of cider and returned to play, all while the match was in progress.

Most 'locals' had a darts team and this created a club atmosphere. A weekly subscription was paid and at the end of the season a bus trip was arranged for players and families to a sea-side resort. This was a tremendous treat for the children because apart from Sunday school outings, it was the only opportunity of seeing the sea.

On arrival, the men would take off jackets and ties, roll up trousers to the knees and have a paddle. Their baggy trousers were hitched about three inches below the arm-pits by a substantial pair of braces. After eating sandy sandwiches they reclined in deck chairs to fry themselves in the sun.

On one such visit to Barry Island I remember the group returning to the bus in the evening with scarlet faces, red noses, shining bald heads and uncomfortable shins. It had been noted that one fellow was missing, but no one really worried. It was assumed he preferred a nearby smoke room to the sea-front. However as we boarded the bus he still failed to appear. Search parties were sent out and sometime later he was discovered locked in a public toilet. He had apparently been trying to escape for most of the afternoon. The poor fellow was not allowed to forget that experience. His only consolation was that he slept soundly that night, whereas the majority were kept awake with agonising sunburn.

Very few people had cars and team spirit was fostered by the fact that for away matches the whole team and supporters travelled on a coach. When the game was completed, each side competed in a friendly manner for a gallon of beer. The starting total was 1001 and the winning team was the first one to finish on a double. I felt very proud at the age of eleven to be able to book the scores and subtract them quickly enough to be praised by adults. I did not owe this ability to the learning of tables in school but by watching and playing the game so often that I knew all the scoring combinations by heart. How interesting that the bar man's sport is becoming both a national and international television attraction.

HOMING SOCIETY

Every Friday evening the pigeon club or 'homing society' as the professionals call it, met under the direction of Mr. Sebert Key. Young birds were purchased or bred and after a number of local races the inexperienced group decided to join a federation.

Throughout the flying season the pigeon fanciers met in our garage. Each coveted red chequer, mealy and blue bar was inspected, handled and admired with great affection. A special rubber ring was fitted on one leg of each bird before it was ceremoniously popped into a large wickerwork basket. Many young owners were reluctant to part with their birds because they feared it would be the last time they would see them.

In the foreground is a 'whisket'. This was the name given to an earthenware jar encased in a wicker basket. These were used by boys who were employed unofficially to carry cider from the local public houses to the quarries.

Foremen and quarrymen outside the Victoria Inn, Clee Hill in 1930.
Left to right from the back row:- Thomas Clee, Wat Burton, Will Greenhouse, Will Gittens, Charlie Clee, Bert Brown, Will Didlick.
Front, Sid Trow, Sam Genner, Jamie Inkman, Ern Brown, Will Mantle, Jim Wiltshire and Jackie Turner.

1939 on the lawn at the Dhu Stone Inn.
Left to right back Row:- Pinkie Breakwell, Landlord Dick Jenkins, Marjorie Jenkins, The Author Alf Jenkins (aged three), Mr. Didlick, Bert Crowther, Billie Crowther.
Front, Sammy Davidson, Sam Harris, Dick Beddoes, Yahee Beddoe, Bill Didlick.

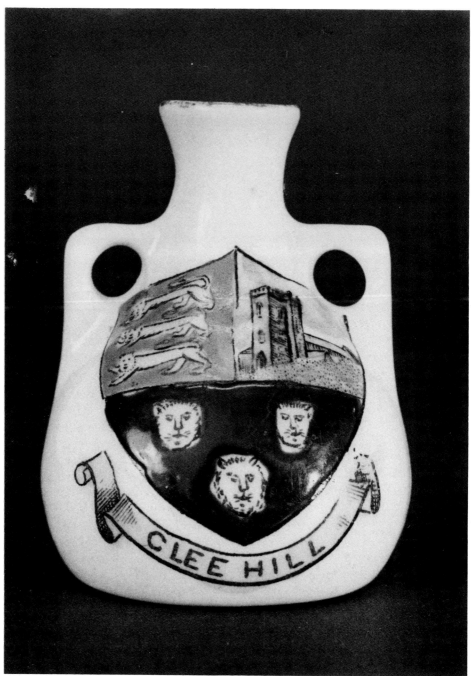

This photograph of a piece of pottery owned by Mr. John Morris of Ludlow shows the Clee Hill Castle. This old fortified house was demolished to make way for the Magpie Quarry in the early 1900s prior to the usage of the Detton overhead ropeway.

1962. Clee Hill Snow in Bitterley Lane.

Snow at the Dhu Stone 1962.

Dhu Stone Inn in 1962 snow.

How we take an indoor toilet facility for granted. The snow of 1962 made
a journey to the outside loo even more uncomfortable.

1947, when the author had many weeks away from school. He is seen here with his father Dick Jenkins and sister Marina standing on the roof of buildings completely covered with snow.

Clee Hill School 1912. Infant teacher Miss Selly on the left.

1910 Clee Hill School.

Clee Hill School 1930s. In the back row the teachers include
Mr. Owen, Miss Manley and Miss Selly.

CLEE HILL WESLEYAN CHAPEL AND SCHOOLS

Clee Hill School and Wesleyan Chapel where the Infants class was held. (1903). Now a private house.

Dhu Stone 1930s. The New Buildings are seen in the background right. A tarmacadam plant is in the centre background. On the extreme left are the drum house (the large brick building with a chimney) which operated the winding gear for the Dhu Stone - Bitterley incline, the railway mens' equipment sheds and the signal box.

Dhu Stone Works, Clee Hill.

Dhu Stone Railway and works. On the left are the drum house which controllec the railway incline, the tarmacadam plant and a little of the New Building Terrace. In the immediate background is the loading wharf and further away the quarry incline.

Angel Hotel on the Angel Bank (1918). This was where all our local auctions were held.

1930s. Clee Hill Village carnivals which used to be held on Clee Hill football ground. It was quite common to see at least two thousand people attending these occasions and local football matches too.

The Royal Oak Tug o' War Team of 1932 which included the local policeman and church organist.

Little Billy Martin's brass band, which was mentioned in the Clee Hill carnivals. Little Billy is seen in the front row extreme right.

One of the many Clee Hill football teams organised by the quarrymen, The Broad'uk Harriers. This 1932 team played 13 games and won them all. One of the rules for their fixtures was to include 4 boys.

The successful Knowle Rangers footballers of 1928.

The basket was sealed, labelled, the number of entrants clearly noted and then taken in my father's car to Ludlow station. It was quite a sight to see dozens of baskets lined up and to hear the coo-ing of hundreds of pigeons echoing around the busy platform.

Saturday's liberation time was well known and everyone hoped for a fine day. Interested people watched local pigeon lofts for many hours hoping to see a bird plunge from the sky and enter its trap.

When the racer arrived, he had to be caught and the rubber ring removed. This was folded, inserted in a thimble and placed inside a clock which marked the time of arrival on a special paper disc. Experienced fanciers will know of the frustration when a pigeon alights on the loft but sits stupidly by the entrance for what seems an eternity. Of course if he tries to encourage the bird to enter, it often soars into the air once again.

In those days the club could afford only one clock. This was positioned on the wall outside my home. It meant that many fanciers had to run at least one and a half miles with thimble in hand, across rugged countryside to register the time of arrival.

At nine o'clock the same evening all members met to open the clock and inspect the registered times. Some fanciers had reason to celebrate but the serious talk was a detailed analysis as to why many birds had not arrived home, the fact that others had refused to enter their traps or what the result might have been if Arthur hadn't fallen while making his run to the clock.

Because of the many railway closures, federations now have their own huge transporters and every member has his own clock but I've no doubt the interest and excitement is just as great.

SATURDAY EVENING

Saturday night was always a jolly time. Every person seemed to have his own party piece to offer. The usual procedure was for one person to sing a song, recite a poem, tell a joke or play an instrument. When he had finished everyone else was encouraged to emulate him with the instruction, 'Sing, say or pay.' The melodian was a favourite instrument and I well remember such tunes being played as The wild colonial boy, My grand father's clock and Give me a nail and a hammer.

Certain individuals did not sing or say but had the most peculiar way of entertaining. One fellow stood tense and upright, then proceeded to fall flat on his face without bending his limbs. This was no mean feat on a quarry tiled floor. Another picked up a sizeable table in his teeth.

So it was that these good people worked extremely hard for very long hours during the day and entertained themselves so simply and enjoyably in their own locality. Television, the motor car, upholstered seats and expensive drinks seem to have destroyed the ability we had to create such fun.

LIGHTING

An oil lamp certainly added something to the atmosphere of the public house. Although not a terribly bright light, everyone managed to play cribbage, dominoes, quoits and darts. Problems did however arise during a darts match if two doors were opened at the same time and the light blew out.

My mother managed to do all her sewing by the light of the fire or an oil lamp and this was never lit until the room was practically dark. Traditional habits die hard and when I visit my mother I still find that she sits in the twilight, forgetting that the flick of a switch would transform her surroundings. How much electricity we would all save in this modern world if we were prepared to switch on only when absolutely necessary.

RAT CATCHING

In my childhood days we did not have rodent officers and the like but vermin was just as great a problem.

Sunday mornings during summer and autumn were traditionally rat-catching sessions. A group of locals, armed with stout sticks and accompanied by sharp, little terrier dogs, congregated in our yard and looked for signs of rats around the pig-sty, barn and cow-house. The terriers sniffed and searched ceaselessly until a rat was detected. When one broke into the open, adults would shout and children scream.

I remember on one occasion a rat darted into the fire-place under the washing boiler with a terrier in hot pursuit. He got fast and could not move in any direction while the rat climbed the chimney, appeared out of the chimney pot and scampered across the roof.

My most memorable recollection was when one dashed across the yard and on being cornered ran for the nearest cover which happened to be a bell bottomed trouser leg. Up the leg he darted to be grabbed just above the knee by the terrified fellow. Miraculously the rat was killed without the man receiving a bite. Through fear, the hair on the back of my neck literally stood on end and has resulted in me having an intense dislike for rats. Consequently I never go into a deep litter shed or likely spots where rats may be without wearing wellingtons and ensuring that my trousers are well tucked inside.

SUNDAY LUNCH-TIME

On Sunday lunch-time the customers were transformed. Even for us who knew them so well, it was difficult to realise that they were the same people we had seen during the week in their working clothes and grimed with dust.

Everyone turned up in Sunday best. Some had bowler hats, others flat caps. Some even wore the well remembered, detachable collar with a tie while others had a clean 'Clee Hill collar and tie', the knotted handkerchief or muffler. Facial features were revealed which were unnoticeable during working hours.

Although we always welcomed the trade, my mother got distressed when she thought of the spoilt Sunday lunches and burnt offerings that awaited so many because they did not return home at a reasonable time.

One Sunday morning, Sammy Clark had been chimney sweeping for Harry Downes. He made large quantities of home made wine and unfortunately persuaded Sammy to consume more than a reasonable amount. As closing time approached Harry escorted the inebriated, soot-covered Sammy into the bar and seated him in an inconspicuous spot. Harry ordered a pint of cider and my mother assuming the drink was for him, obligingly served. However, Harry positioned the cider by the side of swaying Sammy and discreetly left the premises.

Mrs. Clark knew where her husband had gone, knew of Harry Downes' reputation and because her husband was so long returning, decided to investigate. Unable to find him at Harry's home, she came striding into the bar looking every inch a seething Ena Sharples. She grabbed a pint of cider, unfortunately the wrong one, proceeded to be extremely abusive to my mother and flung the pint out through the bar door. Before one could say 'Jack Robinson' she hoisted her tiny husband by the seat of his pants and the collar of his jacket and threw him to join the pint outside. The room full of amazed men began to rock with laughter, but my mother was a little distressed to be blamed for a situation she had not produced.

WEDDINGS

Weddings were occasions to be remembered. Receptions were held either in the home of the bride or the village hall. I never remember a wedding which had less than six or eight bridesmaids. Publicans and their families were usually invited and it was the custom for all the guests to go to the local public house after the married couple had left for their honeymoon. This, as a rule was not very far. It tended to be like the old song:-

> Where shall we go for our honeymoon John?
> Where shall we go for our honeymoon John,
> John my own true love?
>
> Up the lane and back again,
> Up the lane and back again,
> Up the lane and back again,
> Mary my own true love.

The guests had a peculiar custom of bringing two or three new glazed chamberpots to the public house which were filled up with beer and ceremoniously handed around all the customers to have a drink. The bride's father carried an enamel, gallon jug to all the customers and continually topped up their drinks. For one night in his life he was the most popular person in the area.

NAMES

Large families have lived in the area for many years and the same Christian family names were very frequently used. Inter-marriage was common and much confusion arose when referring to individuals. But families tended to confine themselves to a particular area. It was well known that if, for instance, you were walking in the Hopton Bank, Cleeton St. Mary area and addressed any gentleman you met as Mr. Broome, you would undoubtedly be right.

To avoid confusion of reference the Welsh system of nicknames and occupations was used. Also certain families were given, by the community, a particular Christian name ending. The Warringtons were known as Jacko, Tommo, Willo, Billo, Fredo and Samo. Other nicknames were attached because of mannerisms or occupations.

More I remember are Nutty, Dumpy, Slenny, Mussy, Tody, Smicky, Knocky, Butty and Bingy.

Skinnum, Churnum, Fredum, Gillum and Spareum.

Geobbles, Toodles and Tronkles.

Watter, Jimmer, Fredder, Nobbler, Chootler, Flaxer, Tacker, Mussler, Towser, Fisher and Percer.

Oxo, Muggins, Bronco, Yahee, Piert, Blake, Cute, Poon fire, Fire bucket, Crack and Tarpig.

Many people did not respond unless they were addressed by their nickname. They liked them and preferred them to Christian names. Many others were however, never aware that they possessed a nickname because they were never used in their presence.

Week-end trade was always extremely good and customers filled every nook and cranny of the house, leaving no place for family privacy. Even the stairs were used as a seating area and as children we had to step around people to reach our bedroom. Still, I do not recall that the noise and laughter ever kept us awake.

LOOKING AFTER THE BEER

The beer was always very cold because it was stored in an underground cellar. Like many public houses in those days my home was a beer house. That is to say it only had a licence to sell cider and beer and not wines and spirits. The cider and beer was mainly draught and it was only the more affluent and wives who drank bottled beer.

The cider was arranged on a low stillage. The thirty six gallon barrels had to be placed there for a day or two for the contents to settle before usage. Then my father bored a vent hole into a special bung on the top side and inserted a peg. Finally he would knock in a soaked wooden tap. This was bound with brown paper to ensure a tight fit.

Cider was the most popular working man's drink because it was very cheap and very potent.

A great deal of care and patience was needed to ensure a good, clear glass of beer for the customers. Again the barrels had to remain on the stillage for a couple of days before venting and tapping. The next stage was to connect the barrel to a pipe leading to the 'beer engine', the name given to the hand pumps. Good beer was crystal clear with a white, frothy head on it. The drink looked alive until the last drop was drunk from the pint and the froth would cling to the inside of the glass. Nowadays I drink very lttle but I see none to compare with that quality.

When a barrel was empty the feed pipe was disconnected. At weekends I helped carry many buckets of warm water into the cellar. This was drawn through the pipes until the water was absolutely clear. Then the clean pipes could be connected to new barrels.

There was no such name as 'An off licence' but many people came to the door with a jug or a bottle which was filled and taken home. One or two people I remember well, used to drink one pint while you gave the change and another while the bottle was being filled. Surely they could not have tasted the beer, and the only reason I can give for the speedy consumption, was to make the wives think they hadn't stopped for a drink.

Carpets were not used to cover the floor, Bare tiles were far more practical because there was a great deal of mud from quarry men's boots and the sheep dogs which accompanied the hill farmers. After lunch times and evenings we swept through with a broom, then washed the floors with a mop and bucket.

Before festive occasions we washed all walls and ceilings with soapy water to remove nicotine stains. The smarting of the eyes and the filthy, tarry substance on the cloths deterred me from smoking any quantity of cigarettes.

I expect landlords have always found it difficult to turn the customers out at night and my home was no exception. Frequently when my mother approached the bar with a broom to sweep up, someone would grab it and perform a broom dance. I have not seen this since my childhood but it was similar to a novelty Morris dance. The broom was held at one end and the dancer swung first one leg and then the other, over in time to music. Then he dropped the broom and danced along it, jumping from side to side. This always caused much shouting, clapping and appraisal.

MODERN CONVENIENCES

I have mentioned that no home in the area had electricity, but that was not really a hardship or inconvenience. But, being without mains water certainly affected the daily routine.

On arriving home from school our first job was to walk to the nearest tap some seventy five yards away, with two buckets. Every drop of water for washing, cooking, tea-making and bathing had to be carried. This was a hazardous occupation in the winter because the tap was left dripping overnight to avoid it freezing up. Consequently next day there was often a sheet of ice radiating some distance from the tap.

Water was used very sparingly for domestic purposes. After washing faces it was emptied into a bucket and re-used for washing floors. That for washing clothes was used a second time for bathing. The large weekly washing of clothes always took place on Monday. Water was boiled in a furnace and a wooden dollie used to beat out the dirt of the clothes which were placed in a tub of very hot water. At the end of the day when the clothes washing had been completed the family had a bath. Water ladled from the furnace was put into a long tin bath. We would all have a dip and dry oursleves as quickly as possible because we had to do without heated towel rails and modern comforts.

My home was about 1300 feet above sea level. The roof was not felted or lagged and of course there was no central heating. Therefore during long wintry spells the house became very cold, so cold in fact that quite frequently on a winter's morning, the flannel was frozen into a hard lump in the soap dish and mother had to boil some water to thaw it before we could have a wash. Nevertheless as a family we learnt how to economise and make the best use of our supplies.

Our house roof was a good one but when the wind was howling, snow was forced under the eaves of the attic. After every snow storm my father would help me up into the attic. Between the instructions of telling me to keep my feet on the rafters, I had to shovel up all the snow to avoid it melting and soaking through the ceilings.

Like many other country folk we had enough poultry to supply ourselves with eggs. Nothing tastes better than a newlaid egg, but on occasions the weather was so cold that I found eggs frozen in their shells when taken from the nest boxes.

Having no mains water meant no water toilet. This created added difficulties in a public house. Making a trip to the toilet on a cold winter's night was an expedition in itself. It was necessary to wear hat, scarf and overcoat. One did not dwell longer that was absolutely necessary but returned to a cheery fireside as quickly as possible.

Emptying the toilets was a detestable job, especially when catering for the general public too. I remember men being paid 6d, just over 2p to empty each toilet belonging to neighbouring rows of cottages. This was one aspect of the good old days I was not sorry to see pass.

At the age of seven, after a series of sore throats, it was recommended that I should have my tonsils out. Every other child underwent the same operation in those days. I was sent with a friend to Shrewsbury Ear, Nose and Throat Hospital. The following morning a nurse took us by the hand and led us down a long, bare corridor and placed us inside separate cubicles. I looked around expecting to be operated on but nothing happened. A little later the door was opened and on we went to what I now know was an operating theatre. The surgeon said, 'Have these boys had their bowels moved?' It was then that I realised the cubicle in which I had been standing contained a water toilet. Living in an isolated area of Clee Hill I had never seen one in my life and so had not made use of it.

The cooking facilities in my home were similar to most houses in the area. My mother had a cooking range which was always beautifully blackleaded. This grate had a fire in the centre. On the right hand side was a small boiler which was heated directly from the fire, while on the other side of the fire was an oven for cooking. It meant an early start to the day to light fires and give them time to generate sufficient heat for boiling kettles and cooking. In later years we had an oil stove which speeded up cooking considerably but still it was not as convenient and time saving as modern electric or gas appliances.

ILLNESS

Doctors' surgeries were not as full in those days and I am sure it must have been because of the problem of getting there. Our nearest doctor's surgery was in Tenbury Wells, six miles away. Telephones too were few and far between and meant a long bicycle ride or walk to contact a doctor if anyone was ill. Generally speaking local people were healthy and fit. Most men were lean and strong. There was a fear of going to hospital, partially because when treatment was sought it was usually too late and few patients returned home alive. Secondly, Kidderminster was the hospital most frequently used and seventeen miles seemed a tremendous distance in those days.

Because of these factors and others, every family had its own pet remedies for certain illnesses. Many put an onion inside an aching ear or wrapped a warm sock around it. Now we are told it only aggravates the problem to keep infected ears warm. One gentleman who suffered badly from rheumatism, often thrashed his legs with nettles. Possibly the resultant stinging made him forget about his usual pain. When I had whooping cough as a child, I remember my mother applying goose fat to my chest and covering it with sheets of brown paper. Every week-end we were all made to take a laxative whether we needed it or not. It was as important to be clean inside as well as out. I am sure that much damage was done to tummy linings by this constant week-end ritual. But many country folk did realise the medicinal qualities possessed by herbs and used them successfully on their families and animals.

I am amazed how vividly I can recall the distinctive smell which each house had. In one there would be the prominent aroma of herbs, while in another hops or the smell of a particular brand of pipe tobacco. How acute the sense of smell is in young people and how noticeable it is that particular scents bring back childhood experiences.

On reading an old Ludlow Standard recently, dated Oct. 24th 1840, I realised that the medical facilities of my childhood had improved considerably over the years; to quote:-

'Allow me through the medium of your Independent Journal to draw the attention of the public to the present administration of the New Poor Law as it regards medical relief to the poor of the Clee Hill district of the Ludlow Union. A contract has been entered into between the Guardians of the Medical Officer to attend the poor at 8 shillings (40p) per case. It should be borne in mind that this is an isolated district, that is to say there is no resident medical man in it and the present contractor has to ride 4 miles before he gets to the nearest cottage. As it regards the great bulk of the practice so that when he has had two purpose journeys to the same patient and he very frequently has more, he is out of pocket in the expense of horse hire not to mention the loss of time, fatigue over wretched roads and medicine.

All this however would have been counter-balanced had there been something like the same number of patients to attend as there was when a fixed salary was paid, as then many patients could have been visited in the same journey and this was fully expected by the medical officer.

You will be somewhat surprised however to hear that the Guardians have sanctioned and encouraged the witholding of medical relief to the poor for the sake of economy, and in this district the number of cases for which orders have been given is considerably less than half what it was when a fixed salary was paid. In deed since the 27th September only one order had been given and this in a district comprising of a population of more than 3000. This is economy with a vengeance and the poor are the sufferers. The present medical officer has repeatedly complained of this injustice and the shylock like answer was "It is the bond" and they have compelled him to adhere to it. I would suggest Sir, that if it is any use, no medical relief should be withheld even in apparently trivial cases as there is no knowing what might be the consequences of neglecting a very small amount of illness particularly among the half starved population of the Clee Hills.

I remain Sir, your obedient servant, a friend of the Poor Law.'

Dated October 21st

However, little economic progress had been made by the 1930s. In order to maintain their large families people had to work very long hours and be extremely thrifty to survive. The majority walked at least three or four miles to and from the quarry to work. Their wage was insufficient and had to be supplemented by keeping a pig, a few hens and in many cases a milking cow. Everyone cultivated a large garden to produce potatoes and brassicas. I can remember no one who had just one occupation. In our own case my mother ran the quarry public house while my father was an undertaker, wheelwright, smallholder and cultivated a large garden.

In a peculiar way this spartan way of life developed a certain unity. A common phrase was, "Which pub do you use?" Customers tended to frequent one particular public house. In return for their custom my father would support their businesses and help families if the opportunity arose. There were many ways of doing this, such as giving a piece of fresh pork at pig killing time or sending home some lard or skimmed milk with a customer whose family was in need.

WINTER

Winter brought isolation and long spells away from school. The quantity of snow that fell was probably not much greater than was experienced in lower lying areas, but, the wind created tremendous drifts which soon made our narrow, high hedged lanes impassable.

Obtaining delivery of supplies caused problems and worries. My father and I, with many customers from the bar have often spent two or three days clearing snow with shovels, only to find the wind immediately creating drifts behind us.

Horse and sledge was the only way to bring barrels and cases of beer to the house. As winter continued my home became a provisions store. Milk and bread was left in large quantities so that when husbands braved the weather to have a pint they returned home with many necessities for the family. During icy periods I have seen older people with a pair of old socks over their shoes to prevent them slipping. Drifts were so deep that the roofs of buildings were completely covered and I remember in 1947 beginning our sledge run from by the side of the chimney. We travelled for some considerable distance and came to a halt by being entangled in a clothes line.

Blocked lanes meant a stop to quarry work and men were employed for weeks cutting and clearing quarry roads before stone could be transported. Snow ploughs were no use because narrow lanes had no surplus space into which snow could be pushed; and so men would patiently chop out cubes of snow with shovels and throw it into enormously high piles on each side. Because of their height and compactness these snow mounds often remained until May or June.

Paraffin was a much needed cooking fuel which we sold. My home was two fields away from the Dhu Stone lane and when the lorry could not travel any further, I have seen the driver and his mate carry 200 gallons of the paraffin in 5 gallon tins to my home. Twenty journeys each in a blinding snow storm was an endurance test. The reward at the end was warm buttered toast, mulled cider and a glass of parsnip wine; but I'm sure no incentive would persuade people to do likewise nowadays.

My father made sure that a shovel and broom were left indoors each night at wintertime. Occasionally it was impossible to open doors in the morning. Farmers had great problems and I well remember having to toil for hours to clear snow from our cattle shed. However the most time consuming job was carrying drinking water to our milking cow. I have never seen a bucketful disappear so quickly. I would often carry ten or twelve buckets to her and the last one would be drunk as quickly as the first.

As snow storms began, hill horses and sheep ran for shelter under the quarry stone crusher bins. Weeks later, great numbers of suffocated animals were discovered.

Ice was a greater hazard than snow. The area was bathed in freezing fog for days on end and our homes were in semi-darkness. I often heard older folk say, 'We'n at tu av a buz ta goo ta Ludlu ta sa the daa light.' (We'll have to have a bus to go to Ludlow and see the day light). The build up of ice was astonishing and I have measured a diameter of seven inches formed around fallen telephone wires. When the sun appeared, trees tinkled and glistened like chandeliers. The tough hill grass looked like a lunar landscape and made many varied sounds as your boots brushed through it.

Sometimes the freezing mist settled in the valleys below. As the clouds billowed along beneath us, I imagined them to be a rolling sea. The occasional tall conifer resembled the mast of a ship and small hills became islands.

The year 1941 was particularly icy. My father took me to check the condition of our sheep and it was difficult to distinguish them from their frozen surroundings. Rain followed by low temperatures had frozen their fleeces to the ground. My father had to cut round each animal to release it. To our surprise we found that the grass was soft and green where the sheep had lain. It was impossible for them to stand and in no time at all they had slithered to the bottom of the field.

Men walked great distances to work only to find that frost and snow made work impossible for weeks on end. Quarrymen told me that the greatest hazard was the effects of frost on the stone, especially at Titterstone's Funnel of Eruption.

SCHOOL DAYS

Many present day schools are spacious, pleasant places to work in and the services provided by the authorities are far superior to what they used to be.

I often reflect on the difficulties we had to endure as children. Most of us walked considerable distances to the village school. Older brothers and sisters and neighbours' children helped the tiny ones along. I had an older sister who pulled me at such a speed that my feet were often airborne. Nevertheless we were glad of support and help. Frequently my wellingtons were pulled off by the snow and we were forced to walk with our backs to the biting wind.

We arrived at school in tears, not because we disliked it but because as fingers and ears warmed through, the aching was unbearable.

Wet hats, coats and gloves were placed to dry on fireguards around open coal fires. By the end of the day our gloves were as stiff as boards and it was only with great difficulty we were able to force our fingers into them. Still, that was better than putting on a cold, wet covering. Wet trousers remained on the person to dry and without a doubt this has led to many aching limbs in old age. Most children had a knitted balaclava helmet, which fitted tightly over the head and extended down under one's coat onto the shoulders.

The main school building had two rooms and the infant class was conducted in a nearby chapel. The older children sat in long rows with three or four children to each, very long desk. Classes were divided by wooden screens but I do not recall being disturbed by children on the other side. However, I do remember that many children continually had 'candles' running from their noses and discharging ears was a common complaint.

We all detested having to go across the playground to the draughty, bucket toilets in inclement weather, and I am sure that many small children soiled themselves in preference. Children were not cleaned up if they found themselves in that predicament but were sent home with their trousers in a recognisable brown paper parcel.

The headteacher, Mr. Owen, was a short, stocky man with a shining bald head and heavy moustache. He was good humoured and wherever he went he carried his large, black umbrella. Village children walked home for dinner but those who came considerable distances carried their lunches in zebra striped tins which Woolworths stocked in those days. Liquid refreshment was a bottle of cocoa or tea wrapped in a woollen sock, in an attempt to keep it warm. We sat at desks and ate our sandwiches while the headteacher did likewise. This gave us the opportunity to chat to him in a slightly more informal way than we were allowed to in class, but nevertheless with great respect. Mr. Owen was strict but fair and would never shy from using his cane if he felt it was necessary.

In summer the stirring sound of the hounds could frequently be heard. Someone would say, 'Tham kum/in up the Nuv/vers bel/ol/lu.' (They're coming up the Nuvvers in full cry). This was too great a temptation for many of the determined older boys to resist. Away they ran to pursue the pack and of course the cane would await them on their arrival at school next day.

Discipline in school was good and there was very little bullying. Few fights broke out in the school playground mainly because of the fear of the cane. But rivals were often heard to say, "I'll see you across Andrew's lane after school." Word of the impending fracas would pass around. Everyone left school in the normal way but many congregated a little later along the lane. The battle was excitedly watched with opposing gangs verbally supporting their champion. Finally amid bloody noses, torn clothes and nettle stings a fair winner was declared and the grudge almost certainly forgotten. I hope if the new residents in the lane have differences they are able to settle them in a more civilised way than we children used to.

We were given regular gardening lessons but the school had very few tools. If you were keen to participate it meant carrying a rake or spade all the way to and from home.

The junior teacher was the thinnest, most severe looking lady I have ever seen. As a result of facing the elements, everyone had a weather beaten complexion. This person's face however was absolutely colourless, something which puzzled me greatly. She ruled us with a rod of iron. My most vivid recollections of her class were table chanting and handwriting lessons. The better pupils were allowed to assist the poorer ones but woe betide anyone who did not produce the perfect shaped letter. The offender was grabbed by the hair, or ear and hauled to the front of the class. Miss Manley ceremoniously took the wooden-backed blackboard cleaner from its hook. Under her arm she firmly gripped the culprit's non-writing hand and belted the cleaner across the knuckles with the speed of a woodpecker. Every winter I had chilblains on my hands which once bled as a result of the battering.

While being subjected to the punishment the receiver stood behind and very close to the teacher. On one occasion I remember an exasperated pupil kicking Fanny Manley. We were all momentarily reduced to laughter but the lad was punished severely. In her favour I must say that I won numerous handwriting prizes at grammar school but I am sure I could have attained the same standard far less painfully.

The teacher of the infants was a homely, happy person by the name of Miss Selly. She was a most understanding person and a first class musician. We loved her dearly and respected her greatly although her discipline was firm. Over the years she taught at least three generations. When a thunderstorm reared its ugly head all the tiny tots were told to sit on the floor, under the desks, say tables, sing nursery rhymes or play percussion instruments.

Miss Selly had a brother who frequently rode by school with his horse and squeaking coal cart. A favourite trick of the older boys was to hang on the back of the cart as the horse struggled up the hill. Mr. Selly must have had eyes in the back of his head because his long whip would flash like a serpent's tongue over his shoulder and effectively cut across the boys' fingers. That did not deter them, the far greater and more humiliating experience was to be reprimanded by Miss Selly next day. Her manner was gentle and her etiquette impeccable and we in turn responded to her with absolute reverence. How different from this age in which the majority of children have little or no respect for older people. This attitude distresses me considerably. I do not blame teachers, who from my experience work unceasingly to cultivate reasonable, acceptable standards, but I do criticise society which in this modern rat race does not spend sufficient time to inculcate necessary ideals and support its teachers.

One evening I went to the village shop to buy some sweets. The proprietor had sold out of my choice. He said, 'I shall have some in on Friday.' My reply was, 'O.K, thank you.' Before I could turn around I heard the well-known voice of Miss Selly saying, 'O.K, who ever taught you to answer in that manner?' With obvious shame-face I was persuaded to re-phrase my reply.

Our route home from school took us past Treen House where Mr. Fred Edwards lived. He was the well respected owner of Clee Hill Transport, a local haulage firm which employed many people. His lorries transported huge quantities of stone from the quarries and laid new road surfaces with the help of his steam rollers. To us, Treen House was a most distinguished home with beautiful surroundings and the luxury of a tennis court.

We continued up the hill, through an uneven field known as the Pit Ground. The remains of Key's Quarry and numerous bell pits could clearly be seen. In summer the old, filled pit heads formed small, natural ponds. We would sit by the water's edge and collect frog's spawn. Even lunch boxes and wellingtons were used as containers.

Most boys and girls too wore boots in those days. We never failed to amaze our parents by the speed with which steel tips were kicked off and clusters of boot nails worn down. It was very seldom that we visited the cobbler. Instead my father kept a large sheet of thick soling leather in his workshop and frequently at week-ends I found him cutting out new soles for my school boots and tacking them securely in place. In winter the ponds were covered with thick ice. After testing it carefully, a considerable number of boys and girls of varying ages slid across in quick succession, finishing up like a collapsed rugby scrum on the far side. In my mind I can clearly recall the repetitive scrape made by the metal tipped, well studded boots, intermingled with shouts of delight from children.

The footpath continued from the pitground along the side of the G.W.R. railway spur which ran from the Dhu Stone via Clee Hill village to Craven Place. A clearly displayed notice said, 'Trespassers will be fined forty shillings.' But it was accepted practice to walk that way because there was no alternative route. A small shunting engine passed frequently along the line, pushing eight or ten trucks.

Its speed was not great and long blasts from the shrill whistle ensured that we had plenty of time to move to safety. If there were only two or three of us in sight, Mr. George Price, the engine driver would give us a ride. I used to love to pull the whistle cord and put a full shovel of coal onto the blazing fire. It gave me a tremendous sense of power and like many more boys of that age, made me long to be an engine driver.

With the train safely passed we walked in a crocodile fashion, balancing on a railway line.

Nearer the Dhu Stone, there were always long lines of railway trucks waiting beneath the quarry wharf to be filled with either stone or tar macadam. Written in bold letters on their sides were the words Clee Hill Quarries, Field and McKay and Clee Hill Granite Co. Closer inspection revealed destination cards held in position by extremely strong mousetrap-like clips. I could not resist pulling them back to read the details and I was proud to discover that stone was being sent from our local quarry to practically every county I had ever heard of; and so we passed the engine shed where our friendly shunter was housed for the night.

Nearby was the weighing bridge. By the side was the entrance leading to the controls and steps leading out onto the tipping wharf above. This entrance was known as the glory hole. We loved to run up and down these steps and generate a reverberating ring with our boots. I can clearly hear the sound whenever I think of the place. A little further on and immediately above my home were the workmens' tool sheds, the signal box and the drum house which controlled the rate at which loaded and unloaded trucks moved up and down the incline railway to Bitterley and on to Ludlow.

Due to one or two accidents and the increase in road transport which enabled goods to be delivered directly to their destination, this incline closed in the late 1950s and since then all trace of this hive of industry has disappeared.

SCHOOL HOLIDAYS

I never recall suffering from the common complaint of being bored nor my parents wishing me back at school because I was a nuisance to them or had nothing to do.

Family holidays were an unknown luxury and one often heard the expression, 'Thaa bin/nu fer the likes O we.' (They are not for people of our social status).

There were always jobs to be done such as cleaning out the cow shed, feeding poultry or carrying water. In Spring one of our fields at least, was covered with tumps of farmhouse manure and my father tried to persuade me to spread some of them at a rate of three old pence a tump. I thought it was one of the hardest jobs I had ever attempted but the results worked wonders on the grass.

Small holders around the Clee Hill had very few farm buildings and our calves were kept in a small, warm, semi-dark shed during the winter. As warmer days arrived, the calves were released to graze in the fields, but, we did not just

67

open the door and let them bound into the sunlight and open spaces. This new found freedom and strange surroundings frightened them so much that they charged through the nearest hedge and harmed themselves considerably. I was shown how to attach a halter to each calf and lead it around the field. At first the frisky, loveable creatures kicked up back legs, snorted, backed away, tried to break free and often stepped on my feet unintentionally, but by repeating and progressively lengthening their exercise for a few days it was possible to release the calves with safety.

Soon they found their affectionate mother and she allowed them to suck her. We required all the milk we could get for our family needs and so father fitted a gruesome looking nose band on each calf. They were made by pushing a number of long nails through leather straps. Consequently when the calves tried to suck their mother and gave her a bunt to persuade her to release her milk, she jumped sky high. If we were sitting in the long grass producing noises with a long blade of grass or making daisy chains, it did indeed look as though the cow had jumped over the moon as the nursery rhyme tells us.

In those days hay was not baled but it was piled loosely into a barn or rick. After some months it became very compact. Daily, my father sent me to fill bags of hay for the cattle but before I could do this I had to separate a small quantity from the bay by cutting it with a large hay knife.

To encourage the calves to eat hay we used to chop it into short strands. For this we used a machine called a chaff cutter which was an unwieldy machine with a large wheel which incorporated a blade. It chopped the hay beautifully and your fingers too if you were careless.

Many smallholders had fields which joined onto common land and therefore they were allowed to put one and a half head of stock there for each acre of land they owned or rented. Cattle were extremely difficult to confine to small enclosures after they had roamed on common land. The normal practice was to tether them by a long chain or rope until they were tamed.

At milking time I watched my father sitting on a small, three legged stool. He turned his flat cap back to front, pushed his head into the cow's side and pulled gently on the teats. The milk shot in fine jets to the bottom of the enamel bucket, making a distinct, hollow ring. As the quantity of milk grew, a white froth formed on its surface. A treat for me was an enamel cup filled directly from the cow and drunk untreated, not pasturised, sterilised or pulverised and still warm. I'm sure that is not allowed nowadays and perhaps the majority of people would find it distasteful.

Milk was taken to the dairy. Some was strained and taken to the house for drinking, some put in small galvanised buckets for the calves and the remainder poured into a separator. As the name suggests, this machine separated the milk from the cream. I thought it an ingenious construction and was intrigued to see skimmed milk appear through one spout and rich, yellow cream through another. This was stored in a bucket covered with muslin cloth and added to each day until mother had sufficient quantity to make into butter. The skimmed milk was used for numerous purposes in the home including cooking. Before we had a separator the fresh milk was placed in a large, shallow bowl and allowed to stand. Next day a flat spoon was used to 'skim' the settled cream from the surface, leaving the skimmed milk, or milk without cream behind. Hence its name.

I loved to feed the calves and during the holidays I persuaded father to let me have a bucket of bread and milk and walk quietly into the calves' cot. One would rub his wet nose against my hand. I put my fingers inside his mouth and with the calf nearly sucking them off, lowered his head into the bucket to drink. My hand enabled me to regulate the speed at which the calf drank. I was told it harmed him to drink too quickly.

Saturday was the time for butter making. Cream was poured into a large churn which was positioned vertically. The top was screwed on to make sure that its rubber seal fitted snuggly around the edge. An awkward, crooked handle was turned slowly and the churn tipped over. After a few rotations, a valve had to be pressed to allow air and gas to escape. I turned the handle for what seemed an eternity with no sign of butter forming; but what a thrill it was to suddenly feel the butter clotting and the weight falling from side to side as the churn turned. The lid had a glass inspection panel and when small blobs of butter clung to the sides I knew it had formed sufficiently. With the churn again fixed in the vertical position, butter milk was drained off and the lump of fresh butter remained. This was lifted out and placed in a large, round, shallow container which had two wooden handles. Two flat wooden patters were used to remove all the excess moisture from the butter. Salt was added and the patters were used to pat and chop the butter into half and pound quantities. Finally lovely corrugated patterns were imprinted by the patters. I have never tasted any product to compare with that beautiful, smooth, home-made butter. No wonder during the war years urban visitors gave practically any asking price for it.

Nowadays, good milking cows make a terrific price in the market, but the loss of one to a farmer does not affect a family as it did in those days. George Broome reminded me how the community raised funds by holding whist drives, dances and making collections to replace the only milking cow owned by a small-holder. I think of his words as he added, "Folks come in to our community and tell us how to live and what we should do with our common land. I resent that. We know how to live. In our younger days we used to have to work to eat, now you eat before you work."

Country children see the miracle of birth when they are at a very young age. I cannot remember how young I was when I first saw a little calf being born but it amazed me how quickly the mum could lick it dry and seem to inject it with strength, so that within minutes it would be standing and moving confidently around the cow shed. Then by instinct, the new born calf would find its way to mum's udder and settle to its first meal in a strange new world. My mother referred to this rich milk as 'boistings'. She used some to make into beautiful puddings but my father always made sure that the little calf had his fair share because it contained certain ingredients which helped prevent disease.

The birth of piglets seemed a much less painful and easier process to me; one little pig appeared after another until finally the nizgul or runt arrived. These were the names given to the last born of the litter. My father fixed bars around the sty before the young were born. Although sows are good, protective mothers, they seem to flop down with complete disregard to the safety of their little ones. The bars allowed the piglets to escape with safety and avoided them being squashed between the sow and the walls. When the sow was finally settled, each piglet found a teat or drill and I would watch with pleasure as twelve or fourteen tails swung rhythmically to the sound of contented sucking, squeals and grunts.

We always had a few cats at home, partially as pets but also to catch mice and rats. Wherever there is hay and grain there is never a shortage of vermin. I quite liked mice and often watched the timid little creatures scurrying across the manger. I felt sorry to see our pet cats transformed into vicious killers carrying tiny mice to their kittens but I never felt any pity for those detestable creatures, rats. Occasionally however we would run to tell mother that a cat was carrying a kitten by the nape of its neck. She had great difficulty in convincing us that the kitten was not being harmed but that it was nature's method of transporting a blind, helpless creature.

On warm summer days our hens became broody. My parents used all sorts of ingenious deterrents, but we children usually persuaded them to allow us to place a clutch of twelve or fourteen eggs under one hen. Then we began to count the days, ticking off each one on the calendar as it passed. Each morning mum turned the eggs under the clucking, wary hen. When the twenty first day arrived we would run to the cub and listen intently for the cheep of little chickens. Carefully we removed an egg and put it to our ears. Unbelieveably, we sometimes heard a chicken cheeping inside the unbroken prison. An occasional tap could be heard too and soon a little hole appeared and out popped a beak. Gradually the hole enlarged to reveal a wet, bedraggled chicken. With the help of the mother hen's body heat, this near lifeless creature was soon transformed into a cuddly, fluffy, yellow ball. Soon the proud mother would strut around the field calling her brood to search for food. If a cow or cat appeared the hen would squawk. All the frightened chicks would run underneath her as she fluffed up her wings and feathers to an enormous size. By doing this she could cover all the chicks completely.

We always had rabbits as pets and while I was still very young my favourite one died. I obviously did not realise the permanency of death because I took my rabbit and placed him in the oven beside the fire to warm him up, thinking this treatment would revive him.

I spent a great deal of time wandering on the hills. Towards Horseditch, near the Hoar Edge was a mass of whimberry bushes. The whimberries were not easy to find but we never returned home until our jars were full and our mouths and tongues a deep, tell tale blue. What a delicate, delicious taste those whimberry pies were, especially with a little fresh cream added. I was saddened recently to see that all the bushes had been grazed down to the stalks. I can only assume there is insufficient grass because the common land is overstocked.

I never thought the hills beautiful because they were marred by quarry waste and scars from industry. Nevertheless I do not know a spot from which such an extensive view may be seen anywhere in the British Isles. Titterstone is unique. I would turn to the four corners of the compass and see a tremendous distance in each direction. Gazing south I watched trains winding their way across well wooded countryside from Shrewsbury, through Ludlow and on to Leominster and

Hereford. Ludlow a thousand feet below looked so tiny. Even the remains of the mighty castle and majestic steeple of St. Laurence's church appeared insignificant. I reflected that I went to school at the bottom of Mill Street. Looking from this mighty peak how small the problems became; how minute the individual. What a wonderful place to sit to make me realise that I was no more important in the eyes of the world than a grain of sand.

I could turn over in bed and see a distance of sixty miles. There was no need to listen to the weather forecast. Locals could predict it quite accurately. Storms were seen brewing miles away and it was interesting to watch the prevailing winds drive them along the valleys between the many ranges of hills. I could tell that Hereford was having a cloudburst while Tenbury, Abberley and Worcester were enjoying sunshine. My mother would hang out her washing and estimate quite accurately how long she could leave it on the line before a storm reached the area.

We often played around the quarries and got our clothes covered with tar. Most children had iron hoops made by the quarry blacksmith. They were bowled along with the help of an iron hook, shaped like a shepherd's crook. When new or unused, the hoops were rusty but when they were shiny and smooth we could run at top speed with them rolling by our side.

Sometimes I sat in our sally tree and made whistles. I wonder if boys still make them? A piece of young sally was cut about 8cm long from a branch. A knotch was made on one side and the bark tapped all around with a knife handle. Gradually the bark loosened sufficiently to be pulled off in a complete cylinder. The remaining wood was flattened on one side and bark replaced to make quite an effective whistle.

Another simple toy was made by threading a piece of string through both holes of a large button. When this was suspended in the middle of the string it was twisted a number of times and then stretched. This caused the button to spin at tremendous speed, making clockwise and anti-clockwise rotations alternatively. Sometimes we used serrated tin lids for the same purpose and we could generate sufficient speed to cut through pieces of paper.

My dog was a good friend and companion. We wandered together for miles over the hillsides following the well worn, narrow tracks made by the sheep. These were regularly cleared from the hills and it was more interesting than any Western film to see horses, riders and dogs converging from all directions to sweep the bleating sheep in front of them. These cow boys were excellent horsemen. While their ponies were galloping they jumped on and off them with thrilling skill. One gentleman named Norman Broome had a wonderful pony called Stardust. He would gallop like the wind and had tremendous spirit, but when he was not working he was friendly and docile and I have seen his owner lead him up to the bar of our very restricted house.

On our jaunts in early Autumn I saw smallholders whose properties were on the edge of commonland, cutting and hauling bracken to use as winter bedding for their cattle. When snow covered the ground my dog and I followed the tracks of rabbits and hares. Rabbits never ventured far but hares travelled considerable distances and when disturbed often doubled back to return over the first tracks they had made.

I frequently refer to the remoteness of the Clee Hill area and the way in which members of the community supported each other, but they were volatile and independent too. Family feuds were deeply rooted and occasionally it was necessary for the law to intervene. My father was one of the very few people in the area who had a car. No bus service existed off the main roads. Consequently our car served as a taxi and I remember my father having to make four journeys to Ludlow to take and bring home the accused and accuser in one case.

We had some relations who lived twenty miles away at Martley and my sister and I continually pestered father to take us to see them. This he occasionally did but the distance seemed so great that we usually stopped halfway for a picnic. This must be difficult to believe in an era when many commute greater distances to work every day.

The Clee Hill word for an alder tree was a waller. Near the Dhu Stone was a large coppice called The Wallers where we spent many hours playing fox and hounds. In the blackberrying season we wandered through these trees and beyond, armed with a large stick to knock down nettles and enable us to pull the blackberry briars within reach. There was much more rough land about in those days and hedges were not trimmed so neatly. There was never a shortage of blackberries and my sister and I could soon fill a bucket each. Some were used for blackberry and apple pies and the remainder we carried to the main road to sell to the Blackberry Man. I was never sure whether he sold the vast quantities for jam or dyes.

The nearest stock market was held at the Angel public house on the Angel bank. Very few people hired transport to take their stock for sale. Whole families could be seen driving cattle through the lanes. All was well until a cottager's dog suddenly barked from behind a hedge or a field gate was left open. Then curious animals stopped to investigate or bolted off in the wrong direction. The chase would begin. Drovers and dogs ran for miles to bring the strays back to the main group. What exhausting work it was, but not so daunting as not realising sufficient money at the sale and having to drive the animals all the way home again.

The most awkward task was taking a sow and piglets to market. Sometimes we carried a bucket in front, rattled it and shouted, 'Joey, Joey', or 'Stew, stew, stew.' What stubborn, obstinate creatures pigs are. They never seem to go where you want them to.

But it was an experience to watch people who really knew how to handle animals. A milking cow led with a halter closely followed by her little calf; shepherds walking ahead of a flock with an obedient, well trained dog following at a discreet distance. These are sights to remember and cherish. The volume of traffic would make them impossible nowadays.

The market was a social occasion. Gossip and news were exchanged and the auctioneer knew the community well enough to call individuals by name and say the most outrageous things. I was fascinated by the speed with which he could utter his words when selling an animal.

We looked forward to the Clee Hill fair with its brandy snap, hot dogs and toffee apples. A regular competition was singing for a pig. The idea, not an easy one to execute, was for each competitor in turn to hold a piglet in his arms and sing a song, without the pig squealing. The song began, 'Who'd give a dollar for a thing like that? Do you think I've got a donkey under this old hat.' The winner on more than one occasion was Tommy Smith, a cherry minder from the low country. The weather was always cold and windy with occasional heavy snow falls. Locals always complained about it, but the well known fact was that the weather would never improve until the May Fair had left Clee Hill.

I enjoyed the May Day celebrations. Our village school chose a queen and attendants. When the day arrived the queen was dressed in regal costume and the attendants in knicker bockers and tops of Lincoln green. A band, decorated horses and children in fancy dress accompanied her in a memorable parade from the school to the village football ground, where the queen was crowned and celebrations followed. The local brass band was an essential part of the festivities but the band leader ruled his players in an unorthodox manner. While playing at the flower show, one member who had partaken of a few drinks put his instrument down in the middle of a tune. The conductor marched up to him and struck him so forcefully that he was knocked out. No one seemed unduly distressed and when the victim recovered he sat up, picked up his instrument and continued to play as though nothing had happened.

In those days our summer holiday extended well into September and a special week was allocated in October. If this had not been so, there would have been a great deal of absence from school because many families travelled to lowland farms to assist with the potato harvest, while others travelled to Worcestershire for hop picking.

I mentioned earlier how the mist frequently settled in the valleys like the rolling sea. In early Autumn these mists gradually cleared and the sun broke through and began to dry the late dew. I still refer to similar weather as hop picking weather.

Early in the morning, we accompanied friends to a waiting bus or lorry and travelled what seemed an endless distance to the hop yard. There we shared a crib. This was the name given to a sacking container into which each group of people picked the hops. Farm helpers came around on a regular basis and cut down the hop strings leaving a pile of hops for us to clear. We picked furiously to help fill the crib as soon as possible. As lunch time approached, the busheller came to each crib with a large basket which when filled held a bushel of hops. The pickers counted carefully how many bushels were removed from the crib and there were always heated arguments if the busheller pushed the hops into the basket, so taking a greater quantity to fill it.

Working outside always gives one an extra appetite and we would eat ravenously. But the taste of hops was unbearable and if we carelessly rubbed our eyes without washing our hands, the smarting pains were quite severe.

Large groups of Black Country romanies were always seen in the hop yards. They lived for weeks in open sheds along side the farm houses. Many were very pleasant people but because we did not understand their way of life we were afraid of them. The police did not understand them either and very few days passed without fights taking place between locals and romanies with the police endeavouring to intervene. As a result of smoky fires and primitive living conditions, the skin of the gypsy children was weather beaten and dark. We watched them and listened to conversations with interest. One particular snippit I remember amused me. A mother shouted, 'Mary, where's the pudding cloth?' The reply was, 'Round our Joe's sore heel.' The mother, 'Will you tell our Joe if he doesn't bring the pudding cloth here, he'll have no pudding for his dinner.'

As a special treat when I was a little older I was allowed to go to Cleobury Mortimer or Ludlow cinema on a Saturday evening. The return fare in the 1940's was sixpence (2½p) and the cinema ticket fivepence (Approximately 2p). No one had a television and everyone looked forward to seeing prominent events, such as the Grand National or a World Title boxing match on the Saturday evening Pathe News. The night lights of Ludlow were bright and friendly but it was a different world when I stepped off the bus at the top of the Angel bank - not a street lamp anywhere. Normally the stars gave sufficient light to enable me to see my way home but when the hill mists fell it was impossible to see your hand infront of you. On one occasion I found my way up Tommy Martin's lane, through his farmyard and into his field. My intention was to follow the hedge and climb over a stile onto the Dhu Stone lane. However I missed the stile and found myself in the corner of the field. I walked back and forth along the hedge but I could not find the stile. Fear was beginning to grip me so I endeavoured to retrace my steps to the farm and start my route again. In so doing I fell over an object which got up and scampered away. A receding bleat told me it was only a sheep. After what seemed an eternity of groping and stumbling I eventually found the lane and made my way safely home. How different from modern city life.

WORLD WAR II

World War II took place during my childhood days and although the sparsely populated area of Clee Hill was not plagued with constant raids, the war had its effect on our community.

Physically and geographically these hills are surrounded by extensive low areas and therefore it is not surprising that aircraft having navigational problems crashed into the quarry faces. This brought the war to our door step and it was a depressing sight to see a large bomber smashed to smithereens and scattered over a wide area. Perspex from crashed aircraft was acquired and used to make small brooches and model aircraft. Another craze at that time was the modelling of aircraft from coins. I wonder what happened to them all?

The lack of electricity caused great problems in rural areas, but during those years the whole country was plunged into darkness. Cars were not allowed to use headlights and owners painted wide, white lines around the edges of the mudguards and along the running boards. Large stones were painted white along the verges of our country lanes. House lights could possibly attract the attention of enemy aircraft and each household was ordered to make blinds to fit against its windows and avoid any light escaping.

It was impossible to forget war because practically every young man from the area was in the forces. Some local families had three or four sons away at a time and sadly many of them never returned.

I have on many occasions stood outside my house. The immediate surroundings were pitchblack but in the distance frequent explosions could be heard and in far away cities search lights were seen lighting up the heavens in an attempt to track down enemy aircraft.

Food and clothing were strictly rationed. Only small quantities of butter, cheese, sugar and other foods were obtainable weekly and each member of the family was issued with a ration book. Each page contained a number of coupons which had to be submitted at a shop before commodities could be purchased. Even clothes were rationed and it took a considerable time to save sufficient coupons before a suit could be bought. I treasured my sweet coupons like gold. I was allowed a quarter of a pound of sweets per week and once my coupons had been given to the shop keeper, there was no way of obtaining more.

Our family was lucky enough to have its own milk, butter supply and eggs in the summer. The black market was rife and city people were continually asking for butter and prepared to pay handsome prices, but my mother parted with very little because it was one luxury she wished her family to retain.

I wonder how many remember the dried egg powder? I disliked it intensely, but not quite as much as the dried milk we were issued with in school. When made into a drink it was tolerable but the taste and stale smell seemed to linger in school cups and virtually polluted the class room air.

Children's toys were unobtainable and such common things as tomato sauce and tins of fruit were impossible to buy. Italian prisoners of war were brought to work in the quarries. Some of them made most ingenious toys and we were thrilled to receive jumping men and acrobatic clowns from them.

Towards the end of the war, tall, lean American soldiers were billeted at the Dhu Stone. They had most impressive equipment. Their work was to quarry stone and reduce it to required sizes with mobile crushers then transport it to American air bases for building runways etc. Many of these friendly people visited my home but as well as buying beer they brought with them huge urns of black coffee. They wore very well made uniforms, beautiful fur lined boots and long gauntlets. Local quarrymen were poorly clad in comparison.

Children were always asking the Americans for spearmint. We were lucky living in a public house because they gave us generous quantities. However, they obviously disliked the continual requests from the general public because nearly every lorry was soon seen displaying notices saying, 'No gum chum.'

On one occasion my father and I were invited to the camp. When visiting the cookhouse and stores my eyes opened like saucers when it was explained that the mountains of tins were filled with luscious peaches, pineapple, pears and other mouth watering fruit which we were unable to buy in shops.

Inspite of their luxuries they missed home cooking and quite frequently they brought rabbits to my mother which they had shot or run over. She skinned and stewed them and in the evening the soldiers came along armed with their mess tins and ate the cooking with relish.

These men were soon replaced by coloured Americans. One evening I answered a knock at the back door. When I opened it I could see no one. Then, suddenly I saw two pairs of eyes moving in the dark. I ran with fear into the house, but I was soon to discover that they belonged to two coloured, amiable American sentries. This coloured contingent did not remain with our community long, and we were saddened to hear reports soon afterwards that most of them had perished in the English Channel.

AUTUMN
THE PIG KILLING SEASON

Many of the quarrymen had to use 28 pound hammers all day but still found the energy and time to dig and cultivate a kitchen garden. The produce gained, helped supplement the comparatively low wages. When the fervour of summer receded and Autumn began, everyone's attention turned to the bacon pig.

Every household had a small sty at the end of the garden usually constructed of railway sleepers. They cost from one shilling (5p) to half a crown (12½p) in those days. The topic of conversation in the bar would be, 'How's the pig doin?' Everyone made it his business to peer into everyone else's sty and compare sizes. Animals exceeding twenty score were very common.

Pig killing began in November and neighbours tried to stagger the slaughtering. This enabled them to supply each other with fresh pork for some weeks. Without the facility of modern deep freezers it was virtually impossible to keep fresh meat for any length of time.

All the household scraps were put into a large barrel known as a wash tub. Surplus skimmed milk was added and this formed the major part of the pig's diet, and after feeding a pig every day for a year the animal became a pet. Occasionally the owner threw a few lumps of coal over the sty door because it was supposed to be a good medicine.

When the day for killing arrived it was a sad occasion especially for the children but it was a necessary happening because the carcase provided the family with bacon, ham and lard for a whole year. The first essential for pig killing was a good stout bench. My father was a wheelwright and carpenter and he made numerous benches in late summer and early autumn. He used thick elm for the top, usually five or six centimetres thick. Holes were bored for the legs. These were shaped with a draw knife and wedged in position. Through the rest of the year the bench was a useful piece of furniture in many homes.

A group of men from the bar of the public house, probably four or six, were asked to help kill our pig. Early in the morning the boiler was filled with water and a good fire made. When killing time arrived the water was boiling. A rope was lassooed around the pig. It was forced to the bench and turned over on its side and roped. The helpers positioned themselves along the bench, holding the pig firmly. The butcher inserted a knife into the pig's throat and as the animal began to bleed so a front leg was moved up and down to help pump the blood from the carcase.

The eerie squealing of the pig is something I will never forget. This was an experience I disliked intensely. The art of pig killing was to bleed the animal as much as possible so draining most of the blood from the meat. This improved its keeping qualities.

Our butcher, whose name was Sammy Goodman, was a terrible teaser. On one occasion when I was a small boy he threatened to put me in the scalding tub. I was absolutely petrified and ran into the house with my hair literally standing on end and hid behind my mother's apron.

Another experience which distressed me was to see our bullocks being castrated. With a quick flick of the horns the operator would fell an animal on to its side and then proceed to remove the testicals using red hot irons. It was an agonising process to watch and I am glad that there are more acceptable methods nowadays.

Occasionally pig killing brought its drama. One year as the pig was nearing the bench it suddenly lurched forward and broke away. One poor fellow was left hanging on to the end of the rope as the terrified pig darted through the gate and straight over the 'mixun' (dung heap).

The dead pig had to be thoroughly cleaned. Dad filled a wooden tub with boiling water. The pig was heaved into the tub. Only one half fitted in and it looked rather grotesque sitting up with steam rising all around. Circular metal scrapers were used. These made a distinctive rasping sound as the hair was removed from the pig's skin. The butcher used his knife to do the same work. The blade was razor sharp and sliced through the tough hair with ease.

The clean, pink pig was carried into the old 'brew house' and a 'gambol', a piece of knotched wood, was slotted through the achilles tendon of each back leg. A rope was tied around the gambol and the pig heaved up to a beam, high enough for the head to be a few inches from the floor. It was no easy task to hoist up a 400lb pig so we had a wooden roller attached to the beam to act as a pulley.

The butcher cut down the full length of the pig's stomach and removed the entrails. Small intestines were known as 'chitlins' and as children we had the unsavoury job of helping Dad clean them. This was done by fixing an open end of the intestines onto a running tap and squeezing the faeces through the tubes. Before leaving the pig to hang for two days, the butcher fitted a wooden stretcher inside the cleaned body. This held the carcase open to help it cool and dry.

The butcher returned two days later to cut up the carcase but before this was done the pig was weighed with the aid of a special scales called a steel-yard. This was a long tabulated rod weighted with a metal ball at one end and counter-balanced with hooks at the other. Our pig usually weighed about sixteen score (16 x 20 lb). This was small compared with most in the area. Soon there were baths and buckets filled with joints of meat. Some of them were distributed to neighbours and our family in turn received joints from them. Refrigerators and deep freezers were non-existent therefore it was impossible to keep all the joints for one's own family.

The leaves of fat were rolled out and given to mother. She chopped them into small cubes and melted them down. The resultant fat was poured into large earthenware containers, known as steens to cool and solidify into lard. The remains of the fat made lovely, chewy scratchings. The bladder was blown up and left hanging by the back door to dry, so that eventually we could use it as a football.

CURING BACON

Hams and flitches (sides) were placed on a cold slab and completely covered with saltpetre to penetrate the meat. On top of this a thick layer of salt was spread. After a month or so this was cleaned off and the meat wiped down before being suspended from hooks in the warmest, driest room in the house. This happened to be our kitchen and because it was a small room the curing bacon was positioned directly over our table. The meat soon dried but for a week or so we were plagued by salty globules dropping onto our food.

Practically every part of the pig was eaten. We all enjoyed pig's ears, chiterlins and trotters. These had to be eaten while they were still hot because the more they were allowed to cool the more sticky the meat became, so much as that it was difficult to open and close our mouths.

During the weeks after pig killing there was not a minute to spare and my mother seemed to have an endless stream of urgent jobs including making sausages, faggots, black puddings, brawn and pork pies. The bacon pig was invaluable to every family in the area. If one died it was an absolute disaster because the main supply of meat and fat for the year was lost.

CHRISTMAS TIME

As a family we spent a great deal of time decorating the public premises and we enjoyed immensely the carol singing and fun. My only regret was that because of extra work it was almost impossible to find time to have our Christmas dinner together. My mother ordered large quantities of mince pies from Tommy's Bakery and these were handed around the customers on three or four occasions during the Christmas period.

Each Boxing Day we were visited by a group of local men called the 'Niggers.' Having blacked their skin and donned very colourful clothes they made a very early start and visited every public house in the locality. One member played a row of tin whistles and another played bone clappers. These were usually made from ribs. There would be a melodian, an accordian and probably a banjo. The group sang, danced, changed shirts and drank great quantities too.

We attended church regularly and I never experienced any conflict between our faith and living in a public house. The customers sang with sincerity and pleasure and I'm sure it was to recapture the thoughts and values they had acquired and loved in their childhood.

SPRING AND SUMMER OCCUPATIONS

Winter is at least a month longer on Clee Hill than in the surrounding valleys and it was with relief that we always welcomed the cuckoo, pussy willows, daisies, dandelions and other signs of spring.

The improvement in the weather was the signal for seasonal jobs such as repairing stone walls around the hill enclosures and hedge laying. My job was to carry a supply of willow stakes to the skilled hedge pleacher. I watched with interest as he trimmed the sides, thinned out the hedge and chopped the remaining young trees sufficiently to be able to bend them over and weave them between the evenly spaced stakes. On completion the pleacher would dig along each side of the hedge and cover the lower part of it with soil to hold moisture and encourage new thick growth at the base.

Like other smallholders in the area my father prepared some of our grass for mowing. Quite regularly someone would ask in the bar, 'Ăst thē pŭt thē ǎăh up yŭt?' (Have you put your fields ready for hay yet?). Gates were closed and fences repaired to prevent sheep and cattle breaking in to eat the fresh shoots of grass. By July the crop was fit to cut and I was always excited to see Mr Ben Price and his son Stan arrive with the mowing machine and horses.

Before mowing began, my father cut carefully around the gate entrance with a scythe and fed every blade of grass he cut to the cattle. Nothing was wasted. The gate was opened, the machine driven on to the clear area and prepared for work. After fitting in a freshly sharpened blade the driver urged the horses forward. The blade flew from side to side almost faster than the eyes could follow and the rhythmic clicking of the machine could be heard all the way round the field. As evening approached the working horses plodded along side the last remaining, standing row of grass. The machine came to a halt and as jets of cold breath emerged from their nostrils the horses were tethered for a well earned rest. With the machine having been prepared for the homeward journey the Prices went into the public bar for a 'few pints'. By now darkness had fallen. Stan and his father walked out, perhaps a little unsteadily and seated themselves on the machine shafts. The gentle jogging and rough terrain often made them drop off to sleep. By habit and instinct the horses found their way home to Random, a very isolated farm near the slopes of Titterstone. It is a miracle to me how the owners reached home safely having dozed for part of the journey.

When the sun had baked the grass on the upper side we worked our way through the rows turning them with rakes. Often someone followed behind and 'tedded', that is shook the green wads with a pike. After a day or so of constant sunshine and fresh breeze the hay was sufficiently dry for two or three rows to be pulled into one. Before the damp of evening arrived the hay was pulled into small tumps called cocks. These gave some protection to the crop should rain suddenly arrive.

We were never short of help and gathering in the hay was quite a social occasion. Plenty of cider and sandwiches were available for young and old alike. Because our small barn was not far away a horse and cart was not used to carry cocks to their destination. Instead we used two long, stout poles which were pointed at each end. These were carefully pushed under each cock of hay and placed about a metre apart. Two carriers positioned themselves between the poles, one behind the cock and one in front. At a given signal both lifted together and walked instep towards the barn. Any sign of the hay toppling caused the rear carrier to shout, "Right hand up," or "Left hand down," in order to counteract the movement. Of course we children were a little hasty and not really strong enough. More often than not the cock would suddenly lurch and topple to the ground. We heartily laughed, lay on the hay and kicked our feet in the air. The adults would scold and abuse us for 'negligently destroying their preparation.' But if we did not let this happen too often, we mixed pleasure with work and our help was appreciated.

When harvest was completed my father would lean on the gate and gaze with contentment at the cleared fields. Occasionally he would day dream, allow his eyes to look further afield to the Radnorshire Hills, the Black Mountains, the Brecon Beacons and watch the beautiful red sun sinking slowly. This was one of the few occasions in his life when he allowed himself this privilege, but he was soon jolted back to reality by pressures of work.

The gathering in of the hay signalled the end of harvesting on Clee Hill. The binder and threshing machine were not seen because the cold and wet did not allow grain to be grown so high above sea level.

WORKING WITH WOOD

I began my career as a woodwork teacher. This was a natural thing for me to do because my father was a wheelwright and carpenter and a knowledge of the nature of timber had been part of my life from a very early age. When I was not pre-occupied with the happenings in the house, I was invariably in dad's workshop. In addition to repairing furniture, rakes, spade handles, axes etc he was mainly occupied with making farm gates, coffins and cartwheels.

As soon as I was able I assisted him in many ways. He hardly ever had a drawing but usually thought a great deal and then started to work. The traditional wheelwright and carpenter's craft has more-or-less disappeared and it is worth recording the details of constructions I remember so well.

GATE MAKING

Most of the farm gates made at home were nine or ten feet wide. As with most work it was the preparation of materials and marking out which took the time.

For a nine foot gate my father chose English oak or larch or a combination of both, depending on the quality of work in hand and money available.

To understand the sequence of constructing a field gate one must know the names of the various parts. (see Diag. 9). The heavy end from which the gate hangs is called the heel. The light end is called the head. The lower cross pieces are called bars while the sloping bar is the jack and the vertical bars are laces.

Firstly dad chose a heel of oak 5″ x 3½″ thick and a head of the same material 3″ x 2″. Then a top rail of oak. This was a tapered piece of wood 3½″ x 4″ at the heel and tapering to 2½″ x 3″ at the head. (see diag 10). The remaining bars, jack and laces were either larch or oak. The bars were 2½″ x 1½″ and the jack 2½″ x 1″.

The heel and head were placed side by side and the position of the rails and bars marked on the edge (see diag 1). These two pieces were placed 9 feet apart on two benches. They had to be parallel. Marks were made vertically along side heel and head (see dotted lines on diags 1 and 2). A long strip was placed across the diagonals from position 1 and 5 and heel and head were moved until diagonals were equal. A gate made to this shape would have formed a rectangle. After a gate has been used for sometime it often sags and the head drags on the ground. To avoid this dad used to set the head above the heel by about 1″ (see diag 3), and so make a parallelogram. He placed the top rail and bars across from heel to head over the marks 1,2,3,4 and 5 and marked lines alongside each one and underneath vertically. The bars and rails were removed, the heel and head turned on edge, all marks squared across, mortice positions made (see diag 4) and tenons gauged round bars and top rail.

Mortices for the top rail and bar number 4 were made right through heel and head. The underside of each mortice was tapered and the tenons made to match. This ensured a drive in fit (see diags. 5 & 6). The tenons of the top rail and bars were then cut. Occasionally the top rail was knotched at the heel end to minimise sag (see diag. 6). At this stage I often helped dad to drive the rails and bars into position (see diag 7). The jack was placed in position and laces too. These pieces were always put on the side of the gate which faced the road, known as the face side. When finally fixed they lay flush with the top rail.

The positions of the jack and the laces were marked and the mortices too. These were chopped to half the depth of the top rail and the jack knotched into the heel by the bottom bar (see diag 9). Bridle joints or one shoulder tenons were cut on the jack and laces to make a flush face side fit (see diags 8, 8a & 9).

When every member had been jointed into position dad made some oak dowels about ½″ (1 cm in diameter). He bored holes through heel and head at A, B, E, F and C (see diag 9). The oak dowels were driven home and pulled the joints up tightly. Where jack and braces crossed the bars, holes were bored through and bolts inserted. The gate was now completed. All that remained to be done was a visit to the blacksmith to obtain hanging fittings. I have illustrated some of the fittings used. If the width of a gate exceeded 9 feet, dad designed a diamond lace. That meant having two cross straps on either side (see diag 9d).

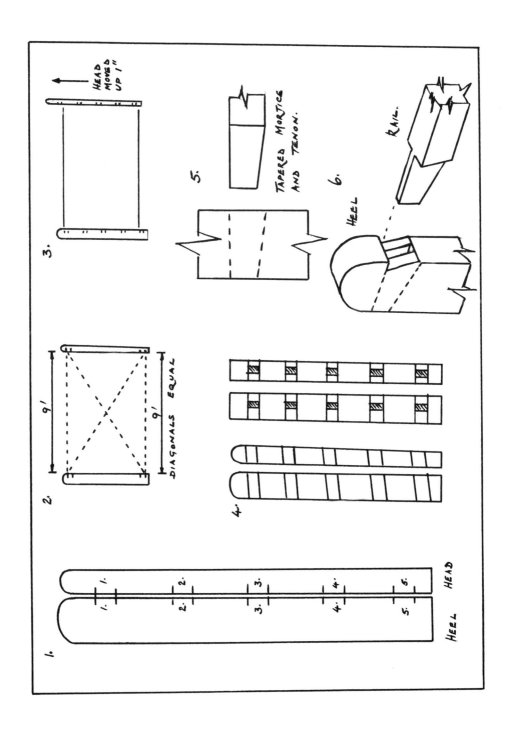

HEAD MOVED UP 1"

3.

5.

TAPERED MORTICE AND TENON.

6.

RAIL.

HEEL

2.

9' 9'

DIAGONALS EQUAL

4.

1.

1. 1. 2. 2. 3. 3. 4. 4. 5. 5.

HEEL HEAD

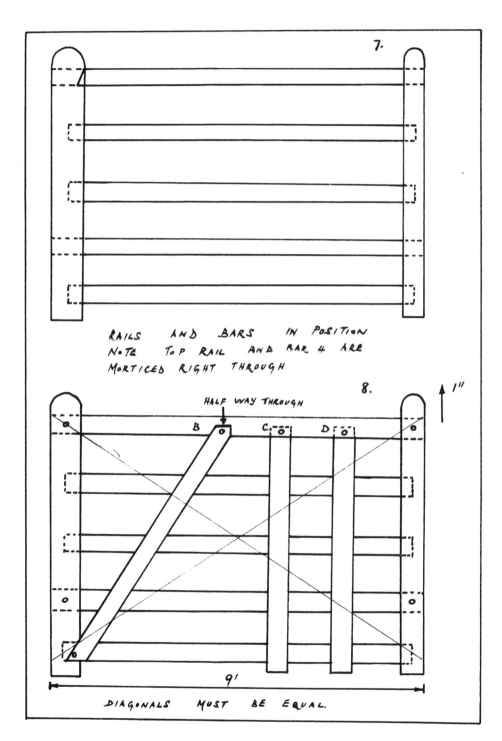

7.

RAILS AND BARS IN POSITION
NOTE TOP RAIL AND BAR 4 ARE
MORTICED RIGHT THROUGH

8.

HALF WAY THROUGH

B   C   D

1"

9'

DIAGONALS MUST BE EQUAL.

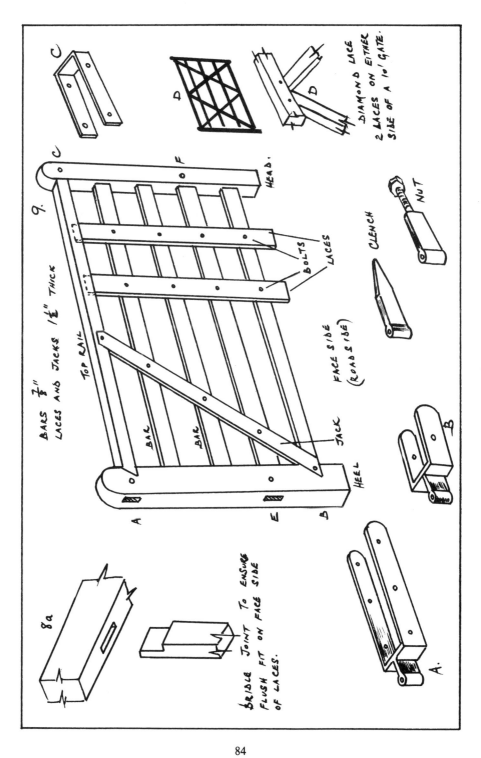

C

D

DIAMOND LACE 2 LACES ON EITHER SIDE OF A 10' GATE.

D

9.

C

F

HEAD.

NUT

CLENCH

BARS 7/8" LACES AND JACKS 1 1/2" THICK

TOP RAIL

BOLTS

LACES

FACE SIDE (ROAD SIDE)

BAR

BAR

JACK

HEEL

A

E

B

B

8a

BRIDLE JOINT TO ENSURE FACE SIDE FLUSH FIT ON FACE SIDE OF LACES.

A.

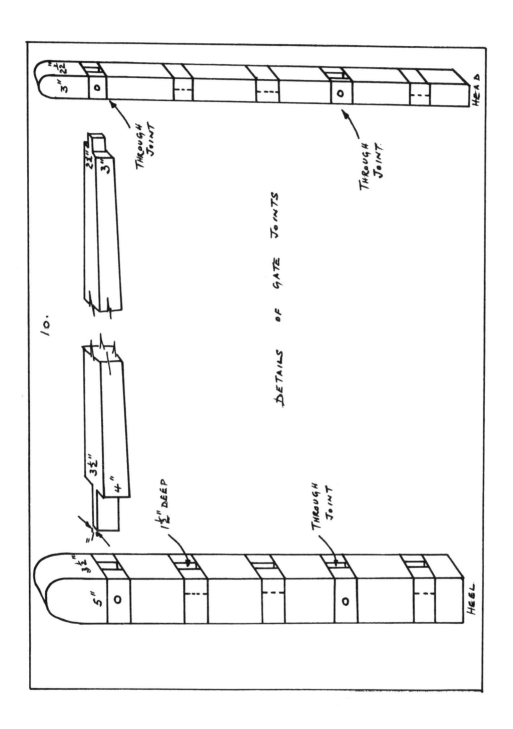

DETAILS OF GATE JOINTS

THROUGH JOINT

THROUGH JOINT.

THROUGH JOINT

THROUGH JOINT

HEAD

HEEL.

$3''$ $2\frac{1}{2}''$

$2\frac{1}{2}''$ $3''$

$3\frac{1}{2}''$ $4''$

$1\frac{1}{2}''$ DEEP

$3\frac{1}{2}''$

$5''$

10.

85

UNDERTAKING

In a rural community everyone knows everyone else. This was certainly the case when I was a child on Clee Hill. My father was the local undertaker. When someone died he was most considerate, sympathetic and understanding because he experienced the sense of loss as much as the rest of the community.

I remember attending a funeral when I was a small boy. The new vicar was from an urban area. In his sermon he sympathised with the bereaved but said 'Other people in the community, the undertaker, business people etc. are so involved in this busy life, they do not share your loss.' Can you imagine the reaction of my father? The new vicar quickly had a lesson in rural relationships.

Many cottages inhabited by the quarry workers were often situated a great distance across common land, well away from a good road. Therefore it was necessary for dad to ask for volunteers in the public bar to help carry a coffin to such isolated homesteads.

Anyone who has a Welsh ancestry is well aware of the 'feast' which follows a funeral and the tradition of laying the corpse in the parlour for all to view. This was the accepted tradition on Clee Hill. Many visitors were expected at the home of the bereaved and so there had to be a plentiful supply of food and drink. Each visitor after expressing his sympathy was given refreshments.

When a family came to see dad to do the undertaking he was invariably asked to take a case or two of beer when delivering the coffin. We drove to the edge of the common land, then began carrying the coffin across the rough hillside. It was often necessary to stop for a well earned rest, and of course a few bottles of beer were produced from the coffin. This was done as a matter of course with not the slightest thought of disrespect.

It was not uncommon to find that the cottage had no stairs but just a ladder leading to the bedroom. It was impossible to get a coffin up the ladder and so the corpse had to be strapped to a board and brought down and laid in the coffin in the parlour.

On the day of the funeral close relations or friends were chosen as bearers. The coffin was carried to the road side and then escorted on a wheelbier to the nearest church. Out of respect every neighbour attended.

Gravedigging is not an easy occupation and it was certainly more difficult in the churchyards on the slopes of the Clee Hills. After digging a spade's depth one immediately hits clay, rock or water. The gravediggers in those days were usually quarrymen who wished to supplement their wages. Just imagine walking three or four miles to and from work, using a 28 lb hammer all day and digging graves by lamplight. I remember dad telling of one such man who said he had had a very good week financially because he had dug three graves at the rate of half a crown each (12½p).

Coffins were either made from elm or oak. My mother often asked me to go to the workshop and cut some morning sticks. There was always a pile of elm off cuts by the vise but I soon found that it was nearly impossible to split the twisty grain of the beautifully marked elm. It was extremely difficult to plane with a hand plane and obtain a cabinet maker's finish because of its wild nature. Natural seasoning too did not give it sufficient stability to be used for furniture. However with modern kiln drying techniques, mechanical planers and sanders Ercol has produced first class furniture with this most beautiful of timber.

Now we have the ravages of the Dutch Elm disease and Herefordshire and Shropshire, once famous for wyche elm, have been practically denuded of this wonderful tree. No doubt in the near future English elm furniture will be rare and very expensive.

I watched my father make many coffins and I have made quite a number myself too. I expect methods of construction are very different nowadays. There was no machinery in our workshop and the main tool was a hand saw. When cutting out the top or bottom of a coffin my father occasionally paused. I would ask, "Why do you stop dad?" I soon found out when I was a little older how very tiring it was to cut out these shapes from one inch thick boards.

Firstly my father selected a 'set' of elm or oak boards according to the length of the dead person. Then he marked out a cross on the piece for the bottom (see diag 1). A-B would be a little wider than the shoulders of the deceased. The base marking was completed as in diag. 2. This shape was sawn out with a hand saw and the shoulders rounded with a spokeshave. Each end of the base had to be planed at an angle (see diag. 3) and the head and foot nailed on.

The next stage was the most difficult part of the construction. The sides were cut to width but left longer than the base. Opposite the shoulders A and B a number of pencil marks were lined perpendicular to the edges (see diag. 5). Saw cuts were made along these lines halfway through the thickness and on each side of the saw kerfs (cuts) sloping edges were cut with a long paring chisel (see diag 6). These chamfered saw cuts allowed the sides to be bent around the base.

Our bending process was rather primitive but very effective. The two prepared sides were placed together on two benches (see diag 7). A piece of wood 3″ x 2″ was placed along A near to the saw kerfs. Then an upright pole B was wedged firmly under the roof beam of the workshop. My mother produced two or three kettles of boiling water and this was poured slowly onto the kerfs.

The ends of the sides were gradually raised as C shows and a substantial batten pushed under the boards onto the supporting bench. After more soaking, additional battens were placed under the boards (see diag 8) until the required amount of bend was achieved. The sides were left to set and any surplus moisture wiped away quickly from the underside of the boards to avoid staining the grain.

After an hour or so the boards were removed to be nailed onto the base and ends, (see fig 9). Overhanging ends at A and B were cut off and all edges planed up. This done, the coffin was turned upsidedown and placed on an uncut lid. A clear mark was made around the coffin about 6 mm away from sides and ends, then the lid cut out. Edges were planed and the lid screwed into position.

I always enjoyed helping with the final stage of construction which was the tacking of a decorative moulding around the edges of the lid and base. My father used a sharp well-worn penknife to shape the corners of the moulding and this he did with great skill.

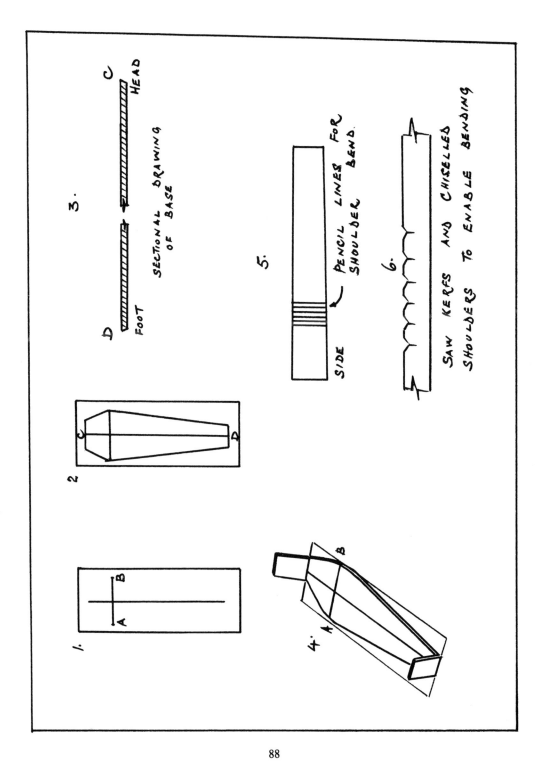

3.

C

HEAD

SECTIONAL DRAWING
OF BASE

D

FOOT

2.

5.

PENCIL LINES FOR
SHOULDER BEND.

SIDE

6.

SAW KERFS AND CHISELLED
SHOULDERS TO ENABLE BENDING

1.

B

A

4.

A

B

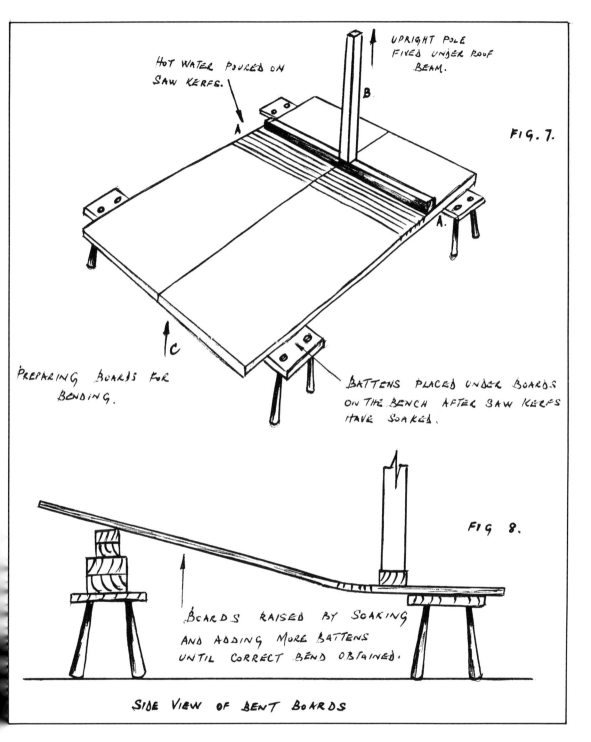

HOT WATER POURED ON SAW KERFS.

UPRIGHT POLE FIXED UNDER ROOF BEAM.

B

A

A

FIG. 7.

C

PREPARING BOARDS FOR BENDING.

BATTENS PLACED UNDER BOARDS ON THE BENCH AFTER SAW KERFS HAVE SOAKED.

FIG 8.

BOARDS RAISED BY SOAKING AND ADDING MORE BATTENS UNTIL CORRECT BEND OBTAINED.

SIDE VIEW OF BENT BOARDS

FIG. 9.
SIDES NAILED IN POSITION.

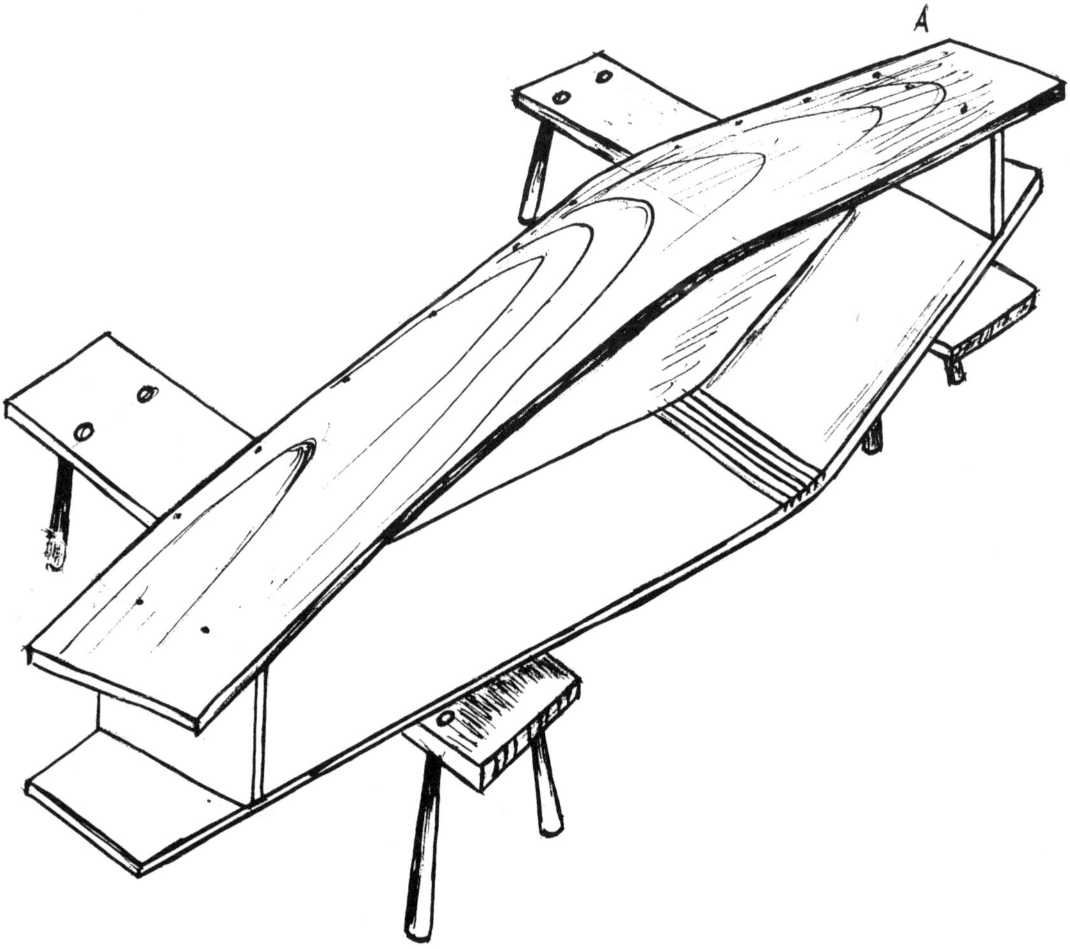

A

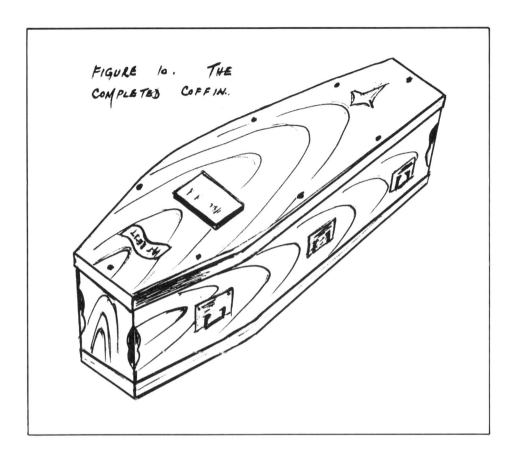

FIGURE 10. THE COMPLETED COFFIN.

Sanding and smoothing the coffin before wax polishing was a tedious job but if well done made all the difference to the finished product. After a couple of hours wax polishing, it was time to waterproof the inside using pitch. I prepared this by breaking a block into small lumps and putting them into a large pot over an oil stove heater. I would be very surprised if customers in a public house bar are able to smell the strong aroma of pitch wafting around nowadays. The molten pitch was poured round inside the base and along the saw kerfs, so making a perfect seal.

To complete the outside appearance metal fittings were clipped and bored in position.

Finally came the internal lining. Clean, soft, new wood shavings were placed to form a pillow under the material. The whole of the inside was covered and padded with great care and beautiful mauve tassells draped around the edges. The result was artistic, beautiful and dignified.

Occasionally two or three funerals occurred more-or-less at the same time and because of our lack of working space it was possible for a visitor to be suddenly confronted with a coffin in our sitting room, stretched across the arms of a settee.

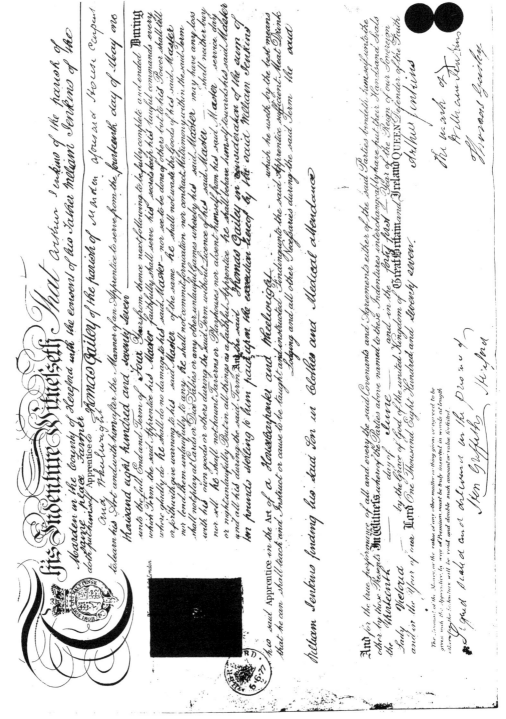

This Indenture Witnesseth That Arthur Jenkins of the parish of the
Magdalen in the County of England with the consent of his father William Jenkins of the
same place Farmer doth put himself Apprentice to James Gailey of the parish of Marden aforesaid House Carpenter
and Wheelwright to learn his Art and with him after the Manner of an Apprentice to serve from the fourteenth day of May one
thousand eight hundred and seventy seven unto the full End and Term of Four Years from thence next following to be fully complete and ended During
which Term the said Apprentice his Master faithfully shall serve his secrets keep his lawful commands every
where gladly do He shall do no damage to his said Master nor see to be done by others but to his Power shall tell
or forthwith give warning to his said Master of the same He shall not waste the goods of his said Master
nor lend them unlawfully to any. He shall not commit fornication nor contract Matrimony within the said Term
shall not play at Cards or Dice Tables or any other unlawful Games whereby his said Master may have any loss
with his own goods or others during the said Term without License of his said Master shall neither buy
nor sell. He shall not haunt Taverns or Playhouses nor absent himself from his said Master's service day
or night unlawfully But in all things as a faithful Apprentice he shall behave himself towards his said Master
and all his during the said Term And the said James Gailey in consideration of the sum of
ten pounds Sterling to him paid upon the execution hereof by the said William Jenkins

the said Apprentice in the Art of a House Carpenter and Wheelwright — which he will by the best means
that he can shall teach and Instruct or cause to be taught and instructed Finding unto the said Apprentice sufficient Meat Drink
Lodging and all other Necessaries during the said Term He the said

William Jenkins finding his said Son in Clothes and Medical Attendance

And for the true performance of all and every the said Covenants and Agreements either of the said Parties bindeth himself unto the
other by these Presents In Witness whereof the said Parties above named to this Indentures interchangeably have put their Hands and Seals
the Fourteenth day of June — and in the Forty first Year of the Reign of our Sovereign
Lady Victoria — by the Grace of God of the united Kingdom of Great Britain and Ireland QUEEN Defender of the Faith
and in the Year of our Lord One Thousand Eight Hundred and Seventy seven.

Arthur Jenkins

Signed Sealed and delivered in the Presence of

Hen Griffith   M Ford

The several in the Margin or the value of any other matter or thing given or agreed to be
given with the Apprentice, in way of Premium must be truly inserted in words at length
otherwise the Indenture will be void and double such amount or value forfeited.

The Words
William Jenkins
Howard Greville

MAKING CART WHEELS

The name wheelwright and making wheels are synonymous to me. The construction of a wheel is a great art and my father often reminded me that as an apprentice he had to assist with the making of every part of many wheels over a period of four years before he was allowed to make a complete one himself.

I have included a copy of Indenture of my Grandfather Arthur Jenkins dated 1877. From the contents it is obvious that not only was the craft apprenticeship arduous but that conditions included many restrictions in private life too.

One has only to romanticise a little and recall the rough usage cart and wagon wheels were subjected to, to marvel how they managed to stay in one piece for so long. Remember there was no glue nor bolts in the construction, just good workmanship.

Some wagon wheels were a tremendous weight, being about 4 feet 6 inches (137 cm) high and often taking many days to complete. Very skillful hard work was necessary, all for the reward of a few pounds. With his ability my father would have no doubt commanded a tremendous income nowadays.

Great interest is being taken in this craft and the revival of rural museums etc, and many wish to know the detailed construction of a wooden wheel.

There are three main parts, the hub, spokes and outside rim known as the felloes (see fig 1). There are usually twelve spokes and six felloes to a cart wheel but seven felloes and fourteen spokes to a light wheel. It is absolutely essential that all the timber to be used is thoroughly seasoned. If not it will shrink and expand while in use and the wheel will fall apart.

My father always chose wyche elm for the hub, oak for the spokes and either ash for light wheel felloes and ordinary elm for cart wheel felloes. After the devastation of these wonderful trees by the elm beetle it would be virtually impossible to find suitable timber nowadays. The hub, or stock is best cut from the trunk of a tree about 18 inches in diameter. A number about 18 inches to 20 inches long should be cut at the same time. The bark must be removed and a hole about 1 inch in diameter bored through the centre of each log. They are then stacked in an open-sided shed where the air can circulate freely for at least twelve months. The same must apply to all timber used by the wheelwright.

When seasoning is completed the hub is turned to the required shape on a lathe. An iron band is placed on the front and rear. These prevent the hub from splitting when the spokes are driven into the mortices (see fig 2). It is important when turning a hub to mark two face lines around with a chisel about ½ inch apart. The use of these two lines will be seen later (see fig. 3).

The nose of the hub is flattened and placed on a flat surface. The circumference is measured and divided by the number of spokes to be used in the wheel. A pair of dividers is used to step around the centre. By trial and error the points are adjusted until the marks are accurately placed. The points of the dividers are dug in deeply because those marks show the centres of the intended mortices. (see fig. 3).

FIG 1.

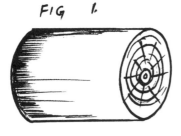

HOLE BORED IN THE CENTRE.
1" IN DIAM. BARK REMOVED,
AND LEFT IN OPEN SHED FOR
AT LEAST 12 MONTHS.

HUB CUT FROM A WYCHE
ELM TRUNK ABOUT 18"
DIAM.

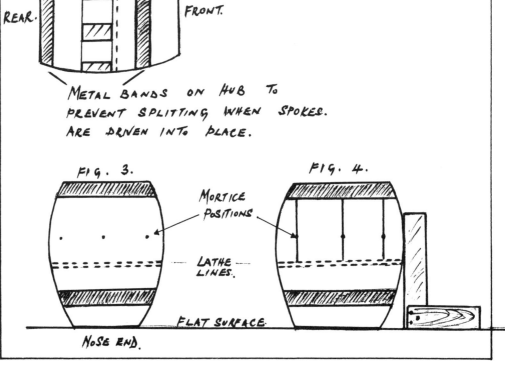

FIG 2.

REAR.   FRONT.

METAL BANDS ON HUB TO
PREVENT SPLITTING WHEN SPOKES.
ARE DRIVEN INTO PLACE.

FIG. 3.   FIG. 4.

MORTICE
POSITIONS

LATHE
LINES.

FLAT SURFACE.

NOSE END.

A try square is slid along the flat surface to touch the hub. Pencil lines are drawn vertically alongside the try square blade and through the divider marks (see fig. 4).

Before any more work is done to the hub the spokes must be shaped. The lengths of the spokes depend on the diameter of the wheel. If it is 4 feet 6 inches the spokes must be half that, i.e. 2 feet 3 inches by 3½ inches wide by 1½ inches thick. The timber must be straight grained, well seasoned oak.

First a centre line is drawn along the base and up the face side and a line squared round 4 inches from the foot (see fig. 5). Then the footing, that is the shaping of the shoulderless tenon on each spoke, is done. This is a complicated process and each tenon has to be shaped to a wedge shape for a drive in fit (see fig. 6).

Each spoke is mounted in a special cramp for shaping with a draw knife, and a spokeshave (see fig 7 and 8). A drawknife is a wonderful tool to enable you to acquire a rough shape quickly.

The hub is held firmly by placing it on a framework called a tram (see fig. 9). This framework has a number of holes bored along each side. A felloe with two holes drilled through at A and B is placed on the tram against the side of the hub. Finally two ropes with heavy weights are draped over the hub and attached to bolts A and B. This completes the fixing of the hub.

Each spoke foot is clearly numbered then placed over the centre lines. The shape of the mortices is obtained by marking around the spoke tenons. To minimise the possibility of splitting the hub, the spokes are staggered, one being brought to the lathe line C and the next one flush with the lathe line D (see fig. 9 and 11). This pattern is repeated right around the hub.

When the spokes are fixed they have to be dished or speached, i.e. sloped out (see fig. 10). This is necessary to avoid a wagon wheel touching the bed or cart side, when it is turning. It is also to help avoid soil clogging between the wheel and the wagon bed.

Obtaining the speach or slope is difficult and needs much care. A ¾ inch auger is used to bore the rear of each mortice right through to the centre of the hub, then a 1¼ inch auger is used for the front of each mortice in the same way (see fig. 11a) A special chisel called a bus is used to chop each corner of the mortice (see fig. 12). Now the mortices have to be cleaned out to the centre of the hub. Remember every alternate mortice is bored and cleaned to the forward lathe mark first, then those to the back lathe mark afterwards, to avoid splitting.

A thin lath called a staff is fixed to the plugged centre of the hub. It must be screwed firmly but allowed to rotate when pushed. Attached to the end of the staff is a thin piece of whalebone. My father used to use a stay out of mother's corsets (see fig. 10). The whalebone is fixed through the staff to coincide with the speach and this varies to the type of wheel.

When a mortice is chopped a thin lath is inserted at the front and held in position with a mortice chisel. The staff is rotated to see if the whalebone touches the lath (see fig. 13). This is called heading the mortice and tenon. The slope or speach has to be checked after almost every blow of a chisel because once it is too great it is impossible to push the spoke back.

95

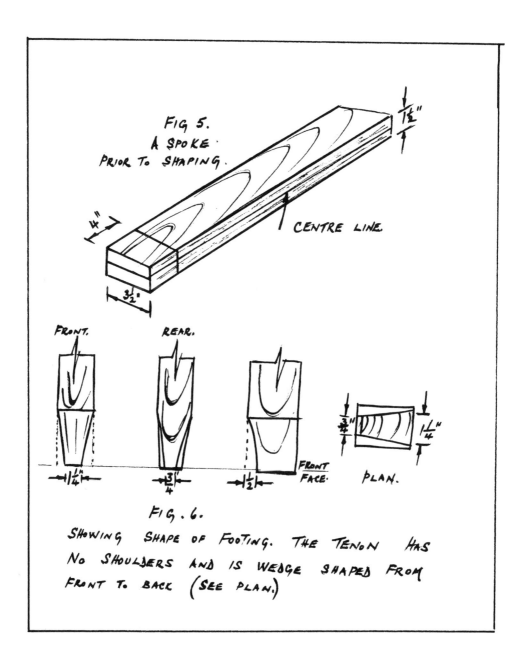

FIG 5.
A SPOKE
PRIOR TO SHAPING.

$1\frac{1}{2}$"

4"

CENTRE LINE.

$3\frac{1}{2}$"

FRONT.
REAR.

FRONT
FACE.

$\frac{3}{4}$"
$\frac{1}{4}$"

PLAN.

$1\frac{1}{4}$"
$\frac{3}{4}$"
$\frac{1}{2}$"

FIG. 6.
SHOWING SHAPE OF FOOTING. THE TENON HAS
NO SHOULDERS AND IS WEDGE SHAPED FROM
FRONT TO BACK (SEE PLAN.)

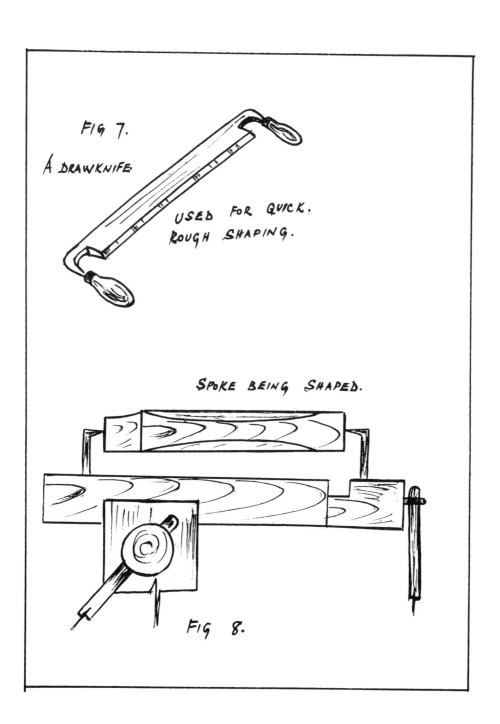

FIG 7.

A DRAWKNIFE.

USED FOR QUICK, ROUGH SHAPING.

SPOKE BEING SHAPED.

FIG 8.

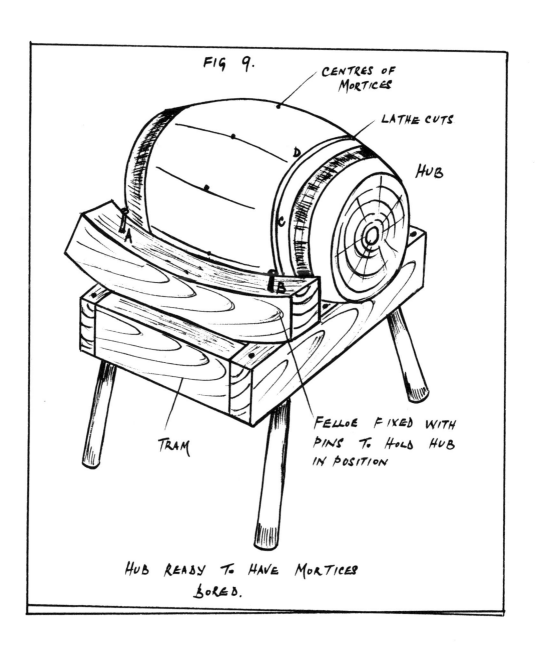

FIG 9.

CENTRES OF MORTICES

LATHE CUTS

HUB

FELLOE FIXED WITH
PINS TO HOLD HUB
IN POSITION

TRAM

HUB READY TO HAVE MORTICES
BORED.

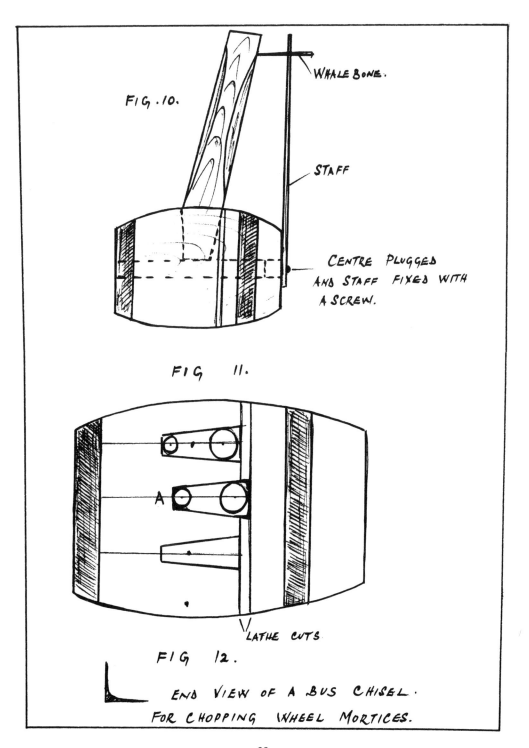

FIG. 10.

WHALE BONE.

STAFF

CENTRE PLUGGED
AND STAFF FIXED WITH
A SCREW.

FIG 11.

A

LATHE CUTS.

FIG 12.

END VIEW OF A BUS CHISEL.
FOR CHOPPING WHEEL MORTICES.

The wheelwright has to make the mortice $\frac{3}{8}$ inch less in length both at the surface and at the base of its depth to ensure a drive in fit and he uses calipers to check these measurements frequently. The width has to be an easy fit otherwise the hub will split open.

Now the tenon is ready to try, and to help it drive, my father used to dip the foot in a bucket of water.

Driving home; A heavy, flat headed hammer is needed. The spoke is placed at the mouth of the mortice and given a gentle tap. It must be ensured that it is about ½ inch from the whalebone. With each strike, as the tenon enters the mortice so the spoke should draw nearer the whalebone. When right home it should just touch (see fig. 10). My father tried numerous materials to measure the speach but the whalebone from mum's corset seemed to be the only thing that would spring without snapping.

When all the spokes were driven home the height of the wheel was determined by marking the radius on the staff. At that distance a line was squared from the staff across each spoke. A second line was squared 4 inches below the first one, this being the depth of the felloes (see fig. 14). These were always 6 inches wide and 4 inches deep on a wagon wheel. They were cut from a felloe pattern of a circle 4 feet 6 inches diameter and had to be of elm (see fig. 15).

A tang or tongue was cut on each spoke to enable the felloes to fit on them. The tangs were tapered slightly to enable the felloes to drive on easily. A face board template was attached to the staff to mark the distance of the tangs from it (see fig. 16 A and B).

The tangs were sawn on each spoke all round the wheel. They were 1½ inches thick on a wagon wheel (see fig. 16 B and C).

On light wheels the spokes had sawn tenons on the foot and round tangs on the felloe ends. Therefore they differed considerably from wagon spokes (see fig. 17 and fig. 6).

The wheel was placed on the tram with the face towards the floor. The felloes were fitted around the wheel by placing them on the tangs. Each felloe had to span two spokes. When the felloes were first placed in position they would not butt together (see fig. 18 A), therefore a lath had to be placed across the diameter of the wheel to pass across the felloe ends to obtain the correct angle. The felloe ends were sawn to this angle but the last pair had a $\frac{3}{8}$ inch gap between them. This allowed final tightening in the last stage of assembly. Every felloe and corresponding spoke had to be numbered clearly.

The shape of the tang had to be transferred to each felloe before the mortices could be cut. This was a complicated process. Firstly pencil lines were drawn along the underside of the felloes and along either side of each spoke (see fig 19). Then lines were squared around the felloes from the bottom of each tang. Fig. 18 D helps to explain how this was done.

The felloes were now bored and morticed. It was necessary to widen each mortice on the felloes outside so that a wedge may be driven in to hold the tangs firmly in place.

The centre of each end of every felloe was found and bored with a bit $\frac{7}{8}$ inch in diameter to a depth of 2½ inches. Oak dowels were made and inserted in one end of each felloe (see fig. 18 D). It had to be the corresponding end of each felloe right round the wheel. A saw cut was made down the centre of each tang. Finally the inside edge of each felloe was rounded off with a spokeshave (see fig. 18 C). Care had to be taken to see that each dowel drew into the ends of the felloes as they were knocked home. A dab of paint on each one aided a slipping fit. My father always went to great pains to ensure that every dowel was slightly shorter than the depth of its marrying mortice (see fig. 18 D).

It was virtually impossible to persuade the felloes to enter the tangs without using a special clamp, called a coupling, to pull each pair of spokes together slightly. This was a wooden pole, shaped at one end, with an adjustable chain at the opposite end (see fig. 20). The chain was wrapped around two spokes and connected to the pole by means of a bolt. A second pair of hands was needed to lever the pole forward. When the pair of spoke tangs were opposite the felloe mortices the felloes were tapped on a little way. The same procedure was adopted all round the wheel.

The wheelwright walked round the wheel tapping each felloe until they were all seated on the shoulders of the spokes. Oak wedges were made and knocked into the mortices on both sides of each tang to hold the felloes firmly in position (see fig. 20 A).

To enable a cartwheel to turn, a tapered, hollow cylindrical box had to be fixed into the centre of the hub. Its centre was chiselled out and the box driven in place with a heavy hammer and a block of wood. This prevented the metal burring and distorting. The box hole was made larger on one face to allow wedges to be driven in all round to hold it firmly in position. It was absolutely vital to make sure the box was accurately placed in the hub centre otherwise the wheel would not turn accurately. The box slid onto a cylindrical arm which was joined onto a flat bar. This bolted to the wagon axle (see fig. 22).

My father always turned the cart bed upsidedown to rotate the wheel, adjusting the wedges and tapped them gently until he was convinced he had obtained an even rotation.

Before fixing a wheel it was absolutely vital to ensure that both wheel arms were lined up correctly on the axle. Occasionally my father found that the new wheel did not rotate in line with its old partner and usually the cause was the incorrect positioning of the axle arms. (see fig. 22).

Every wheel had to have a rim to protect it, hold it firmly together and to assist its rotation. The broad wagon wheel was fitted with iron strakes and a narrower wheel with a metal band.

Before strakes were fitted, the half of each felloe nearer the face of the wheel was bevelled and the strakes to fit this sloping edge were also bevelled. This enabled the soil to fall from the wheel when working on ploughed land (see fig. 22 A). Each strake was 3 inches wide and about ½ inch thick and had to be long enough to span from the centre of the felloe to the centre of the next. (see fig. 22B). The strakes were heated, nailed onto the felloes with special nails and cooled quickly in a bosh. This was a metal tank filled with water which allowed a wheel to rotate on its axle and so dip the strakes to cool. The sudden contraction of the metal caused the joints at the ends of the felloes to pull tightly together.

It will be recalled that when the felloes were knocked home, a small gap of about $\frac{1}{8}$ inch remained between two of them. The reason for this was as follows. When the penultimate strakes were fitted the strake nails were left slightly proud. This enabled a 'samson' to be fitted across the felloe to be covered (see fig. 23 A). The very large nuts were screwed on with the help of a long handled spanner. Gradually the gap between the felloes closed. At this point the last strakes were heated, nailed in position and cooled quickly in the bosh.

Banding a wheel. Narrower wheels were fitted with a continuous band around their circumference. A long straight strip of iron the width of the felloes and $\frac{5}{8}$ inch thick was chosen. A chalk mark was placed on the wheel and the metal strip. The wheel was rotated until the chalk mark again touched the metal. The distance between the chalk marks showed the circumference of the wheel. One inch was added to allow for 'cutting and shutting', the expression used for joining the rim. The long straight strip was fed through a bending machine (see fig. 24). A long bar was fitted through the centre of the central cog wheel and rotated. This wound the steel through the bender and gave the necessary curvature.

The ends were brought together and thickened with a hammer (see fig. 25 A). They were then 'lipped' to form a joint, held together and centre punched to help them grip each other. Two men then lifted the band into a clean forge fire and the lipped ends were heated until they became sticky. Great experience was required to know the correct heat. Too much burnt and melted the metal, too little did not allow a joint to be made.

When the correct glow was achieved the rim was removed from the fire, placed on an anvil and hammered together. Before the ends were forge welded, the blacksmith had to ensure that the length of the metal band was the thickness of the metal ($\frac{5}{8}$ inch) less than the circumference of the wheel. The completed rim was placed on a circle of bricks, and a fire of woodshavings and wood was built around it. This was kindled until the rim had expanded sufficiently to drop over the wheel. Meanwhile it was placed on a metal platform. This had a long metal bolt attached to its centre which passed through the hub. The wheel was secured to this bolt by means of a large nut and washer (see fig. 26). The hot band was lifted by two or three men using long tongs and placed in a tilted position over the wheel (see fig. 27 A). Metal dogs (see fig. 27 B) were placed over the outside of the felloes and the band was levered gradually to drop completely over the wheel. The band was hammered gently all round until it fitted snuggly onto the felloes.

A number of filled water cans were placed conveniently and the contents quickly poured onto the rim. The sudden contraction caused the wheel joints to pull together tightly. Lastly, holes were bored through the rim into which were knocked blacksmith's nails. These had to be so placed to avoid the dowels which joined the felloes.

I remember great problems occurring when a rim was made slightly too small. It had to be taken off, heated and stretched with swages before being re-fitted.

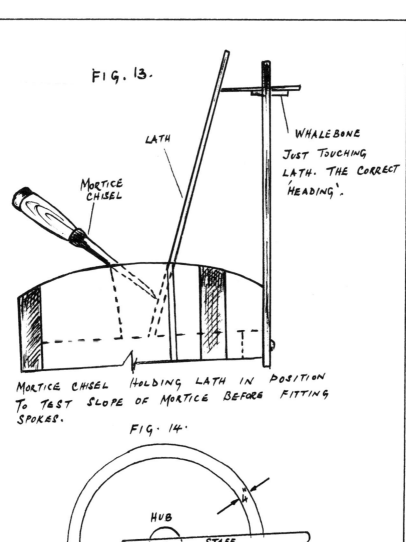

FIG. 13.

MORTICE
CHISEL

LATH

WHALEBONE
JUST TOUCHING
LATH. THE CORRECT
'HEADING'.

MORTICE CHISEL HOLDING LATH IN POSITION
TO TEST SLOPE OF MORTICE BEFORE FITTING
SPOKES.

FIG. 14.

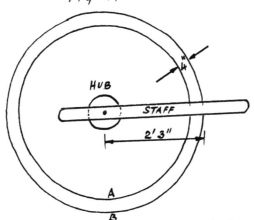

HUB

STAFF

2'3"

A

B

STAFF ENABLES WHEEL HEIGHT TO BE
MARKED ROUND SPOKES. CIRCUMFERENCE A
AND B SHOW WHERE FELLOES WILL REST
ON SPOKES.

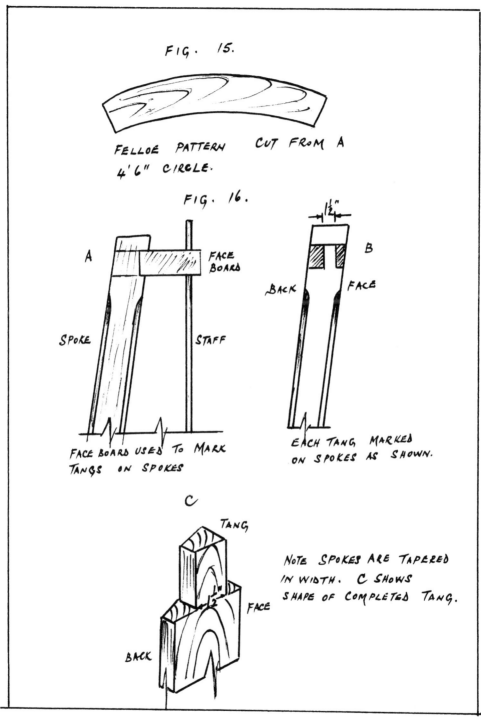

FIG. 15.

FELLOE PATTERN CUT FROM A
4' 6" CIRCLE.

FIG. 16.

A

FACE BOARD

SPOKE   STAFF

FACE BOARD USED TO MARK
TANGS ON SPOKES

$1\frac{1}{2}$"

B

BACK   FACE

EACH TANG MARKED
ON SPOKES AS SHOWN.

C

TANG

$1\frac{1}{2}$"

FACE

BACK

NOTE SPOKES ARE TAPERED
IN WIDTH. C SHOWS
SHAPE OF COMPLETED TANG.

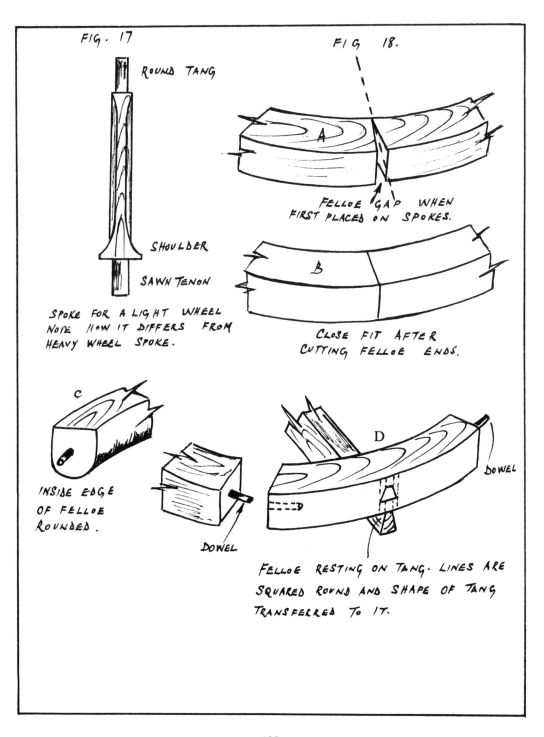

FIG. 17

ROUND TANG

SHOULDER

SAWN TENON

SPOKE FOR A LIGHT WHEEL
NOTE HOW IT DIFFERS FROM
HEAVY WHEEL SPOKE.

FIG. 18.

A

FELLOE GAP WHEN
FIRST PLACED ON SPOKES.

B

CLOSE FIT AFTER
CUTTING FELLOE ENDS.

C

INSIDE EDGE
OF FELLOE
ROUNDED.

DOWEL

D

DOWEL

FELLOE RESTING ON TANG. LINES ARE
SQUARED ROUND AND SHAPE OF TANG
TRANSFERRED TO IT.

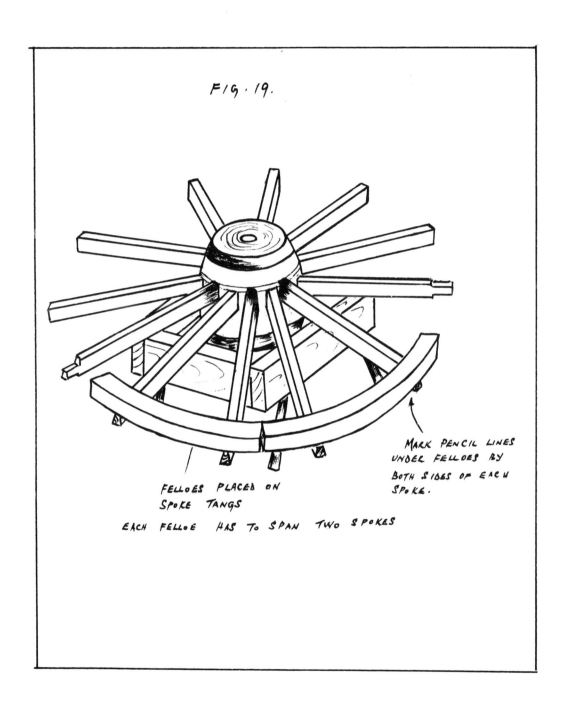

FIG·19.

MARK PENCIL LINES
UNDER FELLOES BY
BOTH SIDES OF EACH
SPOKE.

FELLOES PLACED ON
SPOKE TANGS

EACH FELLOE HAS TO SPAN TWO SPOKES

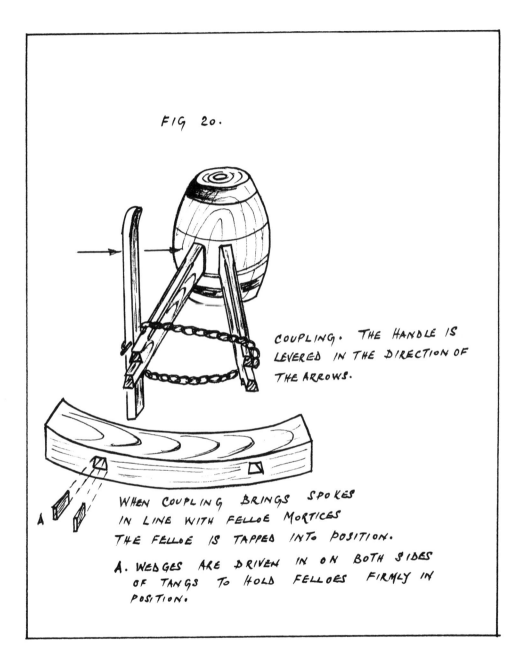

FIG 20.

COUPLING. THE HANDLE IS
LEVERED IN THE DIRECTION OF
THE ARROWS.

WHEN COUPLING BRINGS SPOKES
IN LINE WITH FELLOE MORTICES
THE FELLOE IS TAPPED INTO POSITION.

A. WEDGES ARE DRIVEN IN ON BOTH SIDES
OF TANGS TO HOLD FELLOES FIRMLY IN
POSITION.

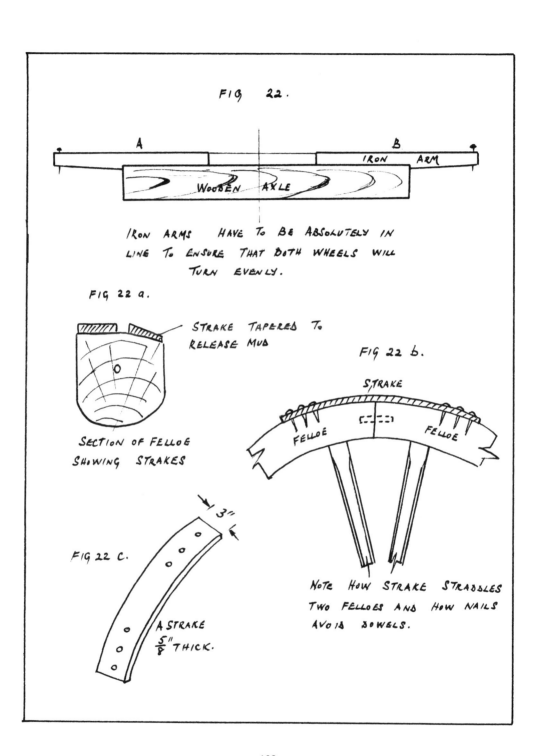

FIG   22.

A   B
                                          IRON   ARM

WOODEN   AXLE

IRON ARMS   HAVE TO BE ABSOLUTELY IN
LINE TO ENSURE THAT BOTH WHEELS WILL
TURN EVENLY.

FIG 22 a.

STRAKE TAPERED TO
RELEASE MUD

FIG 22 b.

SECTION OF FELLOE
SHOWING STRAKES

STRAKE

FELLOE   FELLOE

FIG 22 C.

3"

A STRAKE
$\frac{5}{8}$" THICK.

NOTE HOW STRAKE STRADDLES
TWO FELLOES AND HOW NAILS
AVOID DOWELS.

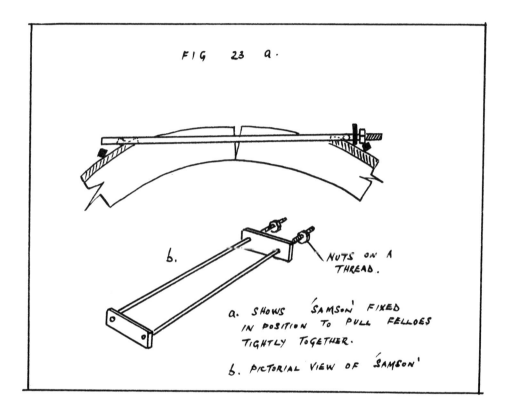

FIG 23 a.

b.

NUTS ON A THREAD.

a. SHOWS 'SAMSON' FIXED IN POSITION TO PULL FELLOES TIGHTLY TOGETHER.

b. PICTORIAL VIEW OF 'SAMSON'

Occasionally rims became loose in summer time. This necessitated my father removing the rim, cutting it and shutting it to make it slightly shorter, then re-fixing it onto the wheel. I have no idea what a wagon wheel would cost now, but my father worked seemingly non-stop for a whole week to make a wheel in the 1930s. He charged about £4 for the finished product and that included all the materials. Looking back it doesn't seem a great deal on which to raise a family.

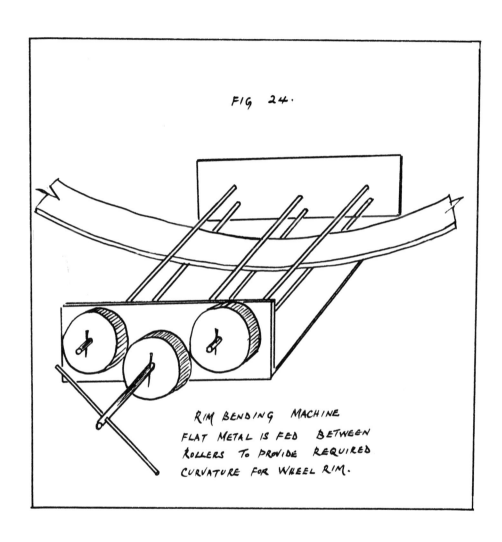

FIG 24.

RIM BENDING MACHINE
FLAT METAL IS FED BETWEEN
ROLLERS TO PROVIDE REQUIRED
CURVATURE FOR WHEEL RIM.

110

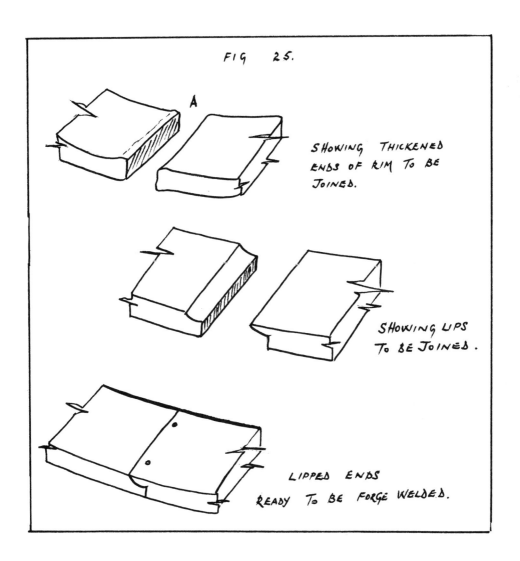

FIG 25.

A

SHOWING THICKENED
ENDS OF RIM TO BE
JOINED.

SHOWING LIPS
TO BE JOINED.

LIPPED ENDS
READY TO BE FORGE WELDED.

111

FIG 26.

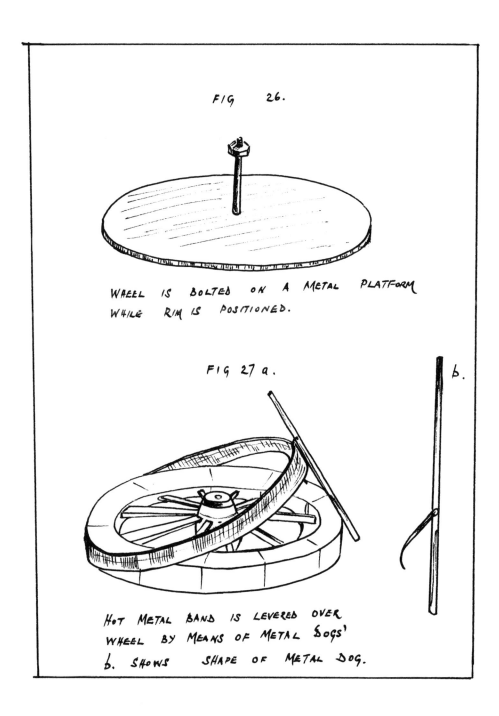

WHEEL IS BOLTED ON A METAL PLATFORM
WHILE RIM IS POSITIONED.

FIG 27 a.

b.

HOT METAL BAND IS LEVERED OVER
WHEEL BY MEANS OF METAL 'DOGS'
b. SHOWS SHAPE OF METAL DOG.

Clee Hill Dialect

In the year 1840 the population of the whole of the Clee Hill Area, according to the Ludlow Standard Newspaper, was about 3000. Assuming that family units were at least four in size the number of adult men would have been approximately 500 to 750.

The main occupations were farming, coalmining and lime quarrying. The Area was bleak, barren and inaccessible because of its hilly terrain, climate and lack of decent roads.

Stone quarrying began in earnest in 1863 and from that date until the year 1900, between 1500 and 2000 men were employed in the Clee Hill Quarries.

The Clees until that time used the typical North Hereford, South Shropshire accent and dialect. Suddenly however there was an influx of workmen numbering about 1000 to satisfy the industrial needs.

These men came from the Black Country, Gloucestershire, Herefordshire, Wales, Worcestershire, Nottinghamshire, Yorkshire and Scotland.

Once these people began working on Clee Hill they were comparatively isolated. Transportation was slow and the journey to Ludlow and back, a distance of ten miles would have taken a day. Even in my childhood, that was the 1930s to 40s, very few cars were seen In the Area, a trip to Tenbury Wells or Cleobury Mortimer was a major event and Kidderminster was as remote as Australia. The only time I heard of anyone visiting that large town was to go to hospital. Most of the required provisions were brought by horse and cart or via the Bitterley-Dhustone railway spur, to the Good's Shed, an unloading depot situated at the top of the lane which still has that name, near Clee Hill Village.

And so the Clee Hill dialect developed, which was a conglomeration of the dialects from the areas mentioned previously. It certainly was unique for a dialect to have such a rich mixture and to have such a short life span.

The hey day would have been between 1890 and 1939. During this period everyone, both inside and outside the family unit would have spoken in the Clee Hill dialect.

However in the 1930s many influences affected this isolated community. The last of the coal pits closed. Radio, television, cinema, improved transport, the 'scholarship' (or 11+) and the Second World War opened up the Area. Greater mechanisation meant fewer workmen were required in the quarries to produce virtually the same amount of stone and a considerable number of people began to commute to Highley, Cleobury Mortimer, Tenbury Wells, Ludlow, Kidderminster and other places. Housing development has continued and the new inhabitants have assisted the change.

Clee Hill folk had always been a race apart and the dialect was a contributory factor to this. They discovered it was not socially acceptable away from Clee Hill and children who travelled to Ludlow and Cleobury to school were ridiculed. I know this because of my own personal experience. Everyone therefore cultivated two standards of speech, a dialect for home use and Queen's English for the outside world. Unfortunately all these influences have accelerated the decline of the Clee Hill dialect.

Early in 1979 the B.B.C. Archives showed a considerable interest. They wished to obtain a family group or a number of quarrymen having an informal chat in the dialect. I informed them the decline had been so rapid that this was not now possible and that even the old natives of seventy and eighty years of age had been influenced to such an extent that their mode of speech was a very much diluted dialect.

Sadly, I predict that in another decade it will no longer be possible to hear the Clee Hill Talk. This urgency has prompted me to formulate a glossary of some of the words which were in common use when I was a child.

Those who have seen Herefordshire Speech by Winifred Leeds and Dialect and Local Usage of Herefordshire by Andrew Haggard will find similar words, but often pronunciation was different and so was the usage. A few examples illustrate the point.

Clee Hill (CH)   Herefordshire (HER)

(CH)   tăng - to beat. I'll tăng yer̄ id. I'll beat you across the bottom.
(HER) tang = to make a noise to attract a swarm of bees.

(CH)   grăf/ter̂ = a hard worker.
(HER) graff = to dig with a spade.

(CH)   ĕft = plenty, a great deal.
(HER) ĕft = a great weight. Similar usage in Somerset.

(CH)   lĭs/sŭm = athletic and muscular. Often referred to elderly working men who were very fit. (Sŭr/ri ĭnt that ŏd quarry mŏn lĭs/sŭm). Good gracious isn't that old quarry man fit.
(HER) lis/som = active.

(CH)   per̂/gĭ = bad tempered.
(HER) perky = obstinate.

(CH)   făg/gŏt = small pieces of wood to help start the fire.
(HER) faggot = a bundle, and in Gloucestershire an old faggot was an insult to an old lady.

(CH)   lĭk/er̂ = fat running from cooked meat.
(HER) licquer = lard.

Some words are similar or have the same usage:-
(CH)   băn/nŭt = walnut. Used also in Somerset and Gloucester.
(HER) bannut

(CH)   ar/gĭ/fī = argue.
(HER) argufy = argue. Similar in Yorkshire, Somerset and Norfolk.

Dr. J. D. A. Widdowson, Director of The Centre of English Cultural Tradition and Language at the University of Sheffield stated on a B.B.C. programme that only local people can detect the subtle differences in usage and pronunciation. He stated that Clee Hill people use the word wristers. This is a plural of the Old Middle English word wrists. In fact the Clee Hill word is wrisses (rĭs/sĕs). He therefore unintentionally illustrated this point very clearly.

114

A common expression on Clee Hill was (Ĭnt it kōd. I'll krōodle up to thă). Isn't it cold. I'll cuddle up to you. Mr. Peter Windows, a producer of Woman's Hour assumed that (to thă) was a girl's name. Mr. Windows gained my respect and admiration because he had the necessary sincere interest with which to gain the confidence of country people.

Dr. Widdowson also substantiated my claim that people a few miles away had difficulty in understanding the Clee Hill Talk, by stating that a detailed survey of dialect had been carried out at Diddlebury. This village is eight miles away and many of the Clee Hill words are unknown there.

Some words and phrases brought by the imported quarrymen remained virtually unchanged. Oddern appern (ŏd/dĕrn ăp/pĕrn) meant a sack apron or woollen cloth apron as it does in the north. Fire new, meant unused and absolutely new. This was and probably still is a Potteries expression.

My glossary applies to what I call the bracken area of the Titterstone, Dhu Stone and Clee Hill. Here, hill farming consists mainly of grass, hill sheep and store cattle.

Gwendoline Jackson's work, The Shropshire Word Book, published in 1882 gives a wonderful insight of rural life in Shropshire as well as a comprehensive survey of the county's words. It is a must for anyone interested in dialect. My own knowledge confirms that her descriptions of country folk are very accurate, but she quotes at least two hundred words stated to be in regular use on Clee Hill. However I never heard any of them used or referred to when I was a child. This puzzled me greatly initially because it did not seem feasible that every one of these words could have disappeared from the daily scene between 1882 and 1936.

Some examples are:-

pous = a mixture of crops of grain.
red row = the stage of reddish tinge barley.
rōp = reap.
scrawly = twisted, entangled grain.
strickless = corn measure.
wazzle = barley beaten down by birds.
yar = a cider hair used in the process of cider making.
must = ground apples.
odd mark = portion of a particular farm for a particular crop.
piles = the awns of barley.
brōo/ĭt = a bit of good herbage.
aw = ear of oats.
bull stud = a bull that has been gelt.

These few words are a fraction of the large number directly connected with the sort of arable and fruit farming which because of climatic conditions could never have thrived on Clee Hill. One has to go below the bracken line to Bitterley, Caynham, Nash, Cleobury Mortimer and Stottesdon. Many of the words were in fact taken from Auctioneers' catalogues of farm sales at Stottesdon. Therefore I do not consider them to be Clee Hill words. I can say that all the words in this glossary have been heard in use during my childhood on the top of the Clee Hills.

Conveying the pronunciation to a reader who is not familiar with a dialect or accent is an extremely difficult problem. I have attempted to spell all Clee Hill words phonetically and to assist accuracy of pronunciation I intend to produce a dialect tape to be used in conjunction with this glossary.

I have differentiated between long and short vowels as follows:-

ă	as in apple
ā	as in ape
ĕ	as in egg
ē	as in peep
ĭ	as in ill
ī	as in island
ŏ	as in often
ō	as in open
ŭ	as in up
ū	as in uniform
êr	as in burn
ōo	as in cool
âr	as in part

The division of syllables is shown by an oblique stroke eg chĭl/lŭn.

Clee Hill people lengthen short vowel sounds to produce the well known Western Counties drawl. I have shown this by doubling the short vowel letter and placing the short vowel symbol above, eg:- hay bay = ăh băa (ăa as in the sound of sheep, is the drawn out or extended vowel sound). Others are spăad = spade, găat = gate, grĕevs = graves and so on.

Some words do not conform to any of these sounds and these are illustrated by placing an explanation in parentheses after the phonetic spelling eg:-

awl/ĭs (aw as in bawl) = always.
dowst (ow as in now) = to put out a fire with water, or by beating.

Patterns emerge and the diminutive nu occurs as in:-

bĭn/nŭ	= am not
kŏn/nŭ	= cannot
shăn/nŭ	= shall not
ōod/nŭ	= would not
mŭn/nŭ	= must not.

The letter n is often added for plurals, eg:-

owsn (ow as in now) = houses.
plăazn = places.

I hope this glossary will inspire others to think about their own dialect. I am sure that many villages and isolated areas would produce equally interesting results. Time is short. The direct links via the old folk in their twilight will soon vanish for ever and these beautiful, old fashioned dialects with them.

ăah/doo (aa as in baa)	-	hello
ăat	-	eight
ăa/tĭ	-	eighty
ăay	-	hay
ăay/băa	-	hay bay
ă/bĭd	-	tolerate

(I kŏn/nă ă/bĭd = I cannot tolerate)

above a bit	-	thoroughly

(He knows his job above a bit = He knows his job thoroughly).

āch	-	each
ā/fêr	-	heifer
ăf/fŏr	-	before
ăf/têr/măth	-	grass grown after a main crop of hay.
ăg/gl	-	argue
ak/êr/dŏk	-	acquiduct
ak/êrn	-	acorn
a/lŭng/ă	-	along wlth
ăn/nŭ	-	have not
ăn/tĭ tŭmp	-	ant hill
ănt yŭ	-	haven't you
âr/dn (âr as in park)	-	stubborn
âr/gĭ/fĭ	-	argue

(In Herefordshire it is argufy - similar in Somerset and Yorkshire).

ăsh/n plănt	-	cat o' nine tails

(cane used by a schoolmaster).

ā/sĭ	-	easy
ăs/īd	-	beside
ăs/nŭ	-	haven't you
ăst (hast)	-	have you
ât	-	eat
ā/tĭn	-	eating
ăt/têr	-	after
āvs	-	eaves
āvd	-	heaved, lifted
ăwl/is (aw as in bawl)	-	always
ăxd	-	asked
ăz/gŭls	-	newts

B

bǎad	-	ill
baǎ/thǐ	-	beathy, damp.

(Chaucer used the word bathe, meaning to bask or dry).

bǎ/bǐ	-	baby
bǎk/kǐnd	-	latter part of the year.
bǎk/kǔ	-	tobacco
bǎkn	-	bacon
bǎk/kǔts	-	backwards
bǎl/lǐ	-	stomach

(A good bal/li was a good litter of pigs).

bǎn/nǔt	-	walnut
		(also used in Herefordshire, Gloucester and Somerset).
bârkd	-	when skin is knocked off shins
bârn	-	born
bǎsh	-	to hit someone or knock them about.
bē	-	am or are
beě/sǒn	-	basin
beět	-	food, bait
běl/lǒk	-	to shout loudly at someone.
běl/ǒlu	-	to make a tremendous noise

(associated with hounds and a group running quickly).

běnt	-	coarse grass

(Herefordshire use as the seed stalk of grass or long stems which bend in the wind).

bêrdn	-	an armful or small load

(a bêrdn ǒ ǒod was an armful of wood).

běst/těd mu	-	beat me
bī/dǐ	-	Bytheway
bǐf	-	beef
big sârt/ed	-	conceited, stuck up
bīl	-	boil
bǐn	-	been
bǐ now	-	by this time
bǐn/nǔ	-	am not

(with a different intonation becomes a question i.e. Are they?)

bǐst	-	are you
bǐst/nǔ	-	aren't you
blaǎd	-	cut up the sides of a hedge before laying.

blăth/êr/in	-	continual natter which does not make sense.
blăw	-	blossom or bloom
bō/gĭ	-	a goblin. Quarry or railway wagon.
bŏnj	-	to eat a tremendous amount
bŏnk	-	bank
bŏn/nĭ	-	plump
(a bŏn/nĭ ŏŏm/ŭn = a plump woman)		
bōō/zĭ	-	where the hay for a cow is put above a manger.
bŏr/rĕl	-	barrel
bŏr/rŭ	-	barrow
bŏst (used by quarrymen)	-	to break
bŏst/êr	-	quarryman's hammer
bŏst up	-	a quarrel or fight
bōt	-	bolt
bowz (ow as in now)	-	annoyed
(up in the bowz = lost his temper)		
boy/stins	-	first milk from a cow after she has calved.
bŏx	-	ill
(on the box = meant being away from work, relying on income from club funds)		
brăăk/in up	-	when fine weather ceases
brăă/sêrs	-	braces
brăăns	-	brains
brăzn	-	very forward
brē	-	cattle annoyed by flies
(cattle charging around in summer with their tails in the air)		
brĕĕ/kĭn	-	breaking
brĕ/vĭt/ĭn	-	searching about
brŏd/dŭk	-	hedge bill
brŏk	-	broke
brōōd/dĭ	-	a hen wanting to sit. A young lady wishing to have children
brōō/ŭs	-	brew house
brŭk	-	brook
brŭm/mŭk	-	hacker
bŭk/tĭth	-	protruding teeth
bŭf/fŭt	-	to hit someone around the head a calf bunting a cow's udder.

bŭnt	-	a clout from the head of a sheep or a goat.
bŭt/têr mĭt	-	a shallow tub in which butter was shaped.
bŭt/tĭ	-	a friend, a mate
(used in Herefordshire too) another use = one of a pair e.g. this shoe is a Bŭt/tĭ to that one)		
bŭz	-	bus and to hit someone around the head.
bŭz/gĭns	-	trousers. A pet name for a child.

C

charm	-	a great deal of noise
chāz	-	cheese
chawl (aw as in bawl)	-	pig's cheek
chêr	-	chair
chêrt	-	sharp (a sharp pain)
chêrp/pêr	-	kiss
chĭl/lŭn	-	children
chĭm/mŭk	-	chimney
chĭt/lĭns	-	chitterlings, the small intestines of a pig.
chŏl/lŏp	-	to have a great deal to say for oneself.
chŏmbl	-	to chew up food noisily and in an uncouth manner.
chŏns	-	chance
chōob/bêr	-	football
chōob/bĭn/kĕz	-	football
Chōos dĭ	-	Tuesday
chŭfd	-	very pleased with oneself
chŭnd/dêr/ĭn	-	muttering

D

dăa	-	day
dăb ond	-	very good at doing a particular thing.
dăg/gŭl/dĭ	-	wet, cold weather. The rough coat of a dog.
(in other areas farmers use the expression to describe soiled sheep)		
dăk/kĭ	-	child's expression for a small pig.

dăn/dĭ/păts	-	slippers
dārd nŭ	-	dare not
dās/sŭnt	-	decent
dăsh/ownd	-	dachshund
dĕe	-	day
dĕys	-	days
dĕs/prĭt	-	desperate
dīch	-	ditch
dĭd/nŭ	-	didn't
dĭd/dĭ/koy	-	gypsy, romany, scarecrow.
dĭp	-	deep
dĭst	-	did you
dĭst nŭ	-	didn't you
djo	-	do you
dŏl/lĭ tub	-	tub in which clothes were washed.
doo (oo as in moon)	-	good feast, as at a wedding.
dŏn/nĭ	-	hand
dŏn/nĭz	-	hands
dŏs	-	to sleep rough, to have a nap when drunk.

(a doss house was a place for down and outs).

dowst (ow as in now)	-	to put out a fire with water
drȃrs (ar as in mars)	-	drawers
drȃr	-	draw

('Drȃr us a pint Dick'. Pulling a pint of beer from an old fashioned beer pump).

drĕkt/lĭ	-	later on, directly, soon.
drownd/dĕd (ow as in cow)	-	drown
drŭv	-	drove
drŭvd	-	(I druvd the ship = I drove the sheep).
dŭ gōo	-	don't go
dŭb/bd	-	to bend or blunt the end of a tool by hitting it on a stone.
dŭn nŭ	-	don't
dŭn yŭ	-	do you?
dŭnt yŭ	-	don't you
dŭn/nŭk	-	long handled manure rake.
dŭst thēe	-	do you
dyŭth	-	death

E

ēŭr	-	year
ēĕdg	-	age
ĕĕp	-	heap
ĕft	-	any amount, plenty

('Ĕny a ĕft ŏn ŭm'.) = plenty of them. In Herefordshire and Somerset ĕft meant a great weight.

ĕg	-	to encourage someone. 'Eg im on.' = encourage him.
ĕlder	-	animal's udder
ĕldĕst	-	oldest
ĕl/lŭn	-	elm tree
ĕr/rŭnt	-	an errand
ĕs	-	ashes, or rubbish from the fire.
ĕs/bŏld	-	someone who has been in the house too long.
ĕs/ōl	-	ashpit under the fire-grate.
ĕsp/pld	-	upset, worried and confused.
ēs/mĕnt	-	relief from pain.

('That ointment gave me ēz/mĕnt). Money given to unemployed.

F

făd/dĭ	-	fussy about food
făg/gŏt	-	small chips of wood to light the fire.

(Herefordshire a bundle, Gloucestershire an insult)

fărk (ark as in park)	-	fork
fărkd stĭk	-	forked stick
făr/tĭ	-	forty
fărt/nĭt	-	fortnight
fā/thĕr	-	father
fāy/ĕr	-	fair
fĕĕs	-	face
fĕl/lĭ	-	curved part forming the outside of a wooden wheel.
fĕt/tl	-	in good fet/tl = in good condition.
findĕr	-	fender
fīr īons	-	fire irons tools needed for cooking and making up the fire.
fīr new	-	absolutely new. A Potteries expression.

fĭs/sĕs	-	fists
fĭt	-	feet
fĭth/êr	-	feather
fĭt/tl	-	food
flăam	-	flame
flĕn	-	fleas
flĭt	-	to disappear suddenly, 'do a moonlight flit'.
flĭt/têr mouse	-	a bat
flōo/êr	-	floor
flŭm/mŭxd	-	mixed up, confused
fōd	-	fold
fō/êr	-	four
for/sōok	-	left, forsaken
fŏr/ŭts	-	forwards
for/yŭd	-	forehead
fōt	-	fought
fow/stĭ (ow as in how)	-	stale smelling
frăal	-	dinner or tool bag
frĭt frĭt/tĕnd }	-	frightened
frŭm chatters	-	old potatoes left in the garden and found when digging the following year. Pig potatoes.
frŭmp	-	a discourteous term for a woman who dresses up to make herself look young.
fŭl	-	full
fŭnd	-	found
fŭt	-	foot
fŭt iōn	-	cobbler's last
fŭst	-	first
fŭt răk	-	foot path made by sheep
fyârn	-	fern
fyârn/ĭs	-	furnace
fyow (ow as in mow)	-	few

găl/lŭs	-	very gay, enjoys devilment.
găm/mĭ fŭt	-	a limp or deformed foot.
gănd/zĭ	-	jumper, jersey, cardigan.
gără̆/vănt/ĭn	-	carefree, enjoying oneself, gallivant
gawb (aw as in bawl)	-	mouth
gêr	-	lazy, not feeling like work
gē/ŭm	-	game

(We ăd/n a gē/ŭm but ē bĕst/ĕd mŭ. = We had a game but he beat me).

gĭ	-	give
gĭ/ăt or gă̆at	-	gate
gĭd	-	gave

(also dizziness in sheep. They turn round, loose balance and fall over).

gĭl/lêr	-	very fast ride or a heavy fall.
gĭs	-	give me
gĭs	-	geese
gĭt	-	get
gĭth/êrd	-	gathered
glăd răgs	-	best clothes
glâr fat	-	all fat
glăt	-	hole in a hedge
glē	-	all aglow, referring to a fire usually.
gŏbd	-	stopped up
gŏb/bĭ	̄	fool
golden chăn	-	laburnum
gō̄o	-	go
gō̄o/ĭn	-	going
gŏr/stĭ	-	rough land covered with gorse
grăf/têr	-	a very hard worker

(Herefordshire 'graff' meant to dig with a spade).

grănch	-	chew noisily
grăn/nĭ rēr/ed	-	brought up and spoilt by grand-parents.
gră̆as/ĭn	-	cattle eating grass.
grĕ̆es and grās	-	grease
grĕ̆evs	-	graves
grĭndl stŏn	-	grind stone
grŭb	-	food

gŭts in	-	eat food quickly
gwăan	-	going
gwŭn	-	gone
gyârd/dĭn	-	garden
gyârd/nêr	-	gardener
gyârd/nĭn	-	gardening
gyăt pŏst	-	gate post
gyawp (aw as in bawl)	-	stare with your mouth wide open.

I

ĭnd	-	end

(înd fêr ĭnd = turn something round, placing one end where the other end was).

ĭm/ĭj	-	image
ĭnk/lĭn	-	an idea or indication
ĭn/êrds	-	inside. stomach or intestines of a pig.
ĭn/nŭ	-	am not
ĭnt	-	aren't
ĭsn	-	his
īst	-	hush, keep quiet, 'Ist yer niz' meant stop your noise.
īz/ŭk	-	scythe

J

jăal	-	jail, prison
jăg	-	small load
jăk stŏn	-	jack stone
jawl (aw as in bawl)	-	shake someone
jêrk/ĭn	-	pullover
jêrn	-	keen

('E ĭn/nŭ very jêrn') = not keen, not very enthusiastic to have a go).

jō	-	do you
jŏb/lŭks	-	wattles on a cockerel

(a person with fat cheeks was said to have big job/luks).

jŏmbl	-	tangled mass
jŏm/md fŭl	-	absolutely full

jănders	-	jaundice
jŏn/nĭ raw	-	farm labourer
jŏn/nŭk	-	absolutely true, correct.
just nows	-	later on

K

kā	-	key
kădg	-	continually pestering to borrow things.

(A cadger in Herefordshire was an itinerant dealer).

kăf	-	bent spade for moulding potatoes.
kăg ŏnd/ĕd	-	left handed
kăg wīr	-	barbed wire
kă/kĭ	-	dirty, messy. An expression often used by small children when they wished to go to the toilet.
kā/lĭ	-	sherbert or sweet powder.
kāl/lĭd	-	drunk
kăn/tĭn	-	gossiping or telling tales
kârk	-	cork
kârn/nêr	-	corner
kăst	-	to throw an animal over to castrate it.
kē/ăk	-	cake
kĕl/têr	-	money, wealth
kĕp	-	kept

(I kĕp im wŭm frŭm skōōl = I kept him home from school)

kĕtch	-	catch
kĕtch	-	caught
kĕtch ōt	-	caught hold

(Sŭr/rĭ that frost kĕtched ōt smârn/in = my goodness that frost caught hold this morning).

kĭd/dl	-	dribble a football, dribble from the mouth.
kīnd	-	In good shape. Doing well

(Thī pig's kind = Your pig is doing well).

kĭndl	-	to light a fire, In kindl = a pregnant cat or rabbit.
klă	-	clay
klăk	-	mouth or throat.
klăm/mĭ	-	damp, close thundery weather.

klān	-	clean
klăp	-	to put down quickly. To flop down

(Er klap/pd er be/ind on our sof/fi = She put her bottom down quickly on our sofa).

klā/ŭr	-	clear
klāz	-	division in a cloven foot, claws of a cat.
klĕmd	-	very hungry
klĕt	-	to eat quickly
klĕt	-	having no money. ('I an/nu got a klet').
klĭk/kĭ	-	close knit group of people. clannish
klĭn/kêr or Klĭn/kĭn	-	very good, a good one.
klĭv/vêr	-	clever
klŏm/bêr	-	to climb ('Look at that yuk/in

klŏm/bêr/ĭn on that sŏf/fĭ. = Look at that child climbing on that sofa).

klŏs	-	close
klowt (ow as in brow)	-	large thick piece of cake or bread
klŭb fŭt	-	deformed foot
kŏk	-	a small lump of hay ready to be carried to the barn
kŏl over	-	to make derogatory remarks about someone. talk about someone.
kōl/ŭs	-	coalhouse
kŏn/nŭ	-	cannot
kŏn/sârn	-	concern
kŏn/sāt/ed	-	conceited
kŏnt	-	can't
kŏn thŭ	-	can't you
kŏn/trăp/shŭn	-	peculiar machine or device
kŏŏ	-	can't
kōō/ăt	-	coat
kōōm	-	comb
kōōt (oo as in boot)	-	a silly person
kŏŏtch (oo as in tooth)	-	crouch in the grass
kŏŏ/zĭ	-	concrete or paved path, usually leading to the toilet
kŏp	-	to steal
kōōt/êr/ĭn	-	messing about
kŏp/pĭ	-	coppice or copse

kŏs/nŭ	-	can't you
kŏst	-	can you
kŏŏv	-	calf
kō/vĭ or od kō/vĭ	-	old man
kow/tī	-	chain for tying up a cow
krāk	-	creak
krām	-	cream
krătch	-	manger for sheep or cattle

(someone who was a good eater was called 'a good krătchêr'.)

krĕp	-	crept
krō/kĭn	-	prowling
krŏmp	-	cramp
krōōdl	-	cuddle
krōp	-	creep
krŏt/chĕ/tĭ	-	miserable
krŭd/dĭ	-	curdled milk, touchy person
krŭk	-	crook
krŭk/ĕd	-	crooked
krŭm/mĭl	-	rogue
krŭs/tĭ	-	bad tempered miserable, in a bad mood.
kŭb	-	small shelter for hens, chicks or rabbits.
kŭb/bŭt	-	cupboard
kŭm/mŭn on	-	come on well, improved greatly.
kŭs/sŭnt	-	cousin
kŭs/tŭt	-	custard
kŭt	-	castrate (pigs, lambs, bullocks etc).
kyâr/pĭt	-	carpet
kyârt	-	cart
kyī/mĭt	-	useless

(old Herefordshire meaning of 'kyment' was stupid).

kyō/kĭn		howling
kwoys (oy as in boy)	-	wood pigeons.

L

lăͣd by	-	been put on one side and not been in use for sometime.
lăͣn	-	lain
lăͣs	-	to thrash
lăͣ/sĕs	-	laces
lăͣt/lĭ	-	lately
lămp	-	hit
Lârd	-	Lord
lârn	-	to teach, usually to teach a child not to be naughty.
lăr/rŭm	–	alarm
lăr/rŭp (ar as in barrel)	-	nattering, mouthy
lăthr	-	ladder
lĕf	-	leaf
lĕs/ŭs	-	field
lĭf/fêr	-	prefer. I'd lif/fer goo', meant I'd prefer to go.
lĭft	-	an upper cut. 'I'll lift yu one',
lĭk/êr	-	fat resulting when cooking meat in a pan.
lĭk/êr/dish	-	liquorice
līm/êr	-	to take unfair advantage. Near the

Dhu Stone there is a lane called the Limer's Lane which was an old route from lime kilns. In her Shropshire Word book, Georgina Jackson says, 'The lime burners goo to a public fur some ale, two young uns and an owd un, the owd un tak's car' to sit i the middle, so as the jug passes backuts and forruts, e gets as much agen as the young uns, hence e's a coming limer oe'r him'.

lĭs/sŭm	-	athletics, muscular built. An active elderly person.

in Herefordshire lissum meant active. Quote from Shropshire word book - 'A stratum. when burning lime ''we putten first a lissum o' coal, an then a lissum o' lime stwun.''

lŏf	-	laugh
Lŭd/lŭ	-	Ludlow
lŭng yŭd/dĕd	-	a good memory.

M

măg/pĭ	-	magpie
mâr/nĭn	-	morning
mâr/tl	-	mortal

129

maw/kin (aw as in bawl)	-	scarecrow
měd/sŭn	-	medicine
měek	-	make
měē/kĭn	-	making
mēl/lĭ mowthd (ow as in howl)	-	someone who doesn't always speak the truth. deceitful person.
mĭd/lĭn	-	very poorly
mīnd thŭ	-	mind you
mĭss/ŭs	-	your wife
mĭx/ŭn	-	rubbish heap
mĭz/atĭ	-	very greedy
mĭz/zlĭn	-	light rain
mŏg/gĭ		children's name for a young calf
mŏl/lĭ kŏd/dl	-	to make too much fuss of a child
mŏm/mĭ	-	runny 'it's mom/mi jam.' It's runny jam.
mŏn	-	man
mŏn/nĭ	-	conceited, big headed, arrogant.
mŏŏch	-	hang around
mōō/er̂ (oo as in moo)	-	more
mŏr/rĭd	-	married
mŏr/ŭl ĭmĭj	-	exactly the same in looks. He's exactly like his father.
mōs/sĭ	-	being nosey. Having a good look around when not invited.
mŏs/sl	-	morsal
mŏst/ly	-	usually
mŏt	-	marker for quoits and 'pitch and toss.'
mŏy/thŭrd	-	confused, mixed up.
mŭ	-	me
mŭ/cher̂	-	not much good. 'E innu a mu/cher.' He's not a very reliable person.
mŭf/fler̂	-	a knotted scarf
mŭg/gĭ	-	damp, close thundery atmosphere.
mŭk/kĭ	-	posh
mūl/lŏk	-	rubbish
mŭm	-	not to say a word, to keep a secret.
mŭn	-	must

mŭnch	-	to chew loudly and contort the mouth while eating.
mŭn/nu	-	mustn't
mŭns and mŭnts	-	months
mŭs/tŭt	-	mustard
mŭth/ẽrs	-	bottoms, hops etc of a barrel of beer.

N

năal păs/sẽr	-	gimlet, a small carpenter's sharp tool for starting holes.
năals	-	nails
năăm	-	name
năp	-	to grab or steal. To be caught redhanded.
năp/pĭn	-	Clee Hill quarrymen's expression for breaking stone or shaping it. They used a special hammer referred to as 'a năp/pĭn ŭm/mẽr.

('thẽs dun sŭm năp/pĭn tă mĕk a rŭk līk that ŭn.' = you've broken a great deal of stone to make such a large pile.)

nãr	-	nor
nãrkd	-	disappointed, to hurt one's feelings.
nãrth	-	north
nãrth īy	-	to keep a sharp look out.
nā/tẽr	-	goodness.

('thẽs kōōkd all the nā/tẽr out on it,' = you've cooked all the goodness out of it).

nē/ănt	-	aunt
nĕe/bẽr	-	neighbour
nēd nu	-	need not
nĕr/rŭ ŭn	-	none of them, not one, neither of them.
nĕsh	-	someone who feels the cold.
nī/gŭn	-	night gown
nĭnt/ls	-	knees
nĭst	-	nest
nīz	-	noise
nĭz/gl	-	last one of a pig's litter to be born
nŏg/gĭn	-	a small drink or a piece of bread or cake.

nǒg/mǔn	-	a simpleton
nǒg/mǔn yǔd/dĕd	-	stubborn
nǒk/lêrs	-	binoculars
nǒr/rǔ	-	narrow
nǒr/rǔ gǔt/ted	-	a very thin person
nǒst	-	know
		('Thē nost' - You know)
nǔnkl	-	uncle
nǔs	-	nurse
nǔt/trǐ stǐk	-	hazel stick

O

| ǒd | - | old |
| ǒd/dêrn ĕp/êrn | - | apron made from a flour sack, used by a shopkeeper. |

(Ear-appern was an old Shropshire gleaner's apron).

ǒf	-	half
ǒk/ǔt	-	awkward
ǒk/shǔt	-	hog's head, the name given to a fifty six gallon barrel.
ǒl/lǔ	-	empty or hollow container. To shout loudly.
ǒl ǔl/lǔng	-	from the beginning
ǒm/êr	-	hammer
ǒmp/êr	-	to delay, hamper, worry
ǒm/ǔst	-	almost
ǒn	-	of
		('Skerd on im,' - scared of him).
ǒn/dǐ	-	handy
ǒn/dǐ ǔn	-	a useless person
ǒn/dl	-	handle
ǒn/dld	-	handled
ǒnds	-	hands
ǒn it	-	of it
ǒn/ser	-	answer
on us	-	of us
		('Six on us plǎǎd pitch un toss' - Six of us played pitch and toss)

ŏs/sĕs	-	horses
ōōd	-	wood, would
ōōd/ŭ	-	would he
ōōd/nt	-	wouldn't
ōōd/nŭ	-	would not
ōw/ĭ	-	yes
ōōl	-	wool, will
ōōm/ŭn	-	woman
ōōn/nŭ	-	will not
ŏŏp	-	half ('Ŏop past fōw/ĕr - Half past four)
ōōsh/ŭk	-	an expression used when something moved suddenly.
oost (oo as in wood)	-	will you
ŏŏth	-	with
ŏŏt	-	will you ('Kŭm ēr ŏot' - Come here will you).
ŏpl	-	apple
ŏpl gawb (aw as in bawl)	-	apple dumpling
ōt	-	rabbit hole
ōt a bit	-	wait a moment
ow bĭn yŭ	-	how are you
ow bist	-	how are you
ows/n	-	houses

P

păl/ĭns	-	a good hiding, peelings
păp/pĭ	-	stupid, daft
păst/ĭn	-	a good hiding, a good beating
pē/ăp/ĕr	-	paper
pē/ĕrt	-	very fit
pĕk	-	pick axe
pĕnz	-	base feathers which have been left when poultry have not been feathered cleanly.

pêr/gĭ	-	a bad tempered person
(Herefordshire pergy - obstinate).		
pêr/kĭ	-	a bright wide awake animal or person. Used when one looked surprisingly well after an illness.
pêr/tĭ	-	pretty
pêr/tĭ tīdĭ	-	doing very well
pĭch/ĭn/ōl	-	opening into a hay bay or loft through which loose hay was thrown
pĭg's stĭ)	-	pig sty
pĭg's cot)		
pīkl)	-	pitch fork
pĭch fârk)		
pīk/lĕt	-	a tea crumpet
pīn/chŭns	-	pincers
pĭn/nêr--	–	pinafore
pĭns	-	pence
pĭsn	-	poison
pĭtch/ŭk	-	broken crock
plāch/ĭn	-	laying a hedge
plăăd	-	played
plăăzn	-	places
plāzd	-	pleased
plĕĕs	-	place
plĕĕsd	-	pleased
plĕĕt)	-	plate
plăăt)		
pet/tĭ	-	lavatory
plŭm jêrk/ĭn	-	plum wine
pōk	-	a sty on your eye
pŏn	-	pan
pŏn kē/ăk	-	pan cake
pŏr/ĭsh	-	parish
pŏr/kĭ	-	a plump person
pŏst	-	post
pōoch	-	pouch
pōon	-	hit hard, to give a good hiding, (I'll pōon thă if thē dŭst/nŭ stop

wêr/ĭt/ĭn.' - I'll give you a good hiding if you do not stop fretting).
'Them stŏn tĕĕkn sŭm pōon/ĭn.' - Those stone take a great deal of breaking.

pōon/ĭn	-	hitting, breaking

pŏp/lĭns	-	poplar trees
pŏs/ĭs	-	posts

('Pŭt them pŏs/ĭs ŭg/ĭn thī aăh băă.' - Put those posts against your hay bay).

pow/êr	-	a great deal

('That trāt/ment at Sōōs/brĭ did ĭm a pow/êr ŏ good.' - The treatment at Shrewsbury did him a great deal of good.)

prā/ch	-	preach
pŭg/gĭ	-	tangled (hair)
pŭk	-	picked

('I pŭk a fyo wĭm/bêr/rĭs.' - I picked a few whimberries).

pŭs	-	purse
pŭt	-	put
pŭt about	-	distressed, upset
pyĕp/pêr	-	paper
pyârt/in (ar as in park)	-	parting

R

rab/bit ōt	-	rabbit hole
rās	-	the liver, heart and lights of a pig
rawl (aw as in bawl)	-	to pull up roughly
rāy/der	-	radar
rāy/êrd	-	to bring up

('Gran/ni rāy/êrd.' - To be brought up by grand parents)

răz/ŭr băk/tŭn	-	a bacon pig
rāch	-	reach
rĕĕk	-	rake
rĕĕs	-	race
rĕĕ/stĭ	-	rancid or sour bacon
rĕĕvd	-	turn your nose up, wrinkled

('Ē rĕĕvd at that snăp/pĭn.' - He turned his nose up at that food)

rēk	-	strong smell
rĕn/dêr	-	to melt down fat

('Ēs a good răz/ŭr băk/tŭn. Wēn ă sŭm/mŭt tŭ rĕn/dêr. Ēn shĕk 30 skŏr.' - He's a good bacon pig. We'll have plenty of fat to melt down. He'll weigh at least 30 score')

rĭnkl	-	dodge, a quick way of doing something.
rĭsd	-	risen
rĭs/sĕs	-	wrists

rŏnk	-	unpredictable, wise and crafty person. Food which was not fresh.

('That bĭf smells rŏnk.' - That beef does not smell fresh.)

ro͞op	-	rope
ro͞op/pĭ	-	poor, stringy, poor quality meat which is not tender.
ro͞o/zls	-	influenza
rŏst	-	roast
rŏt	-	rat
rŏw/sht	-	kick something out of a bush or a tuft of grass with your foot.
rŏw/zl	-	to arouse, to wake up.
rŭk	-	heap of stone, a great number of things.
rŭf	-	roof

('Interviewer at the Dole Office:- ('Garbet, haven't you got a door at your house?' Garbet:- 'No, nâr much bloody rŭf.' - No nor much bloody roof.)

S

săd	-	heavy, not risen

('That kē/ăks sad. Ē ăn/nŭ rĭsd.' - That cake is heavy. It hasn't risen)

săl/lĕt	-	salad
săl/lĭ	-	willow tree
sârt	-	sort
sârvd	-	served
sāt	-	seat
săt/êr/no͞on	-	this afternoon
sĕdn	-	say, said.

('So thay sĕdn'. - So they say.)

sĕek	-	sake
seven coloured linnet	-	goldfinch
shăk	-	to sleep temporarily at a place.

('Wē/êrs thē shăk/ĭn?' - Where are you sleeping?)

shăs nŭ	-	wont you
shĕk/ĭn	-	to weigh, shaking.

('I sĭd ĭm shĕk/ĭn them ŏp/ples.' - I saw him shaking those apples. 'Them tē/ăt/têrs o͞ol shĕk a ŭn/dŭt wĕ/ŭt.' - Those potatoes will weigh a hunder-weight.)

shēl/lêrs	-	ripe nuts (always used to describe filbert nuts)
shêr	-	share
shĭnkç	-	should think

shĭp	-	sheep
shĭp/rĕks	-	a path up the hill sides made by sheep.
shĭt/tĕn	-	shame-faced person
shōōd/rs	-	shoulders
shōōd/n	-	should do
shōō/st	-	shall
shŏŏvs	-	shafts of a hay wagon or cart
shōw/ŭr (ow as in show)	-	shorn

('Ast thē shŏw/er thē shĭp yŭt?' - Have you shorn your sheep yet?)

sĭd	-	seed, seen
sĭdn	-	seen
sĭd/lŭnt	-	a sloping field. Land on the side of a hill.
sĭd/tĕ/ăt/ers	-	seed potatoes
sĭd/ŭts	-	sideways
sĭf/fĭ/tĭk/ĕts	-	saving certificates
sīk/ĕn	-	crying profusely

('E wŭs sīk/ĕn ĭs art out.' - He was crying his heart out.)

sĭm/ŏn/lĭ	-	It looks like it. It seems as though.
sin	-	seen

('E wŭs sin this marn/in.' - He was seen this morning.)

sit	-	a great deal

('E could do ŏŏth a sit more fĭt/tl.' - He could do with much more to eat.)

skăt/tĭ	-	a disorganised person. A scatterbrain
skĕl/ĭn/tŏn	-	skeleton
skērd	-	scared
skew/wĭf (ew as in pew)	-	out of shape, out of line with surroundings.

('Er ăts skew/wĭf on er yŭd.' - Her hat is tilted on her head.)

skŏg/gĭn	-	bragging

('Sid wŭs skŏg/gĭn about is răz/ŏr băk/tŭn.' - Sid was bragging about his bacon pig.)

skōōt (oo as in boot)	-	When a person had dug a large patch of his garden he referred to it as a 'good skoot'.
skrăg/gĭ	-	untidy. Often referred to uncombed, untidy hair, or a thin undernourished animal.
skrăt	-	scratch

(a person who worked very hard and made an existence out of very little).

skrawl (aw as in bawl)	-	to crawl about in the same way as a young child.

137

skrēn	-	a long wooden seat with a high back and sides. Sometimes it had a lift up seat lid which revealed a store chest below. Used in draughty public houses.
skrŭmp/pĭ	-	farm house cider. Drunk by most quarry-men because it was much cheaper than beer.
skwāk/ĭn	-	squeaking
skwāl	-	squeal
skwârk	-	solidified tobacco round the bole of a pipe. Quarrymen scraped this out and chewed it.
skwăăt	-	a short stocky person, to squat.
skwĕdj	-	squeeze
skwĕd/jĭ	-	soft boggy ground, the noise when wading through mud.

(When boots were filled with water locals said, 'Mĭ fŭts all skwĕd/jĭ.' - My foot is soaking wet.)

skwĭlt	-	blackhead, any small swelling on the body.
skwĭtch	-	couch grass
sky/ârf	-	scarf
skĭ/ŭrf	-	scurf
slăăts	-	roofing slates

(on the slăăt meant owing money at the shop or public house).

slĕp	-	slept
slĭv/ēr	-	a very thin slice of bacon or bread
slŏp	-	overall, a cow gown
slŏpd	-	to spill or upset liquid
slōp	-	to walk away quietly trying not to be noticed.

('Ē slōp/pĕd off' - He disappeared without being seen).

slŭm/mŭk/kĭ	-	untidy

('Ē/ăts ĭs fĭt/tl slŭm/mŭk/kĭ.' - He eats his food in a slovenly way. 'Ĭnt ē slŭm/mŭk/kĭ at ĭs work.' - Isn't he an untidy worker).

smârm/mĭ	-	a smooth talker, insincere excessive affection.
smârn/ĭn	-	this morning
smŏk	-	smoke; or an overall cover garment worn by women while working.
snĕd	-	handle of a scythe
snīvd	-	overrun with vermin

sŏb/b̥in	-	soaking wet

('Is fĭt wŭn sŏb/in' - His feet were soaking.)

sŏf/fĕ	-	sofa
sō lŭng	-	cheerio, goodbye.
sŏm/pl	-	lack of character, poor quality

('A poor som/pl.' - A poor character.)

sŏnd	-	sand
soo/bl	-	to splash water over ones face, a quick wash.

('Soo/bl thē fĕĕs.' - Swill your face.)

soŏn/ĕ	-	silly stupid fellow
Soos/brĭ	-	Shrewsbury
spaad	-	spade
spīl	-	spoil
spĭf/lĭ/kāt	-	kill
spĭtl	-	handle for a fork or rake
splīt	-	do a bad turn

('Dŭ splīt thē sĕn,' - Don't do yourself a bad turn.)

spŏd/jĭ	-	house sparrow
spŏr/ĭb	-	spare rib
spŏr/rŭ	-	hedge sparrow
spowl (ow as in cow)	-	a cotton reel
spowt	-	hand water pump for domestic water supply.
sprăg	-	a specially shaped piece of wood to put through the spokes of a quarry truck to stop it.
spĭ/ert	-	spurt, the spurts on a potato tuber
stănk	-	to dam up water in a brook
stârm	-	storm
stāl	-	a handle for an axe or hammer
stĕm	-	steam
stĕn	-	a steen, a wide earthenware container in which cream or lard was stored.
stĭ/dĭ	-	steady
stĭp	-	steep
stŏ/gĭ	-	thick, heavy, not properly cooked.

('Sŭr/rĭ, thī ŏple gawb's stŏgĭ.' - Goodness gracious, your apple pie is not properly cooked.)

stŏk	-	a special tool for removing weeds, like a small kaf (see kaf).

Stōk/ĭs Bridge	-	absolutely full up, unable to eat any more.
stŏn	-	stone
stoop (oo as in moon)	-	to tip a barrel to drain it.
styow (ow as in mow)	-	stew
străăn	-	strain
străăt	-	street
strāk	-	an arch of metal forming part of the protective rim around a heavy wooden wagon wheel.
strēe/kĭ	-	streaky
strĕĕt	-	straight
strĕĕtn	-	straighten
strĭng ōt/td	-	unable to run fast, appearing as though the legs were tied with string.
sŭk	-	sweets
sŭm/mŭt	-	something
sŭng	-	song
sŭn sŭk/ērs	-	rays of the sun after a rain storm
sŭp	-	to drink, to sip off a spoon.

('Ē kōn sŭp some skrŭm/pĭ.' - He can drink a large quantity of cider.)

sŭr/rĭ	-	good gracious or indeed

('Dĭst sŭr/rĭ?' - Did you indeed?)

sŭt	-	soot
swârd	-	bacon rind, the first cut of grass around the perimeter of a field.
swĭlk	-	swill, waste products such as skimmed milk, potato peelings etc which were given to a bacon pig.
swĭng	-	singe

('We swĭng/ed the pig.' - We burnt the hair off the pig.)

swĭngl	-	swindle

T

tā	-	tea
tăl/lĕt or tăll/lănt	-	a storage space above a cow shed or farm building, usually for grain or hay.

tăng   -   to beat

('I'll tăng yēr ĭd.' - I'll beat you across the bottom.)

Herefordshire tang was a clatter to attract a swarm of bees.

tăp	-	to repair shoes
târ	-	to tease
tē/ăble	-	table
tē/ăt/êrs	-	potatoes
tĕek	-	take
tĕm/pĕst	-	heavy, humid thundery weather
thă or yŭ	-	you

('to thă.' - to you.)

thăăm	-	they are
thăă/dn	-	they would
thăăn	-	they have
thârn	-	thorn
thăy	-	they
thē	-	your
thē ăst	-	you have
thĕ/ér	-	there
thē/sĭst	-	you see
thēst	-	you would
thĕy/r	-	there and their
thrĕĕp	-	thrape
thrĕ/shêr	-	a machine for separating corn from the ears
thī	-	your
thrŭstl	-	song thrush
thrŏkl	-	throttle

('I kŏn/nŭ ăbīd a kŏ/lêr and tī thrŏ/kl/ĭn mŭ. Gĭ mĭ a mŭf/flêr any dăă.' - I can't bear a collar and tie throttling me. Give me a neckerchief any day.)

thrŏŏt	-	throat
tĭnd	-	light

('Tĭnd mĭ fag.' - light my cigarette.)

tĭtl	-	to dribble a football
tĭt/tĭ	-	feeding bottle or breast milk
tōd	-	told
tŏŏd	-	it would
tŏŏkn (oo as al in talk)	-	talk
tōōt	-	ill
tŏp/pĭn	-	very good, excellent condition

tow/sl (ow as in cow)	-	untidy, uncombed matted hair, rough looking.
trăăps	-	untidy way of walking, walk over without thought and care.

('Dŭn/nŭ trăăps over mĭ floo/ĕr.' - Don't walk thoughtlessly over my floor.)

trănkl/ments	-	odds and ends, bits and pieces
trĕ/ăkl	-	treacle
trŏl/lŏp	-	an untidy woman
trŏnk/kŭl	-	an idiot
trooth (oo as in tooth)	-	truth
trōw (ow as in owe)	-	a trough for pig or fowl food
trŭk	-	have nothing to do with a person

('I ōon/ŭ ăv any trŭk ōoth ĭm.' - I won't have anything to do with him.)

tŭth	-	tooth
tŭ/thêrs	-	the others
tŭm/mĭ	-	food

alternatives were grub, snăp/pĭn and fĭt/tl. These were names given to a quarryman's lunch which was tied up in a spotted, knotted hankerchief.

tump	-	small mound of earth. An anti tump was an ant hill
tŭn/dish	-	a funnel to put beer in a bottle or paraffin in a tin
tŭsh	-	to pull a heavy weight
tŭs/sŏk	-	a small mound of rough grass
twāk	-	twist or turn

('Twāk the wĭl/lĭs knob.' - Turn the radio control)

twĭt	-	to split on someone.

U

ŭf	-	to be offended, to take offence

('Ēs took the ŭf.' - He's offended.)

ŭkd	-	hooked

('I ŭkd the ŏrs tŭ the kyârt,' - I hooked the horse to the cart.)

ŭk/ĭn	-	a second attempt, a second helping of food.

('Ē ăd one nŭth/êr ŭk/ĭn.' - He had a second helping.)

ŭn	-	one
ŭn/dŭt	-	one hundred

up an/ŭnst	-	up against, by the side of

('I pŭt mĭ făȓk up an/ŭnst the kŏͧ/zĭ.' - I put my fork by the side of the footpath.) Scots, Yorkshire and Gloucestershire used - aunt.

up sĭ/down	-	up side down
ŭr	-	row
ŭs	-	me

('Ē it us in the fĕēz.' - He hit me in the face.)

ŭ/wăͧa	-	away
ŭt/chd	-	curled up with cold or fright

(old Herefordshire - hootched)

V

vin/yeȓd	-	vine yard, vine grove
vŏ/vĭd	-	void

('Thī rĕĕs is vŏ/vĭd.' - Your race is void.)

W

wăͧat	-	wait
wăd	-	lump of mown grass in a hayfield which has not dried.
wăg/gĭn	-	wagon, cart or dray.
wŏl īd	-	a person or animal that has one eye which was different in colour to the other; a streak in the eye.
waȓf	-	wharf
wăt/ched	-	watched
wĕ/ăt	-	weight
wē/eȓ	-	where

('Wē/eȓ bĭst?' - Where are you?)

wĕͧet	-	wait
wĕͧe/teȓ	-	water
wĕͧe/teȓĭ	-	watery

('This sty/ow's wĕͧe/teȓi.' - This stew is watery.)

wench	-	girl
wĕr/ĭt	-	fret, worry

('Stop wĕr/ĭt/ĭn Father.' - Stop worrying father.)

wĕsh/ĭn	-	washing

('Ăst thē finished the wĕsh/īn?' - Have you finished your washing?)

wĕsh tub	-	a tub in which clothes washing was done
wĕst/kŏt	-	waist coat

wĕt/chd   -   watched
('I wĕt/chd ĭm krōp by.' - I watched him creep by.)

wăt   -   what

wif/fl   -   wind blowing from every direction
('Dŭnt that snow wif/fl under the āvs?' - Doesn't that snow blow under the eaves)

wĭk   -   week
('It took a wĭk o Sun/dis.' - It took an indefinite amount of time.)

wīld   -   while

wī/lĭs   -   wireless, radio

wĭl/rĭt   -   wheelwright

wĭm/brĭ   -   whimberries or bilberries found on Clee Hill.

wīnd   -   wind

wīnd   -   wine

wĭnd/ŭ, wĭnd/er   -   window

wĭn/nĭ/kĭn   -   whining

wĭns   -   winch

wĭskĕt   -   whisket basket. A woven basket placed around earthenware jars to protect them. Quarrymen used them to avoid beer jars being cracked.
(used as a clothes basket in Herefordshire.)

Wĭs/tŭn/tĭd   -   Whitsuntide

wĭ/thĭ   -   pliable, bendy stick.

wō/lĕt   -   owl
('Kŭst thē er that wŏ/lĕt in the grāāv yard?' - Can you hear that owl in the graveyard?)

wŏl/ler   -   alder tree
Wol/lers was the name given to an alder coppice.

wŏŏk   -   woke

wŏŏnt (oo as in soot)   -   mole

wŭm   -   home
('Bĭst gwāān wŭm yŭt?' - Are you going home yet?)

wŭn   -   were

wŭn/st   -   once

wŭn/tŭ   -   wasn't he

wŭnt it   -   wasn't it

wŭn/nŭ   -   wasn't

wŭn yŭ   -   were you

wŭr   -   war

wŭrm   -   warm

wŭs/sêr   -   worse

('Ows thĭ fāther?' - 'Oh ēs wŭs/sêr.' - 'How is your father?' 'Oh he's worse.')

wŭst   -   were you

wŭz   -   was

Y

yăp/nĭ   -   halfpenny

('Ē'd skin flĕn fêr a yăp/nĭ.' - He'd skin fleas for a halfpenny.)

yăp/pŭth   -   halfpenny's worth

('Gĭs a yăp/pŭth a sŭk plăaz.' - Please would you give me a halfpenny's worth of sweets)

yârks   -   trousers tied at the knees with string. They were usually corduroys, always worn in this style by quarry-men.

yăt   -   hate

yĕd   -   head

Yĕd/êrt   -   Edward

yĕl/lêr   -   yellow, a coward

('Thrĕep ĭm. Dŭn/nŭ be a yĕl/lêr bă/bĭ.' - Hit him. Don't be a coward.)

yêr   -   your

yĕr/ĭn   -   herring

yō   -   you

yōosd (oo as in soot)   -   used

yōw   -   ewe

yōwm   -   you are

yōw/dn   -   you had

yōwn   -   you have

yŭ   -   you

yŭd   -   head

yūk/ĭns   -   young boys

('Dŭnt that yŭk/ĭn kratch.' - Doesn't that young boy eat well.)

yŭt   -   yet

SOME LOCAL PLACE NAMES

Klāy Ĭl	-	Clee Hill
Klĭb/rĭ	-	Cleobury
Kŏr/lĭ	-	Coreley
Kŏrn Brŭk	-	Corn Brook
Dyōos Stŏn	-	Dhu Stone
Fârl/ŭ	-	Farlow
Ŏs Ditch	-	Horse Ditch
Nō/brĭ	-	Knowbury
Sōos/brĭ	-	Shrewsbury
Bĕd/lŭm	-	Titterstone Cottages
Tĭt/tēr/stŏn	-	Titterstone
Kĕĕn/nŭm	-	Caynham
The Gĭ/ăt	-	The Gate Hangs Well
The Krem/lin	-	Craven Arms Inn
The Darkies	-	Dhu Stone Inn

CLEE HILL PHRASES

Ēs as lŭng as a wĭk. — He's very tall.

Dŭ thē trāăps on mī klān floo/êr. — Don't put your dirty boots on my clean floor.

I ăn/nŭ got a klĕt. — I haven't got a penny. I'm broke.

Thēs got. — You have.

Why dŭst/nŭ thē shut thē lăr/rŭp? — Why don't you keep quiet?

Răz/ŭr băktŭn. — Bacon Pig.

I shĭnk thē wănts tă goo an ă thī yŭd looked at. — You want your hair cut.

I got the rooz/ls. — I've got the flu.

Ē wŭn kăld up. — He was knocked over.

Klĕmd tu dyŭth. — Very hungry.

Dŭnt our Yĕd/ŭrt bolt is fĭt/tl. — Doesn't our Edward eat his food quickly.

This tās like ditch wāt/êr. — This tea is very weak.

Ĭnt ē a soon/ni. — Isn't he silly.

A mag/pĭ tăld jacked. — A frock coat.

Ĭnd fêr ĭnd. — Reverse positions. Turn the pole round. Turn a complete circle.

A tŏd bel/ĭd ŭn. — A little fat man.

As dyŭd as a ŏm/mêr. — As dead as a hammer. Dead.

Put thī fŭt into that choo/bĭn/kĕz. — Kick that football.

Tĭnd mĭ fag. — Light my cigarette.

Ēs got no ōt in hīm. — He's very unreliable.

The gorse is in blăw. — The gorse is in blossom.

He'll be comin drĕkt/lĭ. — He will be coming later on.

I'm gwăn fêr a bêrdn ŏ ood. — I'm going for an armful of wood.

Dŭn/nŭ egg ĭm on. — Don't encourage him.

Ēs for/rŭt enough. — He knows too much.

Skrē/ăp thē thrŏt. — Clear your throat.

Thēst ăt tŭ give ĭm a twāk. — You'll have to give it a turn.
(referring to a wireless control).

Ēs bĭn gwăn about ăat mŭnts. — He's been gone about eight months.

I got sŭm/mŭt stuck in mĭ klăk. — I've got something stuck in my throat.

Int ē mŭk/ĭ. — Isn't he posh.

I sĭd ĭm krōp by. — I saw him creep by.

Int ē lĭs/sŭm sŭr/rĭ. — Good gracious, isn't he fit.

Īst yêr nīz, thăm cŭmĭn. — Be quiet, they're coming.

147

Ē an/nŭ got a bit a māt on hĭm. — He's very thin.

Sŭr/rĕ ĭnt ē nŏr/rŭ gŭt/ĭd. — Good gracious isn't he thin.

I'd as lĭv gōo as not. — I'd rather stay at home.

Ēs a dab ŏnd at plāch/ĭn. — He's a good hedge layer.

Slŏp/ĭn off. — Craftily walking away.

Thē dŭst/nŭ wănt tŭ spīt thē sĕn. — You don't want to do yourself any harm.

Sŭr/rĭ, thē ăss/nŭ ŏf got sŭm chŏl/lŏp. — Good gracious, you've got plenty to say for yourself.

Dŭst/nŭ wănt a nŏg/gĭn a chās? - Would you like a piece of bread and cheese?

I kĕt/chd a thorough kōd. — I've got the flu.

Gĭs a chêrpêr. — Give me a kiss.

Ēs the moral image of ĭs fāthêr. — He looks exactly like his father.

Dŭnt our Tŭm minse ĭs fĭt/tl. — Doesn't our Tom chew his food for a long time.

Bĭst thē gwăn ōōth ŭm? — Are you going with them?

Sŭr/rĭ ănt I got the gêr? — Good gracious, don't I feel lazy.

That jŏm's gwŭn all on a mŏm/mĭ. — That jam's gone all runny and sloppy.

Look at that ŏd Kōv/ĭ. — Look at that old man.

Sōobl thĭ fēēs ōōth kōd wātêr. — Swill your face with cold water.

There thē bĭst thē sĭst. — There you are you see.

Thăm kŭm/ĭn up the lĕs/ŭs bel ŏlu. — They're coming up the meadows full gallop.

Ĭnt ē a klĭink/êr? — Isn't he a good one?

There's any a ĕft on it. — There's plenty of it.

Kŭst plăă thē cōom ŭn pyĕp/pêr? — Can you play the comb and paper?

I've just about a lat/ch āv/êr. — I've just about enough for a pint.

Wērs mĭ pŭss? — Where's my purse?

Ē wŭs shĕk/ĭn like a lĭf. — He was shaking like a leaf.

Jĕst thē look ow them ōŏnts av sārvd thĭ gyārd/ĭn. Thăy ănt ŏf āvd it up ănt ŭm? - Just you look how those moles have treated your garden. They haven't half heaved it up, haven't they?

Ēs as ăp/pĭ as a bĭd/dĭ. - He's as happy as a baby.

Gĭs a yăp/pŭth a sŭk, plāz? — Give me a halfpenny's worth of sweets please?

Gĭt thĭ fĭt under the tāābl. — Get your feet under the table.
(this meant to try and marry someone or to be accepted).

Ĭnt it kōd. I'll krōōdl up to thă. — Isn't it cold. I'll cuddle up to you.

So lŭng fêr now. — Cheerio.

A poem by Dennis Crowther

FATHER'S CHILDHOOD DAYS

It wŭs klŏs on 1906
When I fŭst sĭd the light ŭ daă,
and mĭ fā/ther̂ ē stāy/er̂d like a throttled kyăt
At the whisket in which I lăă.
Fŭr a pot bellied yū/kĭn I wŭs fer̂ sure,
I'd got a yŭd like a ŏk/shŭt bŏr/rĭl,
And mi gran/nĭ er̂ sĕd/n, 'Well bless mĭ soul,
Of is fā/ther̂ ē is the mŏr/rĭl.

I ăd mĭ fŭst solid fĭt/tl at ăă/tēn wĭks,
I wŭs wēnd ăf/or I wŭs two,
And ŏŏth only two tĭth I could granch a pork chop,
And bīld sŭk I could āt quite a fyō.
The fŭst words I spŏk wŭs 'Hell to mĭ nŭn/cl,'
I could skwāl like a răz/ŭr băkt pig,
And if I kŏŏd/nŭ get wăăt I wăntd.
I'd tie a knot in mĭ grand fā/ther̂'s wig.

Thē kŭst fol/lŭ the traăl wē/er̂ I'd bin on the flō/er̂,
Fer̂ mĭ bŭz/gĭns thăy never wŭs dry,
I'd krōp up on the kyat and yârk on er̂ tăăl,
Through the ā/er like a bird er̂ ŏŏd fly,
Mĭ nē/ant er̂ ŏŏd sleep ŏŏth er̂ fĭt on the ŏb,
And I'd skyŏm/bl upon to er knee,
And I'd krŏŏdl up into er̂ ăp/per̂n,
Wē/er̂ I could plan mĭ next little spree.

Then when I rā/chd the ĕĕdg of five an a ŏŏf,
Mĭ fā/ther̂ one daă to mĭ said,
Thĭ trēē/sĭs bĭn down tŭ thī shŏŏ/drs,
It's about time that I looked at thī yĕd.
I'll măăk the skў/ŭrf fly ŏŏth mĭ scissors I ŏŏl,
Down thī neck ŏh old Phēb/ĭ ŏŏl shine,
And I'll buy thē a pā/er̂ a lŭng trousers,
I'll be proud tŭ saă thē bĭst mine.

And now that I'm ŏͦt/chd by the ĕs/ōl,

At the āͣg of seventy three,

I ŏf/fen looks back on mĭ childhood,

When nŭth/in wŭs wĕr/ĭt/ĭn me.

Oh! the jovial tricks I got up to,

Thay sē/ŭms like a drē/ŭm fêr aw/āͣa,

And I treasures these thoughts by the fire,

Well thăy passes the ow/ers awāͣa.

GARDENING TIME

A song

by Dennis Crowther

The song tells us that it was a common practice on Clee Hill to borrow gardening tools from each other because hardly anyone had a complete set. Hence work was often hampered because one neighbour had to wait for another neighbour to finish with the tool he required.

Well it's gy/ârd/in time in the country,

With the sīl I must come to terms,

The spŏr/rŭs bĭn wēͤt/in up in the spout

Fêr mĭ tŭ disturb the worms.

I ăd/nŭ lŭng bĭn dig/gin

When sŭm/mŭt mēͤd mĭ lŏf,

I ōp I finishes mĭ gy/ârd/in this sā/son,

Who the bloom/in 'ell bŏr/rŭd mĭ kāͣaf.

Chorus

Well fol/lu me rol di rid/dl oh

Fold di rol di ray,

Fol di rol di rid/dl oh,

Fold di rol di ray.

150

Oh I'll put on mĭ gy/ȃrd/nin gē/ĕr,
Shĕk mĭ gănd/zĭ tŭ row/zl the flĕn,
I'll put mĭ klŏd ŏp/pêrs tŭ wȃrm on the 'ob
An I'll tap ŭm ōŏth leather ŭg/gĕn
I'll get mĭ sĕn up by the fĭndr
And bit mĭ a skyom/ŭk a kĕ/ăk,
And pŭt in mĭ gyȃrd/in a row ŏ shallots,
If no bugger's borr/ŭd mĭ rēĕk.

Chorus

I wonder wē/êr mĭ ăk/êrs gwŭn
I got nothin tŭ call mĭ own,
The kĭst/nŭ see thē ows fêr wĭds,
Ten fŭt êr mōw/êr thăn grōwd,
Thērs a chap a gyȃrd/nin across the road
Ē sĭms tŭ bĭ tēek/in is time,
Ē might as well stop an av a gyawp round,
Kŏs som buggers bŏrr/ud is line.

Chorus

And now I think I'll shut mĭ trap
Pŭt a lock on the kōl/lŭs dō/êr,
Tŭ stop the tē/ĕt/êrs bolt/in
The spy/êrts am draggin the flō/êr,
The gyard/ners in the village
It's very plãen tu see,
Thãan a/tu farm a gyard/nin club
Tŭ find wē/êr the tak might be.

Chorus

151

BIBLIOGRAPHY

1. Dialect and local usage of Herefordshire, by Andrew Haggard. Published by Grower Books.
2. Herefordshire Speech, by Winifred Leeds.
3. A glossary of provincial words used in Herefordshire, published 1839.
4. Shropshire Word Book, by Gwendoline Jackson, published 1882.

SUBSCRIBERS

JOHN CROFTS,	Luston.
HARRY CONOD,	Luston.
HENRY BEAUMONT,	Kimbolton.
MARINA CLENT,	Knowbury.
Mrs. C. C. WILLIAMS,	Milson.
Mrs. G. B. FARMER,	Knighton-on-Teme.
Mrs. G. HAMMOND,	Milson.
Mrs. I. E. SPEARING,	Neen Sollars.
Mr. F. J. MOORE,	Neen Sollars.
Mrs. E. M. LINK,	
Mr. & Mrs. HULLAND,	Upper Langley.
Mr. B. OWEN,	Neen Sollars.
Mrs. K. SHILLING,	Cleobury Mortimer.
Miss D. M. EDWARDS,	Orleton.
Mrs. PAT WAITE,	Knowbury.
Mrs. S. J. RODWAY,	Knowbury.
Mrs. GORDAN HOWELLS,	Knowbury.
Mrs. MURIEL FIELD,	Clee Hill.
Mrs. LINDA EDWARDS,	Clee Hill.
Mrs. PAMELA EDWARDS,	Clee Hill.
Mr. DONALD MARTIN,	Clee Hill.
Mrs. R. WALKER,	Clee Hill.
Mrs. I. BANKS,	Tenbury Road.
Mrs. V. RUTTER,	Clee Hill.
CLEE HILL W. I.,	Clee Hill.
Rev. F. T. RUMBALL,	Eye Vicarage.
Mrs. JEAN PICTON,	Tenbury Wells.
Mr. & Mrs. T. TAVERNOR	Knowbury.
Mr. & Mrs. GEOFF GRIFFITHS,	Little Hereford.
Mrs. V. A. ROBSON,	Burford.
Mrs. D. L. SHEARWOOD,	Clee Hill.
THE OLIVER FAMILY,	Brampton Bryan.
Mrs. M. J. JENKINS,	Orleton.
Mr. & Mrs. D. BROOKS,	Leominster.
Mrs. A. JORDAN,	Tenbury Wells.
Mr. & Mrs. L. H. EVANS,	Ashton.
Mrs. PAT WILLIAMS,	Tenbury Road.
Mrs. IRENE ILOTT,	Tenbury Wells.
Mrs. JIM MANTLE,	Clee Hill.
Mr. & Mrs. J. F. TILLMAN,	Kidderminster.
Mrs. S. K. FRANKLIN,	Tenbury Wells.
Mrs. J. EDWARDS,	Inchmoor.
Mr. D. DAVIES,	Kimbolton.
Mr. & Mrs. J. A. MILLARDSHIP,	Clifford.
Mr. & Mrs. J. CLEETON,	Warrington.
THE EVANS FAMILY,	Eye.
THE OWENS FAMILY,	Tenbury Wells.
Master JAMES PHILLIPS,	Bockleton.
Mr. W. A. TAYLOR,	Orleton.
Mr. DAVID LLOYD,	Moseley.
Mr. & Mrs. R. BROOKES,	Tenbury Wells.
Mrs. MAY BRADLEY,	Clee Hill.
Mr. DAVID BANKS,	Ludlow.
Mr. CLIVE COATES,	Malvern.
Mrs. W. GITTENS,	Coreley.
Mrs. JOY HARPER,	Clee Hill.
Mr. ROBERT WILLIAMS,	London.
Mrs. ANN GARDENER,	Titrail.
Mrs. MARY LLOYD,	Clee Hill.
Mrs. GLADYS GREENHOUSE,	Clee Hill.
Mr. JOHN DAVIES,	Middlesex.
Mrs. J. FRENCH,	Clee Hill.
Miss B. BUTCHER,	Clee Hill.
Mr. & Mrs. W. TUDDENHAM,	Clee Hill.
Mr. C. A. BUTCHER,	Clee Hill.
Mrs. BARBARA PUGH,	Coreley.
Mrs. MARGARET BROOME,	Crumps Brook.
Mrs. VIOLET MEREDITH,	Ludlow.
Mrs. LEON JONES,	Burford.
Mr. W. BREAKWELL,	Onibury.
Mrs. V. E. BRIGHT,	Tenbury Wells.
JACK AND CAROLINE BEESTON,	Titterstone Cottages.
JOHN AND HILDA TROW,	Clee Hill.
Mr. & Mrs. D. W. PLANT,	Ludlow.
Mr. & Mrs. M. J. PLANT,	Titterstone.
Mr. & Mrs. C. G. POWELL,	Hereford.
Mr. & Mrs. S. J. DUNN,	Orleton.
Mr. GORDON LEECH,	Weobley.
J. & E. ALLERTON,	Ludlow.
TERENCE HARRIS,	Ludlow.
MAY JACKSON,	Ludlow.
ALAN & EVELYN JOHNSON,	Ludlow.
LYNNE WATKINS,	Leintwardine.
Mr. & Mrs. K. HALLAM,	Ludlow.
Mrs. D. N. BUNN,	Ludlow.
Mrs. C. L. COOPER,	Ludlow.
Mr. JOHN BEVAN,	Leominster.
Mrs. H. BRISTOW,	Tenbury Wells.
JOHN BARTON,	Cambridge.
L. PREECE,	Coreley.
Mrs. G. SAER,	Broad, Leominster.
Mrs. BERYL PRICE,	Ludlow.
Captain J. M. G. LUMSDEN,	Henley Hall.
Mrs. BETTY EDWARDS,	Dhu Stone Lane.
Mrs. MAY POWELL,	Cleobury Mortimer.
Mr. JOHN BREAKWELL,	Ludlow.
Mr. JIM BREAKWELL,	Australia.
Mrs. BETI LLOYD,	Downton.
CHRISTOPHER BUTTERWORTH,	Farlow.
N. & D. BROWN,	Farlow.
FRANCIS CHINN,	Farlow.
JOHN DEIGNAN,	Farlow.
RICHARD HOWELLS,	Farlow.
ROBERT HOWELLS,	Farlow.
E. M. LINK,	Farlow.
JOHN OLIVER,	Farlow.
JACK STANTON,	Farlow.
Mrs. BRIAN WALL,	Farlow.
IVOR WALL,	Farlow.
Rev. J. T. VIVIAN JONES,	Orleton Rectory.
Mr. & Mrs. H. COLE,	Cornbrook.
ALAN WEBB,	Doddington.
JOHN HUGHES,	Knowbury.
J. J. MORRIS,	Boraston.
Mr. & Mrs. GEOFFREY TAYLOR,	Bedlam.
DANIEL SYMONDS,	Stroud.
HILDA MARY REYNOLDS,	Clee Hill.
Mr. & Mrs. O. HUGHES,	Bleathwood.
Mrs. MARION BASSETT,	Brimfield.
Mrs. MARGERY MARTIN,	Ludlow.
Mrs. JEAN HOLLIS,	Knowbury.
Mrs. PAMELA COLES,	Knowbury.
Mrs. ELIZABETH GOLDTHORP,	Knowbury.
Mrs. ELIZABETH ROBINSON,	Clee Hill.
Mrs. NORA BOOTMAN,	Knowbury.
Mrs. MARGARET TOMLINSON,	Knowbury.

Miss TRUDY PASTON-COOPER, Nash.
ALFRED & FRANCIS WILSON, Ludlow.
HEREFORD & WORCESTER EDN. COMM., Oakfields, Worcester.
ANDREW J. WARRINGTON, Clee Hill.
RICHARD W. WARRINGTON, Clee Hill.
Mr. A. D. BALL, Bitterley.
DAVID & PAULINE CHAPMAN, Cleobury Mortimer.
Miss AMANDA CORBETT, Bedlam.
Mrs. I. M. WALL & ALAN, Orleton.
Mr. J. COLLINSON, Church Stretton.
Mr. RON MORRIS, Church Stretton.
THE COX FAMILY, Orleton.
Mr. JACKIE MORRIS, Ludlow.
M. H. & J. M. VARNEY, Crumpsbrook.
Mrs. Q. M. ALLIBONE, Solihull.
Mr. A. BREAKWELL, Tenbury Road,
Mr. ROBIN BOOTMAN, Ludlow.
Mr. CLIFF PROSSER, Lancaster.
Mr. A. CHIDLEY, Clee Hill.
ERN WALL, Oreton.
KATHRYN M. DAVIES, Cleobury Mortimer.
Mrs. PHYLLIS EDWARDS, Clee Hill.
Mr. H. G. RODEN, Whitton.
Mr. & Mrs. T. TIPTON, Ludlow.
J. & J. H. BERRY, Rochford.
O. WESTWOOD, Halesowen.
Mr. & Mrs. E. L. HEAPEY, Orleton.
Mr. & Mrs. M. L. HEAPEY, Canada.
Mr. W. MOFFAT, Knighton-on-Teme.
Mr. TONY WARD, Leominster.
Mr. DEWI EDWARDS, Leominster.
Mrs. PAT MORGAN, Eyton.
Mr. FRED FOTHERGILL, Pembridge.
Mrs. MARION LEWIS, Berrington.
Mr. A. B. ALLEN, Tenbury Wells.
Mr. A. W. JENKINS, Hereford.
Mrs. M. A. BLOOM, Ludlow.
Mrs. JOAN (PITT) ROLFE, Hereford.
THE GILLARD FAMILY, Rochford.
Mrs. SHEILA BOWEN, Dhustone, Clee Hill.
Miss JOAN CLENT, Clee Hill.
Mr. NORMAN T. LLOYD, Ludlow.
Dr. & Mrs. A. SURPLICE, Newcastle-under-Lyme.
Mrs. JEAN KENNEDY, Ludlow.
THE PERROTT FAMILY, Wigmore.
Mr. E. G. COLLIER, Ludlow.
DAVID BYTHEWAY, Church Stretton.
Mr. GRAHAM LEWIS, Potters Bar.
JACK BYTHEWAY & FAMILY, Salt Lake City, U.S.A.
PHILLIP & SHERRY BYTHEWAY, Washington, U.S.A.
JOHN BOWEN, Leominster.
DEREK BOWEN, Knowbury.
Mrs. JOANNA SHIPP, Bude.
DONALD (MALLY) HARRIS, Tenbury.
GEMMA, SPENCER & SHELLY DAVIES, Tenbury.
EVELYN & LAWRENCE THOMAS,
JAMES SCARLETT BARKER, Ludlow.
DOROTHY HOLE, Launceston.
LENA DAVIES, Ludlow.
Mr. & Mrs. J. D. WATTS, Tenbury.

Mr. & Mrs. ARTHUR FLETCHER, Tenbury.
SYLVIA SHAKESPEARE, Tenbury.
BETTY KEMP, Burford.
Mr. & Mrs. BASIL HOLEHOUSE, St. Michaels.
THE ROBERTS FAMILY, Foldgate View, Ludlow.
Mr. RICHARD BYTHEWAY, Doddington.
JOAN & BILL LEWIS, Rusticarea.
ANN TOMLEY, Oswestry.
SEBERT KEY, Dhustone.
MARGARET & PETER SPAREY, Stanford Bridge.
DEREK & JANE EDWARDS, Hereford.
Mrs. DORIS CATHERINE GENNER, Clee Hill.
ELIZABETH ANN KING, Clee Hill.
P. J. MOSEDALE, Eardiston.
ERIC & PHYLLIS LOWE, Tenbury.
CYRIL & EVI BROUMLEY, Leominster.
SUTTON PHILLIPS, Much Wenlock.
BETTE WAINWRIGHT, East Hamlet.
Mrs. EDIE TOMKINS, Hereford.
Mrs. EVELYN BETTS, Aldridge.
Mr. ARNOLD THOMAS & FAMILY, Bitterley.
ISABEL & TONY DAVIS, Leintwardine.
JOAN & CHARLES MAYNARD, Orleton.
Mrs. M. W. EVANS, Cleobury Mortimer.
BEATTIE STANTON, Dhustone, Clee Hill.
Mrs. MARGARET BATE, Dhustone, Clee Hill.
Mr. GEORGE STANGHAN, Reigate.
DENIS TURTON, Lyonshall.
TED CONNOP, Leominster.
KELVIN OWEN, Kingsland.
GERRY KEEBLE, Leominster.
DON & MARIJKE PREECE, Leominster.
M. & M. C. & J. JONES, Clee Stanton Farm.
THE BISSELL FAMILY, Lichfield.
THE CLEE FAMILY, Ludlow.
JOAN BALLINGER (CLEE), Lichfield.
CHRISTINE ADAMS, Clee Hill.
Mrs. E. BREAKWELL, Crumps Brook.
THE HILES FAMILY, Dhustone.
MARJORIE PURSLOW & FAMILY, Cleobury Mortimer.
THE RICHMOND FAMILY, Australia.
THE WILSON FAMILY, Dhustone.
THE WHITE FAMILY, Dhustone.
THE ROMEO FAMILY, Cleobury Mortimer.
Mr. & Mrs. DUNCAN EDWARDS, Clee Hill.
Mr. & Mrs. TED ANDREWS, Dhustone.
BETTY LESTER (NEE OWEN), The Priory, Leominster.
GRAHAM, HELEN & KAREN JENKINS, Orleton.
BERT PRICE, Diddlebury.
Mr. & Mrs. D. M. IVERS, Leysters, Leominster.
ROSE CORFIELD (NÉE OWEN), Whitefriars, Ludlow.
Mr. COLIN WALKER, Ontario, Canada.
J. B. BROCKBANK, Bridgnorth, Shropshire.
Mrs. RUBY McIVOR (NÉE JACKS), Guildford, Surrey.
Miss TENCH, Blackpool.

Mr. & Mrs. DENNIS EDWARDS, Manchester.
CHRISTINE & MICHAEL RAYNER, Cressage, Shrewsbury.
BERNARD KEY, Dhustone.
DENNIS BUTCHER, Ludlow.
DENNIS & PEGGY MANNING, Toronto, Canada.
MAURICE MARTIN, Knowle.
REG TENNANT, Clee Hill.
JOHN WILLIAM JORDAN, Clee Hill.
Mr. G. J. PRITCHARD (CHIMNEY SWEEP), Leominster.
Mrs. A. THOMAS, Ashford Carbonell.
DOREEN POWELL, Ashford Carbonell.
SHEILA COOT, Ashford Carbonell.
Mrs. B. COOKE, Alfchurch, Birmingham.
Mrs. B. SMALL, The Sheet, Ludlow.
E. G. BAYLEY, Ashford Carbonell.
B. GENNER, Caynham.
NICOLA JONES, Caynham.
Mrs. B. CLARKE, Ashford Carbonell.
Miss E. L. CHITHAM, Bringewood, Ludlow.
Mrs. I. BOWDEN, Ashford Carbonell.
Mrs. M. MOSS, Greenacres, Ludlow.
Mrs. P. A. DOWNES, Tenbury Wells.
Rev. IAN W. WILLIAMS, Lichfield.
DEREK BYTHEWAY, Hopton Wafers.
WALLACE HAMMOND, Coreley.
Mr. & Mrs. W. J. LLOYD, Australia.
Mr. J. E. TENNANT, Clee Hill.
Mr. J. T. LLOYD, Knowbury.
Mr. & Mrs. A. R. GREATWICH, Clee Hill.
Mr. D. WEAVER, Ludlow.
Mr. & Mrs. J. TENNANT, Clee Hill.
Mr. & Mrs. T. HARRINGTON, Wolverhampton.
Mr. & Mrs. H. WEBB, Wolverhampton.
PAUL GREATWICH, Clee Hill.
DAVID J. COOPER, Wolverhampton.
PAUL YUNNIE, Wolverhampton.
MARY WILLIAMS, Orleton.
THE ASTON FAMILY, Rochford, Tenbury.
AUDREY & RALPH PEARSON, Olton, Solihull.
JANET & TREVOR YAPP, Newsagents, Clee Hill.
YVONNE & MICHAEL JOHNSON, Redhill, Reigate.
Miss MARY ROBERTS. Caversham St. London SW3.
Mr. B. J. H. GRIFFITHS, Mallards, Penybont.
Mrs. DOROTHY LLEWELYN (NÉE BEST), Gorse Road, Sunderland.
CLEE HILL PRIMARY SCHOOL, Clee Hill.
OLWEN HELME Ford Farm, Leominster.
THE HUGHES FAMILY Bromyard Rd.
THE BAGLEY FAMILY Bromyard Rd.
Mrs. EUNICE SLATER Whitton.
Mr. RON JORDAN Crumpsbrook
Mrs. MARY BROWN Three Crosses.
Mrs. VALERIE MILLINGTON Kington.
D. M. BROMLEY Knowbury
Mrs. MARY HAYWOOD Knowbury
DAVID A. WILLIAMS Orleton
Mr. BERT FORTEY Leominster
THE COLLIER FAMILY Tenbury

LINDA & ROGER FRYER, Australia.
EDDIE CASEY; Ludlow.
Mr. & H. U. ROBERTS. Caynham Road.
Mr. C. WILKINSON. Presteigne.
EILEEN CLENT, Clee Hill.
THE MARTIN FAMILY, Pool Farm, Clee Hill.
CATHERINE MARY THOMAS, Ludlow.
ELSIE HOTCHKISS, Highley.
MARGERY BALL, Chesterfield.
MARTIN SWAIN PRYCE, Knowbury.
DENIS LEWIS MARTIN, Madeley.
JOAN & FRED WARRINGTON, Clee Hill.
SAM CLARKE'S GRAND-DAUGHTER & FAMILY, Birmingham.
Dr. A. BURNETT, Tenbury Wells.
Mr. RON WILLIAMS, Coreley.
Mrs. MONA CLENT, Clee Hill.
Mrs. D. BROOME, Oreton.
Mr. PRICE, Oreton.
PHILIP MORRIS, Vernolds Common.
D. R. P. JOHNSON A.R.C.
D. C. PLUMMER, Bridgenorth.
H. A. BUBB, Malvern.
K. D. WILLETTS, A.R.C.
D. C. WILLETTS, A.R.C.
Mr. & Mrs. Y. L. BRADLEY, Titrail.
M. JACKSON, Road House Studley.
BRENDA POYSER, Coal Port.
HILARY & ROY GUY, Caynham.
EDWARD M. WILDING, Highley.
E. HOTCHKISS, Nash.
Mrs. HILDA HOWELLS, Hopton Bank.
Mrs. MARGARET ROBERTS, Ludlow.
ROBERT REYNOLDS, Ketley Bank.
Mrs. FELTON, Shrewsbury.
Mrs. JANE OWEN. Ludlow.
Mr. & Mrs. J. REYNOLDS Clee Hill.
BETTY DOREEN DAVIES, Cleobury, Mortimer.
G. & J. VAUGHAN, Australia.
M. GATEHOUSE & D. EDWARDS, Clee Hill.
J. & L. A. GATEHOUSE, Ludlow.
LYDIA (CLENT) ROBERTSON, Birkenhead.
JANET BROWN, Coreley.
Mrs. WEBB, Tenbury Wells.
HARRY MILLICHAMP, Nash.
Mr. PHILL CLEETON, Hereford.
TONY & SHEILA BRICK Coventry.
HAZEL & BILL WOOD, Cleobury Mortimer.
Mrs. R. M. SIDDALL, Cleobury Mortimer.
HEATHER BIRCH, Doddington.
EDWARD MAYOR, Doddington.
Mrs. JANET HUTTON Wigmore
Mr. R. C. FRENCH Leominster
Mr. B. J. WARRINGTON Clee Hill
THE LEWER FAMILY Hollington
V. A. & E. E. CHALINOR Kingsland
G. R. GREGORY A.R.C.,
Dr. COLIN & ANN BROWN Bridgenorth
Mrs. ANGELA BROOME Ludlow
Mr. G. BOUNDS Ashford Carbonell
DESMOND & CASSANDRA JORDAN Rochford
Mr. BASIL CLENT Clee Hill
Mr. ROBERT KEYSE Ludlow
GEORGE WHITEFOOT Woolferton

Mr. GEORGE POYNER	Hopton	Mr. ROY CLENT	Clee Hill
Mrs. WHATMORE	Clee Hill	Mr. DENNIS WILTSHIRE	Kidderminster
Mrs. BARNFIELD	Snitton	Mr. BILL WILTSHIRE	Clee Hill
JOHN & LINDA DAVIES	Richards Castle	ROBERT DAVID WILTSHIRE	Clee Hill
ARTHUR & VI MEREDITH	Ludlow	Mr. HARLEY DANCE	Yarpole
ROY & LIN MEREDITH	Knowbury	Mr. & Mrs. P. OSBORNE	Hopton Bank
Mr. & Mrs. DEREK FLETCHER & FAMILY	Clee Hill	Mr. & Mrs. CLIFFORD MILLS	Coreley
Miss PHYLLIS & MR BERT MARTIN	Clee Hill	D. MANTLE	Whitton
		Mrs. N. P. NASH	Ludlow